HIGH NOON

HIGH NOON

The Inside Story
of Scott McNealy
and the Rise of
SUN MICROSYSTEMS

KAREN SOUTHWICK
for Upside Magazine

New York • Chichester • Weinheim • Brisbane • Singapore • Toronto

Copyright © 1999 by Upside Magazine. All rights reserved.

Published by John Wiley & Sons, Inc.

Published simultaneously in Canada.

Library of Congress Cataloging-in-Publication Data

Southwick, Karen.
    High noon : the inside story of Scott McNealy and the rise of Sun
Microsystems / Karen Southwick.
        p.   cm.
    ISBN 0-471-29713-5 (alk. paper)
    1. McNealy, Scott.   2. Computer scientists Biography.   3. Sun
Microsystems.   I. Title.
QA76.2.M37S68   1999
338.7'61004'092—dc21   99-16031
                                                              CIP

Printed in the United States of America.

10 9 8 7 6 5 4 3 2 1

Contents

Foreword

Holding a Mirror to the Network Revolution

A few companies stand out as mirrors of the incredible change, growth, and technical achievement that have characterized Silicon Valley and the U.S. computer industry. One such company is Sun Microsystems, ably chronicled here by Karen Southwick in a book that tracks Sun from its conception in the early 1980s by a small band of ambitious Stanford and Berkeley students to its position today as a global power in network computing with a market cap of $43 billion.* Along the way, Southwick introduces the reader to the daring businesspeople and technical geniuses who shaped this remarkable success story. And, we follow the development of today's information technology from the early phases of open systems to today's interconnected world of distributed intelligence, "write once, run everywhere" software, and the Internet.

It started with a vision, even if it took a few years for Sun to crystalize that vision in one phrase—"The Network Is The Computer"—a company slogan that mystified many when first introduced in 1985, but today seems almost uncannily prescient about everything that was to come. Back in the antediluvian 1980s, when the microprocessor began to assert itself, we felt the sway of Gordon Moore's law, which stated that the processing power available to our customers would double, at least, every 18 months. It would take another visionary, Bob Metcalfe of Xerox PARC and later of 3Com, to tell us, "All well and good with Moore's law, but you ain't seen nothing yet. The power of any computing device, no matter how awesome the chip inside, will increase along with its connections to a network."

* As of early 1999.

increase along with its connections to a network."

No doubt, the Sun executives, scientists, and engineers encountered in this book were years ahead of their competitors in understanding the potential of networks. Not only did they take Metcalfe's law to heart, they embodied it in hardware and software that would transform individual and group productivity, at first for engineers and scientists, and later for knowledge workers in organizations of every kind. The network not only opened each user to an expanding universe of connected resources, it also allowed organizations to distribute software and processing power across many different networked computers—the key to maximizing the performance and efficiency of the entire computing investment. As this book progresses, the reader can feel the mainstream of computing shift from dedicated mainframes and stand-alone PCs to distributed networks of clients and servers.

For any of these systems to work, of course, different computers and software programs must connect and interoperate. That requires open standards, common interfaces available to every developer with a better idea for a network-ready product. It was this same open-systems approach, pioneered by Sun, that made possible the global standards-based network we call the Internet. Here again, Sun was out in front of the industry curve in seizing the Internet opportunity. The Net first became a way of life and doing business at places like Sun, which were focused on the Internet's underlying protocols and operating systems. Sun's history, as captured in these pages, is part of the history of both Internet business and Internet culture.

Closely related to the Internet is Silicon Valley's unique business culture, which Sun as much as any company has exemplified over the years. Sun's founding quartet of Andy Bechtolsheim, Vinod Khosla, Bill Joy, and Scott McNealy are inspirational prototypes for the legions of Silicon Valley entrepreneurs who have followed, and its brilliant technical contributors, like James Gosling, have rightfully earned legendary status among their peers. Together with their colleagues, they built a company that has come to typify an approach to work and life that might be called the Silicon Valley way: incredibly smart people working incredibly hard in an atmosphere of high risks and high rewards.

Today, computing is entering yet another phase as organizations look for ways to manage the relationships among the myriad people, computers, software applications, on-line services, and devices connected to the Internet. This is a new era of directory-enabled networks that know and serve every user, applications that can be accessed anywhere, and intelligent devices from cellular phones to vending machines that can be managed and controlled over the network. Sun, with new technologies like Java and Jini, is again playing a prominent role in this next evolution of the network, what we might call ubiquitous computing. A new law of relationships is determining success in this new era, where no single vendor can hope to control the user's access to information and resources. The winning hands will belong to those vendors who can help customers establish digital identities and manage this growing complexity.

One of the strengths of Karen Southwick's excellent book is that it takes us on a straight path to the future. By following the progress of Sun, we can see how far the technology and business of networking has come, where it stands today, and why the future promises new innovations and achievements that will once again amaze us. My 14 years at Sun were an incredible delight, with the highs higher than I could have ever asked for. I hope you enjoy your Sun experience via this book as much as I enjoyed mine.

Dr. Eric Schmidt
Chairman and CEO, Novell, Inc.
Sun Microsystems, 1983–1997

Preface

Why *High Noon*?

Who's going to control the future of technology, currently the most influential force for change in business and society? Microsoft is one obvious contender, an alleged monopolist whom the government compares to the Standard Oil of the past. The opposition to Microsoft is now coalescing around one of the most surprising companies in all of technology: Sun Microsystems. From its introduction of the popular Java programming language to last year's deal with America Online and Netscape Communications, Sun continues to deliver breakthroughs in technology and strategy that change the rules of the competitive arena. Sun and its CEO, Scott McNealy, have become serious obstacles to Microsoft's drive for power.

High Noon is the first book to explore the modern Sun in-depth, to examine the intriguing balance between chaos and genius that led to innovations such as Java. It also presents a vivid portrait of the stubborn, charismatic McNealy, as seen through the eyes of friends and enemies, coworkers, and mentors. The Sun CEO, who has long identified Microsoft as his company's biggest enemy, was like a lone prophet shouting in the wilderness for years. Critics dismissed his dire warnings about Microsoft, calling them envious whining about a more successful rival. But today even the U.S. Department of Justice is sounding the same cry. McNealy has become the focal point for those who seek to guarantee businesses and consumers multiple choices about how to access the Internet and where to buy an operating system.

In rich, evocative detail, *High Noon* tells the Sun story—from its shaky beginnings in 1982 to its emergence as a $10 billion powerhouse that will determine how you use technology in the future. Sun's Java is one of the keys to the world in which computing appliances will be everywhere, from your home to your car to your office. And McNealy's determination to dethrone Microsoft has given rise to the pivotal battle in today's business world.

I have been writing about technology and Silicon Valley for more than a decade, first with the *San Francisco Chronicle,* then *Upside* magazine and, most recently, with *Forbes ASAP.* Although McNealy himself declined to be interviewed directly for *High Noon,* I did extensive research, talking to leading Sun executives such as Ed Zander, Bill Joy, Alan Baratz, and John Gage. I also spoke with many current and former Sun insiders, ranging from Carol Bartz of Autodesk to Eric Schmidt of Novell, both of whom were Sun managers before becoming chief executives of their respective companies. The views of Sun allies and competitors, including IBM, Netscape, Hewlett-Packard, and, of course, Microsoft, are represented as well. The result is an in-depth, thought-provoking portrait of a fascinating company whose success epitomizes the excitement that permeates the Silicon Valley scene.

The Introduction describes McNealy as he went to Washington last year to testify before Congress about Microsoft's domination of the computer industry, an event that thrust him onto a national stage.

Chapter 1 takes us back to Sun's beginning, when McNealy teamed up with three other graduate students to found a company that made high-powered workstations for engineers.

Chapter 2 presents an early leadership struggle, culminating in McNealy's elevation to chief executive. It also offers a biography of the Sun leader that shows us how his character became indelibly stamped upon the company and what that has meant.

Chapter 3 demonstrates how Sun combined technological innovation with marketing and strategic ploys to force larger competitors to take note and even follow its lead as computing power accelerated.

Chapter 4 portrays a cocky Sun that has defeated its early rival, Apollo, and burst into the hypergrowth period that will make it a billion-dollar company.

Chapter 5 takes us into Sun's abyss, in which its own brashness, combined with unanticipated market responses, led to a quarterly loss and a reorganization. McNealy emerged from this trial by fire stronger and more determined than ever.

Chapter 6 describes Sun's unusual culture, which combines entrepreneurialism with the resources of a large company, through the eyes of the people and executives who work there.

Chapter 7 focuses on the emergence of Java and how it was saved from oblivion by a handful of brilliant thinkers within Sun.

Chapter 8 shows how Sun's marketing campaign, coupled with the emergence of the Internet, thrust Java into prominence.

Chapters 9 and 10 detail how Java's ability to undermine the Windows operating system escalated the confrontation between Sun and Microsoft, even into the courts.

Finally, Chapters 11 and 12 project how Sun could win its strategic battle and become the technology leader of the twenty-first century.

High Noon is both instructive and entertaining in describing the behind-the-scenes maneuvering of Sun as it seeks to thwart Microsoft and advance its own cause. It provides new perspective on how the complex, contradictory McNealy has shaped his company and fashioned its strategy. This book will appeal to managers interested in applying Sun's innovative tactics to their own companies, as well as to anyone intrigued by the compelling story of this unique Silicon Valley company.

Introduction

Sun Goes to Washington

Scott McNealy was out of his element. So were Bill Gates and Jim Barksdale. In an extraordinary confrontation that could have been lifted from a Frank Capra movie, high technology had come to Washington, D.C.—a venue the industry usually detested. Three of technology's most powerful titans, CEOs all, were squaring off in a public hearing convened by the Senate Judiciary Committee. McNealy had built a fledgling computer company, Sun Microsystems, into a $10.5 billion* behemoth whose hot new Java technology was popping up in everything from the Internet to cable settop boxes. Over the same decade and a half, Gates had led Microsoft to its commanding position in personal computer software and was expanding his empire into publishing, broadcasting, on-line transactions, and the digital home. Jim Barksdale was fighting to keep Netscape Communications, whose browser software had kicked off the Internet era, alive in the face of blistering competition from Microsoft. Senator Orrin Hatch, chairman of the committee, had called this hearing to discuss competition in the software industry, and everyone knew the primary topic would

---

* As of end of 1998.

1

be whether Microsoft was a monopolist seeking to extend its domination of the PC market into the Internet world.

Flashbulbs popped and TV camera crews hit the on switches on their videocams as the high-tech industry's prominent celebrities entered the Hart Senate Office Building, which was packed shoulder-to-shoulder with legislators, aides, journalists, and lobbyists. One veteran lobbyist told the *Wall Street Journal* it was the biggest congressional hearing to hit Washington since the confirmation hearing of Supreme Court nominee Clarence Thomas, who had to fend off sexual harassment charges.[1] Gulped McNealy: "I've never seen so many cameras in my life." But the aggressive leader of Sun Microsystems is not easy to intimidate. Indeed, he would boast during the hearing that Sun was virtually alone in calling attention to the bullying tactics of Microsoft. As he entered the crowded room and sat down at the front table, between Gates and Barksdale, McNealy's wide-eyed expression and serious demeanor signalled the importance of this session.

The hearing on March 3, 1998, was held to discuss "Market Power and Structural Change in the Software Industry." That's why Microsoft, the largest software vendor in the world, and Netscape, the largest vendor of browser software to access the Internet, were there, but why was Sun taking center stage with the other two? Sun, after all, is not primarily a software company. Most of its billions in revenue come from selling hardware—workstations and high-powered computers used to run corporate networks. Sun, it seemed, had crashed someone else's party. But Sun has had a long history of doing just that. From the moment Sun was founded in 1982, it was dismissed by early competitors as a lightweight not even worth the bother of smashing. Far from sinking into oblivion, Sun proved that, by making its own rules and unleashing a take-no-prisoners style of competition, it could speed blithely by the toughest and largest of competitors.

Sun's story is one of a scrappy renegade that made it against all odds. In McNealy, it also is the story of a loner willing to stake his company and his own reputation on intuitive conviction about where technology is headed. Sun brings together a uniquely American blend of disparate personalities, who squabble among themselves but band together to achieve the overarching goal of creating a great company. Even at $10 billion, it is innovative, flexible, and fast-moving, able to adapt to the challenges of the twenty-first century by retaining entrepreneurial structures and attitudes. Its biggest test, however, is ongoing—the direct confrontation with arguably the world's most powerful company, Microsoft.

For Sun to fully exploit its opportunities requires besting or at least slowing down the Microsoft juggernaut. This accounts for McNealy's appearance before Congress and Sun's avid support for the Department of Justice's antitrust action against Microsoft. McNealy has spoken out about Microsoft's alleged monopoly at a time when much of the industry is keeping mum, afraid to run afoul of the behemoth. At the hearing, McNealy and Barksdale laid out the case: The government had to rein in the Microsoft monopoly to prevent it from throttling innovation and choice. The son of an American Motors executive, McNealy drew on the familiar car analogies that pepper his public speeches: "By owning the entry points to the Internet and the electronic marketplace, Microsoft has the power today to exercise predatory and exclusionary control over the very means by which we access this Internet. It's a lot like General Motors having the ability to dictate what type of gasoline you put in your car or what interstate you can drive on, or even how you get on the interstate."

McNealy was uncharacteristically subdued during the Senate hearing, hiding his ready grin and holding his witty one-liners in check. But then, as an acknowledged libertarian, he's more comfortable decrying government interference than asking for it. His presence at the Senate hearing was a sign of how deeply McNealy felt about Microsoft's threat not only to his company, Sun, but to the high-tech industry as a whole. Microsoft has a choke hold on the PC that allows it to dictate what scores of other companies do. "This is about protecting consumer choice in the marketplace, protecting innovation and basically about enforcing the laws of the land," he said in his opening statement. "I also believe in the economic principles on which this country was founded—free enterprise, consumer choice, free and open competition . . . What we want today is enforcement of the laws that are already on the books, in this case the antitrust laws."

In fact, McNealy's passionate belief extends so far that he places a blanket prohibition against using any Microsoft software within Sun, a policy which handicaps his own salespeople. They can't, at least not officially, use common business applications like PowerPoint. Such seeming inconsistencies are typical of Sun, a company built on contradiction. One that many said would quickly fade away after its shaky start. When it did succeed, going public in 1986 as a $210 million corporation, the naysayers still forecasted doom at every turn. Sun would be done in by powerful competitors ranging from Digital Equipment to IBM to Hewlett-Packard to, ultimately, Microsoft and its cohort Intel. So far, Sun has defied them all. It has enlarged the market for its cash cow computer systems. It has developed innovative software that has the potential to transform the company and computing. And, it has largely retained its freewheeling, iconoclastic culture, though it continues to struggle with organizational issues of control and responsibility.

■ THE SUN KING

Ever the contrarian, McNealy parlayed himself and his company into prominence partly by insisting to anyone who would listen, particularly the press, "I am not Microsoft." How far would he go to grab headlines for Sun? A few months before the congressional hearing, on the October 13, 1997, cover of *Fortune* magazine, McNealy obligingly donned a silly-looking cape and a demonic expression to pose as Javaman, a comic book–like character out to save the world from Microsoft's evil empire. Both McNealy and his company are a study in contrasts. McNealy's mastery of the 10-second sound bite (he's referred to Gates and his righthand man, Steve Ballmer, as "Ballmer and Butt-head") has enlivened many a television or magazine report on technology. Not everyone grasps the intricacies of operating systems and source code, but they can understand an old-fashioned, all-out battle between two masters of the technology universe: Gates and McNealy.

Unlike a one-dimensional comic book muscleman, though, McNealy has depth and smarts. He has degrees from Harvard and Stanford universities; he is one of the longest-reigning CEOs in an industry notorious for turnover at the top; and he has positioned Sun to take advantage of a remarkable range of opportunities—with technology that can run everything from a Fortune 500 company's data center to the light switch in your home. After cofounding the company, McNealy has led Sun throughout most of its 17-year history, which makes him a member of an extremely exclusive club. Most founders of technology start-ups reach a point at which the company outgrows their skills, and they give way to veteran managers. McNealy, by contrast, has scaled with Sun, able to refine his strategic sense and recognize new market opportunities. One of the only other founders who has been able to do this as effectively is Bill Gates.

McNealy, who was originally Sun's vice president for manufacturing, became CEO two years after the company's start when Sun's board couldn't find anybody else. His background was in manufacturing, not computers or engineering like most technology entrepreneurs. But McNealy was a quick study who would soon learn to talk about the intricacies of technology from the brilliant engineers who were his cofounders. Beyond that, he has business and people know-how. He focused Sun initially by streamlining production and cutting the cost of workstations, in the process boosting sales and undermining competitors. In the early 1990s, he correctly identified software giant Microsoft, not the hardware companies with whom Sun had traditionally competed, as the looming rival, and refocused the company to move out of the giant's shadow, at least for a while. McNealy "understands strategic principles better than anyone this side of Bill Gates," says Steven Milunovich, a managing director with Merrill Lynch in New York. "Good strategy is about being different and being focused. Sun has always been the 'opposite' company. This renegade approach makes investors nervous but is the only way Sun can add value."

McNealy is so colorful and quotable that he can sometimes be his own worst enemy, shooting from the hip without regard for the consequences. "Scott is the king of the sound bite," says Bret Rekas, a longtime Sun analyst now with a hedge fund, TES Partners, in Minneapolis. "People mistake his posturing for fact. They take it too literally and overreact." Actually, McNealy enjoys playing the provocateur, especially when it gets Sun headlines in the likes of *Fortune,* the *Wall Street Journal,* and *New Yorker* magazine.

Away from the spotlight, McNealy has been the inspirational leader who built Sun into a very real success with basic virtues like hard work, foresight, and determination. He's also good at surrounding himself with talented people, like Ed Zander, Sun's second in command, and Bill Joy, a renowned technology innovator, and then giving those people room to run. "Sun's management team is extremely talented," says Rekas. "They make their bet and live with it." He credits McNealy and Zander with smart decisions, but adds, "it's not just them. It's the whole team."

Sun moved to the top of its workstation market against larger, more established competitors, such as Hewlett-Packard and Digital Equipment. As Microsoft threatened that market, McNealy recognized the need to move up the food chain by broadening Sun's product line. Sun is now a leading vendor of even more powerful computers, known as servers, that run the networks that link corporate desktops together. McNealy's decentralized, turn-on-a-dime management style has given Sun the flexibility to survive in an increasingly competitive market and to force mighty Microsoft to take notice of a company it once ignored.

■ MICROSOFT AND BEYOND

After workstations and servers, Sun's third important technology resulted from its considerable research and development (R&D) prowess. In 1995, Sun launched Java—a programming language that turns the Internet into a computer operating system. The story of how Java was developed is a prime example of how to encourage innovation within a large corporation. Java was the product of a small, elite team of developers who had worked in secret in offices outside of Sun. They were unknown to all but Sun's highest ranks for several years. When the first market for Java—interactive cable TV—failed to pan out, Sun demonstrated its adroitness by recasting Java as an Internet technology. McNealy and company then began a vigorous publicity campaign that won Java attention and supporters. Today, thousands of software developers are writing programs in Java and Sun is the center of a growing web of allies. The largest technology company in the world, IBM, has joined Sun in an alliance to push Java into the corporate arena.

As the twenty-first century approaches, Sun has shown how its new technology promises to fundamentally change how and where we interact with computers. Java strikes at the heart of the twentieth-century personal computer (PC) paradigm, personified by Microsoft's Windows operating system, which is packaged with 95 percent of PCs. Because it doesn't depend on Windows or any other operating system, just the Internet, Java could be Microsoft's Achilles' heel. The stand-alone personal computer was the old battleground, and Microsoft won that war handily. But now the battle has shifted to the Internet, with its 50 million users. And Sun has unleashed a potentially lethal new weapon that is attracting support from a range of different arenas, including cable-TV providers, credit card companies, retailers, and automobile manufacturers. A measure of Sun's success with Java can be seen in the fact that Microsoft has reacted so strongly to it. In late 1997, Sun filed a lawsuit alleging that Microsoft was trying to disrupt development of Java by making its own version and splitting the Java camp.

By deliberately setting itself up as the Microsoft alternative, Sun has staked out a course that flouts conventional wisdom, but could pay off big if technology moves into the new era many pundits are predicting. In the wired world of the future, Internet access, or Web-tone, is as ubiquitous as a dial-tone and the network is everywhere—from the home to the office, from your TV settop box to your telephone, from banking to shopping. Potential customers range from the largest corporations to every consumer. As its reaches out to this vast market, Sun proclaims itself the champion of diversity, in which various technologies from multiple vendors compete for consumer acceptance, with Java acting as the connecting link. Microsoft, on the other hand, is portrayed as the purveyor of Windows everywhere, seeking to extend its monopoly into the Internet world.

■ THE FOUNDATION OF SUCCESS

In many ways, Sun's journey is an example of how to do things right, especially when it comes to penetrating a market, reinventing yourself, and generating innovation. Unlike many of its peers, Sun has managed to catch the wave of two significant paradigm shifts in the technology industry—from centralized computing to individualized desktops, and from individualized desktops to networked enterprise. Now it's poised to catch the third wave—from networked enterprise to ubiquitous computing in the digital home and digital office. It's rare to be able to catch three waves in a row. It's even rarer to be a leader in each, as Sun has been—thanks to McNealy's gutsy, instinctive course setting and the abilities of a superb supporting cast that includes outstanding managers and engineers. "Sun is among the best at continuing to sell the next vision of computing to the marketplace," says Jim Moore, chairman of the consulting firm, GeoPartners Research, in Cambridge, Massachusetts. "What Scott [McNealy] realized early was that a company needs a vision for the marketplace. At first Sun was hot screaming boxes for those who are really hip. Then they were the network computer."

Sun is remarkable not because it dares to oppose Microsoft, but because its history proves that it can take on varied challenges and find a way to win. Sun has the guts and the brains to do what it must to thrive in an unpredictable and at times hostile, environment. It also has the internal awareness and self-confidence to stick with an unpopular, even derided, strategy until it proves itself. "Sun has a very clear sense of who they are," says Milunovich. "That focus is what has made them successful." Sun is in charge of its own destiny because its foundation is solid, with savvy operational management that assures consistent financial performance. That solidity allows the flights of fancy that result in such breakthroughs as Java. Sun is "highly coupled, loosely aligned," as McNealy puts it.

But the Sun story is also one of recouping from missed opportunities and blown initiatives. McNealy's fly-by-the-seat-of-your-pants management style has guided the company more than once into storms of controversy. Sun has always emerged, if not unscathed, at least the wiser for its mistakes. Sun's core qualities of dogged determination, combined with brilliant technical expertise and courageous leadership, were forged during a decade and a half of intense competition and bouts of internal strife. In an industry as mercurial as technology, Sun steers to an inner compass that generally points in the right direction, beating out bewildered competitors who are zigzagging around in search of a course.

Chapter 1

Beginnings

Like the musical genius of a Mozart or a Gershwin, entrepreneurial ability often manifests itself very early in life. As a teenager in New Delhi, India, Vinod Khosla already knew he wanted to start his own company. With a degree in electrical engineering from the Indian Institute of Technology, the intense Khosla came to the United States after he failed with a start-up in his homeland. He received a master's degree in biomedical engineering from Carnegie-Mellon University in Pittsburgh before trekking west to the Stanford University MBA program in Palo Alto, California. This was in the late 1970s, when the recently named Silicon Valley was becoming a mecca for entrepreneurs. Apple Computer's two founders had developed the first real personal computer in a garage, while Intel had just invented the microprocessor. Stanford and the nearby University of California at Berkeley provided the computer laboratories in which countless students honed the skills to make their dreams come true.

After Khosla graduated from Stanford in 1980, he wrote 400 letters to companies that met his criteria: less than three years old, fewer than a hundred employees. He was already demonstrating those qualities of near fanatical determination and attention to detail that would pave the way for his triumph and later his downfall. None of the 400 letters paid off, but a connection at Stanford proved fruitful and, in early 1980, he helped start Daisy Systems, which specialized in computer-aided design (CAD). While Daisy eventually foundered after a promising start, the year-and-a-half he spent there gave Khosla the impetus to found Sun. At Daisy, he was searching for a better computer to handle CAD. The prevailing model required that engineers take turns, or share time, on a larger minicomputer. Few people thought it was feasible to give every engineer a computer with enough power to do CAD or CAM (computer-aided manufacturing), but Khosla recognized that the solution might lie in the new workstation, an individual computer that was relatively inexpensive, yet able to handle complex tasks previously done by minicomputers. Khosla also wanted the workstation to plug into a network of the type he had seen running at Stanford, called the Ethernet, which would allow engineers to collaborate electronically. This was a revolutionary concept at the time.

In 1981, came one of those fortuitous meetings that are the stuff of Silicon Valley legends: a secretary connected Khosla with a graduate student who was working on a project called the Stanford University Network, or SUN. This was fellow immigrant Andy Bechtolsheim, a tall, blond, introverted German, whose appearance and manner contrasted starkly with Khosla's. They spoke to each other in differently accented English, but Khosla grasped that Bechtolsheim had the technology he needed to make his vision of a workstation reality. Bechtolsheim had more modest ambitions: he was licensing his design to local companies for $10,000 apiece. That seemed like a great business while he finished his Ph.D. But Khosla told him bluntly, "I want the goose that laid the golden egg."

Bechtolsheim never did get his Ph.D. He and Khosla wrote a terse six-page business plan outlining how they would build and sell the SUN workstation. Dated February

12, 1982, the plan listed more than a dozen competitors, ranging from minicomputer manufacturers like Digital Equipment, Data General, and Hewlett-Packard, to personal computer vendors like Apple and Tandy. Workstations, priced then from $25,000 to $100,000, were smaller, cheaper, and more flexible than minicomputers, but more powerful than PCs. Another start-up, Apollo Computer of Chelmsford, Massachusetts, founded just two years earlier, had already demonstrated there was a market for workstations. (Microsoft, at the time an obscure vendor of PC software up in Redmond, Washington, was not even on Sun's radar screen, though it had already concluded a crucial deal to provide IBM with an operating system for its PC. For the rest of the decade, Sun and Microsoft would grow into hugely successful companies on parallel tracks, remotely aware of each other's existence.)

Sun was grounded in the notion of open systems and networking. Apollo, its chief competitor, had developed an elegant hardware-software combination, but both of those elements were proprietary. That is, they were unique to Apollo and totally under its control. By contrast, Sun intended to use standardized components. For an operating system, it would use Unix, which was developed by AT&T and widely licensed to universities, research labs, and companies. The Sun hardware was based on semiconductors from Motorola, available to anyone who wanted to buy them. The value added came in how Bechtolsheim put these chips together in the guts of the Sun workstation. Using off-the-shelf components, rather than building from scratch, enabled Sun to price its machines at less than half the cost of the competition. According to the business plan, Sun's machines would carry an end-user price of $10,000 to $20,000, whereas Apollo's cheapest machine sold for $25,000.

On the networking side, the Ethernet link would allow potential users to exchange electronic messages and share services such as file storage and printing. "To me the vision was distributed computing," Khosla says. Because the

Ethernet allowed users to share information, "you didn't need all the computing power in the same place. Technology had changed the economics of the computer." Though open systems and networking are trumpeted today by almost every computer manufacturer, the concepts were new in the early 1980s. Leading computer manufacturers like IBM and Hewlett-Packard each offered separate, proprietary technology that did not interoperate with each other. Customers were forced to make a choice and stick with it, unless they wanted to scrap all those expensive machines and start over. Sun's technology was quicker to put together, much like the Ford assembly line replaced hand-crafted automobile manufacturing, and thus it was more responsive to market changes.

■ SHOW ME THE MONEY

Before Khosla and Bechtolsheim could start their company, they needed funding. In the early 1980s, the elaborate structure of the venture capital community in Silicon Valley had not yet fully developed. Today, aspiring entrepreneurs must have a sophisticated, multifaceted business plan and an oral presentation before they begin parading before various venture capital firms like beauty contestants seeking a crown. In 1982, the venture capital world was smaller and more informal. Armed with their six-page business plan, plus the demonstrable fact that they had a working model of their product running at Stanford, Khosla and Bechtolsheim met with Bob Sackman, a veteran engineer turned investor whom Khosla knew from Daisy Systems. In Silicon Valley, would-be entrepreneurs cultivate a network of knowledgeable contacts they can turn to time and again. Sackman, with 30 years' experience in the electronics industry, had cofounded U.S. Venture Partners of Menlo Park, California. Another potential investor at the meeting was Doug Broyles, representing

West Coast Venture Capital, also of Menlo Park. Within five days, the two venture capitalists wrote checks totaling $284,000 to fund the young company. "It was really on trust," Khosla told Professor Amar Bhide of Harvard Business School in a 1989 case study on Sun. "There was very little due diligence on their part—they just believed in the concept."

The business plan that got Sackman to invest was short, simple, and maybe a trifle naive, but it reflected qualities that would persist at Sun. The stated mission was to "develop, manufacture, market, and support graphics workstations for the CAD/CAM marketplace . . . Maintain lead with the best cost/performance product on the market." Computer-aided design, which created blueprints for products from airplanes to chips, was a market of sophisticated engineers who demanded technical excellence and had no qualms about taking a chance on a new company that could supply it. Although Sun's market has since expanded upward to corporate information managers, the company has never lost its devotion to being a technological leader with its products, rather than being merely an integrator or solutions provider using technology from elsewhere. Ask any of the other top executives at Sun to define the company, and they will describe it first and foremost as a *products* company that controls its own intellectual property.

The tentative two-year forecast by Khosla and Bechtolsheim suggested that Sun would achieve total sales of $4 million in its first full year of operation, fiscal 1983, and $10 million in its second year. In addition, they expected to "manage company growth to produce break-even cash flow by the end of the first year." In fact, the company had sales of $8.6 million in its first fiscal year and $39 million in its second. Operating income was $588,000 in that first year and $3.7 million in the second. Despite its reputation for zaniness on other fronts, Sun has always been a tightly managed company that meets its financial objectives. In 17 years, Sun has had only one losing quarter—in 1989, an important turning point for the company. Read more about this in Chapter 5.

Thanks to Bechtolsheim's work at Stanford, Sun was already known within the scientific/technical community, which would prove to be the basis of word-of-mouth recommendations. "The SUN workstation has been reviewed and acclaimed by the scientific community," the original business plan stated. "Literally hundreds of inquiries have been received without any active marketing." The Sun founders had stumbled upon a community of supporters who would not only buy Sun's technology, but help it to evolve. No hardware or software vendor, no matter how big or powerful, survives without this web of external support. The web includes customers whose needs define how a technology evolves, and software developers who write programs for it. By targeting technical computer users first, Sun gained entree to sophisticated, independent buyers who generally made their own decisions about technology. This was not a new strategy: competitors Apollo, Digital Equipment, and Hewlett-Packard had all used it; Sun, however, would take it to the extreme, becoming a company of engineers selling to other engineers. Sun thus achieved a camaraderie with its customers, who propelled sales with enthusiastic reports. This early model gave the company a solid base upon which to expand.

■ MEN ON BOARD

Flush with seed capital, Khosla and Bechtolsheim could now turn to the problem of staffing their start-up. Khosla thought of a friend he knew from Stanford, someone who was running operations at another Unix start-up, Onyx Systems, in San Jose. This was Scott McNealy, who had grown up in a wealthy Detroit suburb, courtesy of his father's executive position at American Motors, and developed a reputation at college as a party-going jock. Though he attended Harvard and Stanford, McNealy was hardly known for academic excellence. Even today, he'll tell you he majored in "beer and golf." With his toothy grin and self-deprecating manner, the personable McNealy was highly regarded by his college friends, including Khosla.

After Sackman committed the money, Khosla took McNealy to celebrate at the local McDonald's, which suited Khosla's wallet and McNealy's fondness for fast food. Khosla said to his friend, "So when are you quitting your job?" McNealy replied, "You haven't made me an offer." Khosla panicked for a moment, concerned that McNealy would puncture his dream of the two of them working together. Then McNealy, who had the natural jokester's knack for timing, told Khosla: "I will take the job." McNealy, Khosla, and Bechtolsheim were all baby boomers born in the mid-1950s. "We were twenty-something-year-olds running a company," recalls Bechtolsheim, "and we had just met, but we certainly shared the passion" of starting a company.

McNealy—young, unattached, and eager for adventure—joined Sun as a designated cofounder and head of manufacturing. One of Sun's investors, Doug Broyles, was also the CEO of Onyx. Broyles had recruited McNealy there at the suggestion of a mutual friend, Bill Raduchel, who had known McNealy at Harvard and now worked for a customer of Onyx. "Scott doesn't know anything about computers, but he's a real good operations guy," Raduchel confided to Broyles. "He's going to make someone a lot of money someday." Broyles, who would soon become an investor in Sun and join its board, was favorably impressed with McNealy's energy and willingness to learn. "Scott grew up in a manufacturing environment because he'd worked summers for his father," Broyles recalls. "We brought him on as director of operations, and put manufacturing and purchasing under him. Within a couple of weeks, Scott had the 50-year-old manufacturing guy's respect and they were working as a team. Scott went out on the line and talked to people." McNealy's ability to relate to different kinds of people would prove critical to Sun, which has attracted an astonishing array of talent over the years, including many managers and engineers who went on to head companies themselves.

The trio of Khosla, Bechtolsheim, and McNealy worked feverishly over the next three months to develop a prototype of the first product, the Sun-1 workstation, but they weren't completely happy with the Unix variant they were using as the operating system. Fortunately, just across the San Francisco Bay was one of the recognized experts on Unix, Bill Joy, a graduate student at the University of California at Berkeley. The team went over to woo him.

Joy is a bushy-haired, bespectacled genius who still delights in dressing in the psychedelic colors of Berkeley in the 1970s and 1980s. When he's discussing technology, he usually goes off into the stratosphere, way over everybody's head. But Bechtolsheim, who has the same knowledge of hardware that Joy does with software, hit it off instantly with the prospective recruit. He was impressed when Joy walked over to the Digital VAX minicomputer that he was using and casually turned it off. "He was shocked because you couldn't just shut computers down back then," Joy recalls. The tweaks he had made to the operating system—a version called Berkeley Unix, which Joy practically owned—allowed the quick shutdown. Joy was about the same age as the other three, so he shared the optimism of youth. He was also getting fed up with fighting for space and resources at Berkeley. After dinner with the trio, during which he spent most of the time talking shop with fellow tech-head Bechtolsheim, Joy signed on as the fourth cofounder. "I said, 'what the hell'; these guys seem young and naive," Joy recalls, "but I was frustrated at Berkeley and ready to take a chance."

➤ A Team Is Born

The key people were now in place for Sun to build a successful product: Khosla with the ambition and the vision,

McNealy with practical manufacturing and personal skills, Bechtolsheim and Joy with the technical expertise. (McNealy and Joy remain at Sun, while Khosla is now with the prestigious venture capital firm Kleiner Perkins Caufield & Byers of Menlo Park, and Bechtolsheim is an engineering vice president at Cisco Systems of San Jose.) As the driving force, Khosla had grandiose ambitions for what was now called Sun Microsystems Incorporated. (The first name, SUN Workstation, was discarded as too narrow.) "I am a very competitive person and I didn't want to build a small company," he says. "There are companies when they start that are zero million dollars and there are companies that are zero billion dollars. Sun was a zero-billion-dollar company." The analogy he likes to use was that this start-up was a rocket ship that needed to reach orbital velocity. "The moon or bust was our motto," he says. In contrast to Khosla's intensity, McNealy was more light-hearted, joking that Sun "will be the biggest belly flop." You could see the difference already between their respective styles. Joy and Bechtolsheim kept their heads down and concentrated on technology.

But, what Sun lacked was someone to sell the product that Joy and Bechtolsheim were avidly designing. Joy turned to an older, more experienced friend of his at Berkeley, John Gage, then doing consulting for cable companies. Gage, today a grizzled visionary whose eyes still light up over the prospects that technology offers, is another noteworthy character in the company menagerie. A former hippie who helped organize anti-Vietnam War marches in Berkeley and Washington, D.C., Gage can wax poetic on everything from fluid flow dynamics to ethics. His sprawling house, located in an older section of the city of Berkeley, is plastered with old protest posters. He's a bright man who majored in mathematics, but whose real genius lies in his ability to assimilate information from diverse spheres and bring it together. Several years older than the founding team, he brought real-life experience to the table. Says Joy: "I brought John down because Scott and Vinod didn't understand marketing and sales. He was in a different zone," a description of the enigmatic Gage that rings true today.

Now a chief scientist at Sun, Gage "basically sold every machine in 1983," Joy says. He remembers how Gage would divide up the phone messages piled on his desk into various time zones. Gage "would start with Europe in the morning and, as the day progressed, he would move on to different time zones. Once in a while he shoveled everything back into a pile because he didn't have enough time." Adds Gage: "The first year all the sales came from me talking on the phone, saying, 'How many do you want?'" When he joined Sun, says Gage, McNealy and Khosla were a bit clueless about the business world. "Scott and Vinod were trying to hire a vice president of marketing and sales by raiding Digital and Data General—talking to mature people with families and country club homes." Snorts Gage: "They wasted a lot of time." In addition to marketing and sales, he wound up handling technical support and answering all the outside calls. Gage took orders, and Sun built the machines and shipped them.

Sun was typical of many start-ups, chaotic and unstructured, but out of these early days constructs emerged that would solidify and guide the company's evolution. The first was that the company ran lean and mean, and employees worked long hours, usually with far fewer resources than their competitors. "I remember my wife calling about midnight to see when I'd be coming home, and I'd say it's going to be another couple of hours. Then I'd show up at 4 A.M.," recalls Crawford Beveridge, vice president of corporate resources from 1985 to 1991. Khosla and McNealy were both frugal, particularly Khosla. He figured out how many engineers he needed by looking at the smallest viable player (next to Sun) in the market, which he identified as Hewlett-Packard. "HP had 300 engineers" in the division selling workstations, recalls Khosla. "I said I'm twice as good as HP—I need 150 engineers." He adds that the notion of open systems allowed Sun to leverage innovations developed elsewhere, rather than rely solely on proprietary, in-house technology.

The second construct was that non-product-related functions, such as marketing and customer support, were dealt with on a rather ad hoc basis. They were after-thoughts to the engineering-driven technical aspects of the product. As it moved up-channel, Sun would be forced to revise these priorities, but they held for a good chunk of the company's history.

The third construct was that McNealy was the one who talked to employees and dealt with morale issues, which meant that he was emerging as the de facto leader, even though he was vice president of manufacturing and Khosla was the CEO. But Khosla was too driven, and Joy and Bechtolsheim too buried in technology, to relate well to personnel and cultural needs.

■ THE FIRST CRISIS

Sun introduced its first real product, the Sun-2, in late 1982. (The Sun-1 was essentially a prototype.) The Sun-2 incorporated elements that the engineering market was looking for: it ran Joy's Berkeley Unix, which was considered the coolest, hippest operating system of its day, on top of Bechtolsheim's sleek hardware design. So, it was fast, for its time, and relatively easy to use because most engineers are proficient in Unix. The best way to instill customer confidence "is to design products around accepted industrywide standards at all the interfaces where one technology will need to talk to another," McNealy explained in a viewpoint article in the December 16, 1985, issue of *Computerworld*.[1] Unix "is one example of such a standard that can be shared by all the classes of computer equipment from supercomputer to desktop. . . ." The Sun-2 had one more thing high on the target user's priority list: a big 19-inch monitor that allowed for leading-edge graphics capability.

The trouble was that the Sun-2's new monitor, obtained from an outside supplier, emitted so much static electricity that it could short out the whole system. Dave Cardinal, an early hire at Sun in product support, remembers the problem well. At the 1983 Comdex trade show, he was assigned to get nine Sun-2 machines set up for product demonstrations at Sun's booth. "We packed 20 machines to have nine that worked," he recalls. "The whole truck was full of spare material." When someone tried to use the machine, it would often reboot itself due to the buildup of excess electricity. "Out in front John Gage would ad lib his 'reboot speech,'" Cardinal recalls, while in back he and the rest of the small Comdex team worked frantically to get the machine running again. Because the failure rate was so high, Sun had to offer an extended warranty promising replacement of monitors to reassure customers.

That same year Sun recruited Bernie Lacroute, a 14-year veteran from Digital and a French immigrant, to head engineering. One of his first tasks was to fix the monitor problem. "It was a life-threatening situation," recalls Lacroute. He discovered that the monitor would discharge electricity through the connecting cables and zap the machine. "It was like a lightning bolt hitting the CPU (central processing unit) board." Sun couldn't immediately find another supplier, so in the interim Lacroute and his team tried a series of cables that might contain the electrical discharge from the monitor. "Every evening we'd try a new cable out on units on the manufacturing floor," says Lacroute. "We shipped the darn things knowing we'd have to replace the monitors. If we couldn't ship we were dead." The Sun-2 crisis took almost a year to really clean up. "We ended up hiring a couple of guys from HP who finally did it," Lacroute says.

The Sun-2 eventually became a relative success for Sun, selling in the thousands of units and paving the way for the next-generation workstation, which would propel the company to billion-dollar status. Despite its problems, the Sun-2 enabled Sun to develop a manufacturing strategy of building machines quickly to meet specific customer demand. Ship at all costs became the motto, which meant the four founders and everyone else in the company would congregate on the manufacturing floor the last day of a quarter to assemble machines for shipping. Finally, the Sun-2 was the product that Sun used to make a critical deal, one which forced the leading workstation vendors to sit up and take notice of the little upstart in California.

■ GRAPPLING WITH COMPUTERVISION

In the early 1980s, Computervision, based outside Boston in Bedford, Massachusetts, was the leading supplier of complete systems for the CAD market. In late 1982, Computervision set off a free-for-all among workstation companies by announcing that it would shift its reliance on minicomputers to the cheaper workstations, which were now powerful enough to meet the demands of CAD. The choice came down to the new kid on the block, Sun, and the established vendor, Apollo, which had the additional advantage of being in Computervision's backyard. Sun bid with its new Sun-2 workstations, which were lauded by Computervision's engineers, but Apollo landed the contract. Khosla got the bad news in a phone call from a Computervision purchasing agent.

In a move that has achieved legendary status among Sun old-timers, Khosla and McNealy grabbed a red-eye flight from San Francisco to Boston and showed up uninvited at Computervision. This moment was vividly captured in *Sunburst,* a book about Sun's early years.[2] The two young Sun cofounders "planted themselves in the plush lobby of Computervision's headquarters. From there they called everyone they knew inside Computervision, asking for another chance, demanding an opportunity to revise their bid." It was a classic example of the win-at-all-costs

West Coast approach versus the more polished, mannerly East Coast mentality. Apollo and Computervision figured they had a deal; Computervision staff members tried to shoo Khosla and McNealy out of the lobby. Nothing doing. Finally, a Computervision vice president cut a deal with Khosla and McNealy: Get out of the lobby and Computervision President James Barret will call you at the local sales office.

According to *Sunburst:* "When the call came, Khosla knew it was his last opportunity to sell Sun. So he sold hard. Winning Computervision . . . would prove to industry watchers that Sun was real . . ."[3] Sun virtually gave the machines away at cost, a number of people recall, but it won a three-year, $40 million deal with Computervision that established the company as a player. Khosla sprang for a celebration cruise on the San Francisco Bay for the entire company, which consisted of 40 people. The essence of the deal was not the price Computervision paid for the workstations, Khosla emphasizes, but the fact that it would also manufacture and resell them. That meant Sun captured a portion of the gross margin on Computervision's sales with no manufacturing costs on its part. Sun had also effectively blocked its biggest rival, Apollo, from making the deal that might have established its technology as the preeminent standard for CAD/CAM.

Todd Basche, who would later join Sun as a director of desktop systems, was an engineer at Apollo when the Computervision deal was sealed. "I remember being in Apollo meetings where people would laugh at Sun and say, 'It's a bunch of kids at Stanford,' " he recalls. After Computervision, "they changed their tune." He adds, "Basically, Sun sold its soul to get the deal. But we didn't laugh at Sun any more." Basche believes Apollo's machines at the time were more reliable and superior to Sun's. Sun won, he says, for two reasons. First, Apollo's traditional management team was unprepared for Sun's aggressive, unruly approach, and didn't know how to react when Sun snatched the deal away. Apollo's executives could only fume that their rival hadn't played fair. Second, Sun's workstations used Unix, which was becoming a standard in the engineering world. That meant less training and enhanced collaboration with colleagues who were likely to know Unix but would have to learn a proprietary system like Apollo's. If Apollo had been willing to move to Unix, Basche suggests, "it would have been a different story."

Because sales were never huge, the Computervision deal was not a big moneymaker for Sun, but it did something much more important in opening the door for other significant contracts. A year or so later, for example, Sun bid on a contract with the National Security Agency, which had already bought Apollo workstations in the past. "I thought Sun might get 40 percent of the contract and Apollo 60 percent," recalls Gage, who handled the negotiations. "We got 100 percent." The NSA deal underscored the importance of Sun's use of a standard operating system, because federal agencies needed to exchange information and were moving to Unix as the means. Sun was well on its way to a goal no one would have believed possible even months before: overtaking Apollo. Or, as McNealy was wont to say, "*killing* Apollo." Khosla still has a company T-shirt from the time with the word *Sunburn* stamped across Apollo, as well as Digital Equipment and IBM.

■ TROUBLE AT THE TOP

Sun soon learned that for every silver lining like the Computervision deal, there was often a cloud. In this case it was a major thundercloud: a raging dispute between Khosla and Sun's new president, Owen Brown, that was exacerbated by the twists and turns of the Computervision negotiations. The board of directors of Sun, which now included four investors, Sackman, Broyles, John Doerr from Kleiner Perkins, and David Marquardt from Technology Venture Investors (TVI), wanted more experience at the company. In early 1983, Khosla and Broyles flew to Massachusetts to recruit Brown from Digital, where he had nine years of experience as a sales manager. He also had an engineering degree and had served a stint in the Navy, where he was still on reserve duty. Brown, who graduated from Auburn University in 1964, was 42 years old, a decade and a half older than the Sun founders. On paper his credentials looked like a perfect fit with what Sun needed, and Khosla lobbied hard to bring Brown on as president, over some objections from the board. But soon, a rift opened between Khosla and Brown.

"The power struggle with Vinod [Khosla] just got worse and worse," recalls Brown, who now heads his own management consulting firm in Silicon Valley. "Vinod was CEO and I was president. I was going to focus outwardly and he was going to focus inwardly. But Vinod could never just focus inwardly, so there was a constant struggle." In a small company, it was hard to hide that constant struggle. Khosla says another point of tension was that Brown "wasn't particularly action-oriented and not very inclusive of Scott in the decision-making."

To top it off, Brown was away from Sun, on a two-week duty in Norfolk, Virginia, for the Naval Reserve, when the Computervision deal seemed ready to go Apollo's way. Khosla blew his stack, pinning the blame on Brown for what could have been a near-death blow to the young company. Brown says he was involved with the Computervision negotiations and helped cement the deal. "It just so happened that [the two weeks] was when we got word that Computervision had chosen Apollo," he says. Regardless, Brown had violated the Sun ethic, which was that the company came first. Sun has always demanded an intense loyalty and a willingness to do whatever it took to make the company successful. Not everyone wants to work in an atmosphere so prone to overload and burnout, and that was the conclusion Brown drew himself.

Not long after the Computervision deal, Brown went to Honolulu to serve another week of reserve duty. One day when he called Sun to check his messages, he had one from Lacroute, who broke the bad news. Khosla and McNealy had gone to the board and insisted that Brown had to go, or they would leave. "I had made no secret of the fact that Vinod and I were having difficulties," says Brown. It was obvious that the board had to act. "I could have put up a big fight over this and taken a lot of people down, but I decided to resign," he says, leaving Sun in February 1984.

■ GIANT STEPS FOR A COMPANY

Brown was gone, but his legacy remained. From Digital, he had helped to recruit other senior executives for Sun, like Bernie Lacroute as executive vice president and Carol Bartz as vice president of marketing. Meanwhile, Khosla's own credibility was severely damaged in the prolonged power struggle. The board, unwilling to cede all the executive authority to the CEO, elevated McNealy to president. The exacting Khosla, who had the drive and vision that had brought Sun this far, would be offset by the more personable McNealy. The two were friends, former classmates, and even roommates—with McNealy sharing a townhouse with Khosla and his wife. As Sun entered its third year, the power-sharing arrangement seemed like an ideal solution.

In spite of the technical glitches with the Sun-2 and the personality issues with Brown and Khosla, Sun in early 1984 could look back on its first two years with a sense of solid achievement. It was closing in on $39 million in sales in only its second fiscal year of operation. It had won over Computervision, opening the door to a number of other big deals. Its success had forced the rest of the minicomputer/workstation industry, which at the time was concentrated in the Massachusetts area, to take these kids from California seriously.

More than that, Sun had a strategy that would take it a lot further than anyone ever thought it would go. When

Carl Swirsding joined in 1983 to handle creative services, he interviewed with Khosla, who, characteristically, took him to a hot dog place for lunch. "We sat outside and I asked him, 'How big do you think this company is going to be?' " Swirsding recalls. Khosla replied with total conviction: "We'll be $100 million in a few years." This convinced Swirsding that the company had a future, and he signed on. (What Sun actually reached in five years was $537 million.) "I had a sense that these guys had a vision of where they were headed, a perspective of what they would add and how it was unique," says Swirsding.

Sun's business strategy, developed informally and piecemeal and, in some cases, out of sheer necessity, turned out to be right on. First, it put a computer on every user's desk. This gave engineers a freedom they had seldom experienced. Rather than standing in line to use a centrally located minicomputer or mainframe, they could sit at their desk and fiddle with whatever they were designing, and the workstation would immediately show them the new iteration. Apollo invented the workstation, but Sun improved on it by giving engineers a universal operating system that they loved and a hardware design that could be easily reconfigured to meet a fast-moving market. Second, it gave each user a large monitor with a graphical user interface (GUI). Although Apple would make the interface a major selling point in the PC world, computers of the time, particularly those for professionals, relied on long lines of code typed into the machine. Sun's GUI was radical in simplifying the user's interaction with the computer. Third, Sun networked every computer, allowing users to collaborate from their own workspaces. Fourth, it used industry standard parts to build the machine, undercutting Apollo's pricing by half while enabling rapid evolution of the product. Fifth, it pinpointed where it could truly add value—for example, in tuning Berkeley Unix to a higher level.

Finally, Sun would do anything to win. With Computervision, it gave the larger company manufacturing rights to products that would be developed jointly. This was rare

in the early 1980s, when the monolithic, vertically integrated model of IBM and Digital was the norm. From its
infancy, Sun was a disruptive force that would break any
rules it had to to succeed. This kept competitors and allies
alike off-guard, while it gave employees a clear sense of
where Sun stood in comparison with the competition.
"Sun did the big things right," sums up Bechtolsheim. "We
had the right business model—the open system approach
and open attitude toward our customers. Once you get that
right, you can afford mistakes." Fortunately for Sun, the
company had gotten two big things right—its business
model and its new president, because there was more turmoil lurking around the corner.

Chapter

In the Driver's Seat

As 1984 progressed, people within Sun were becoming painfully aware that the company was outgrowing Vinod Khosla's skills as a CEO. It came down to his inability to deal with the primary capital of any knowledge-based company: people. Khosla was a visionary who didn't understand the down-to-earth reality of trusting employees to do their jobs. This was apparent in the 10-month power struggle with Owen Brown. Although he was forced to leave, there were those inside Sun who sympathized with his laid-back, kinder, gentler approach to management. With Khosla, Brown "always had this 28-year-old guy looking over his shoulder," recalls Jonathan Lancaster, who worked in product support. Adds cofounder Andy Bechtolsheim: "Vinod deserves the credit for getting the company together and driving the initial funding, but his bluntness and outspoken criticism weren't appreciated as the company grew. His style matched better to the early stage of the company."

McNealy, who had taken over as president after Brown's departure, was probably in the toughest situation. After all, Khosla had recruited him to Sun in the first place and the two were close friends. Now, because of his personal skills and his ability to relate to other employees, McNealy was emerging as the leader at Sun. It was McNealy, not Khosla, who got up at the Friday afternoon beer busts and gave the energizing pep talks that had everyone mesmerized. "Scott stood on a chair and told us everything that was going on, which company we were talking with, what deals we were closing," recalls Carl Swirsding, who ran creative services at Sun from 1983 to 1990. "Everyone would cheer. It was a family atmosphere." McNealy's enthusiasm kept employees motivated, focused on what the company was trying to accomplish, while Khosla's meddling frustrated his coworkers. He was so detail-oriented that he worried whether people were using too many pencils. At the first annual Sun party, employees presented him with an elaborately wrapped gift— which turned out to be a sharp pencil.

As the complaints about Khosla mounted, the four external board members—Bob Sackman, Doug Broyles, John Doerr, and David Marquardt—realized they had to take action. They queried other executives, who agreed that Khosla had to go. At one meeting, Bill Joy told them, "Just do it, lance the boil." Even McNealy, reluctantly, was coming to that conclusion, although he never put himself forward for the CEO job. Recalls Marquardt: "Scott was always incredibly loyal and supportive of Vinod." But with Khosla bypassing managers and going down to the production line to suggest changes, the company was becoming more like a dysfunctional family. After siding with Khosla during the battle with Brown, McNealy now realized that the situation was getting worse, not better.

■ THE INTERIM CEO

Compounding the dilemma over Khosla was an ongoing delicate negotiation with Eastman Kodak Company, who was prepared to spend $20 million for a 7 percent stake in

Sun and a seat on the board. Kodak wouldn't be happy pouring that kind of money into a company whose leadership was in question. Even though Sun financially continued to grow and gain new customers, internal strife was likely to scare off the conservative East Coast company. Kodak did put its investment on hold when the board informed it of Khosla's impending departure, but came in when it learned McNealy would be named CEO. "We were closing financing with Kodak, and they really liked Scott," Bechtolsheim recalls. "It became clear we could only have one guy running this company and it came down to Scott."

A bitter Khosla was persuaded to leave in the fall of 1984, although he remained on the board for several more years. Even though Khosla walked away with founder's stock worth several million dollars, "with Vinod, money was secondary," Broyles notes. "He's always viewed leaving Sun as a personal failure." But Khosla's heavy-handed tactics had not endeared him to his fellow managers nor to employees. Several Sun old-timers tell the story of the companywide meeting called to inform everyone that Khosla was stepping down. Instead of the expected barrage of questions, only one intrepid engineer raised his hand. "What," he asked, "would happen to Vinod's stock?"

Khosla recalls that his most serious disagreement was with board member John Doerr. "We just couldn't agree on issues like how to run the company, who to hire." Khosla hastens to add that "none of this was personal." In fact, six months later, he joined Doerr at Kleiner Perkins. The passage of time has softened Khosla's perspective on his removal. "I was terrible in dealing with people," he now admits. "In retrospect that's one thing I would change." Khosla liked interacting with and rewarding brilliant, "best-of-breed" people like Bill Joy or Andy Bechtolsheim. With everyone else, "I was just very very impatient," he says. He had no tolerance for the "average person." Fixed on driving Sun to success, he didn't consider employees' feelings at all. McNealy, by contrast, had some of the sensitivity that Khosla lacked. "Scott was very much the glue person, holding things together," says Khosla. "He was more pragmatic, not trying to optimize to the nth degree, while I never stop optimizing."

McNealy got the title of interim CEO. To forestall panic and keep Kodak hooked, board members knew they had to name someone to the top post right away—and McNealy was the only choice. But several board members wanted to recruit a more experienced CEO to lead Sun now that it was poised on the threshold of dynamic growth. "Firing Vinod was the biggest decision for the company in propelling it forward," says Broyles. "But we were polarized. We knew we needed to search for a new CEO." Broyles and Marquardt backed McNealy as a permanent replacement, but the rest of the board didn't agree with them. McNealy's youthfulness worked against him, as did his cocky, insouciant attitude. Meanwhile, out of respect for Khosla, McNealy didn't want to campaign for the job, although he did move out of the townhouse he had been sharing with his friend. That was because both of them needed more space, Khosla says, but they remained neighbors and friends.

■ THE PERMANENT CEO

The board began interviewing candidates for the position of permanent CEO, and settled on Paul Ely, a veteran Hewlett-Packard executive who had the large-company experience that Doerr, in particular, was seeking. Ely "had the look and feel and resume that the board felt was needed to make Sun into a billion-dollar company," Broyles recalls. But Ely, in his mid-forties, was accustomed to a hefty compensation package. And there were concerns about the culture shock, both for him and Sun. "A lot of his strategy came from the minicomputer world. It seemed like oil and water," says Marquardt. "And he wanted a huge amount of stock and salary." Broyles remembers offering Ely in the range of $250,000, along with very generous stock options. By contrast, no one else at Sun was making more than $100,000. "We asked Paul to tell us the minimum he needed; he said he'd need $400,000 just to keep the lights on. That turned the tide. Even Doerr said that's too far from everyone else," Broyles says.

By the time the deal with Ely crumbled in early 1985, McNealy was convinced he could handle the job himself. He had gotten over the blow of seeing Khosla forced out. Says Broyles: "To Scott, Vinod was his friend and they'd started Sun together. At first I think he felt that if he took the job, he would be behind Vinod's ouster." With no other candidate in sight, Broyles and Marquardt pushed to make McNealy the permanent CEO, and the rest of the board went along—but, not without apprehension. "Scott looked young and behaved young," recalls Broyles. "Every time he opened his mouth, people wondered. They would interpret his statements as really arrogant." He remembers an investment banker quizzing McNealy: "When are you going to learn not to run your mouth off when you're talking to someone who buys ink by the barrel?" That was after McNealy told a local newspaper that Sun couldn't afford to make charitable contributions because it was a small, undercapitalized company with large competitors "That got picked up everywhere," Broyles says. "Scott was portrayed as this insensitive CEO."

McNealy eventually overcame these obstacles. "I had my misgivings about Scott," says Marquardt, "but he really stepped up to the plate. The company was growing by leaps and bounds and Scott was growing even faster. He did an incredible job of getting sales focused and organized." The fun-loving college jock proved to have formidable organizational and motivational abilities. No one knew it at the time, but Sun had found its once and future leader, the man who has led it to this day, whose quirky personality is at the root of the company's culture and whose contrarian vision formed the basis of its success.

■ WHO'S SCOTT MCNEALY?

Among the four founders of Sun, Khosla was the original driving force, while Joy and Bechtolsheim were the technology geniuses. McNealy was, on the surface at least, the technology novice. He had some skills in running a manufacturing operation, but knew little about technology. It wasn't even his first choice for a career; he had stumbled into it. Though he had degrees from a couple of prestigious universities, Harvard (economics) and Stanford (M.B.A.), his academic record was undistinguished. During his college years—he entered Harvard in 1972 and Stanford in 1978. McNealy didn't take school very seriously, as he himself admits.

But, colleagues and coworkers underestimated McNealy. It's a common mistake, one that's abetted by McNealy himself. Now in his forties, the Sun CEO still cultivates the "jock" image, aided by his compact build, close-cropped brown hair, and prominent teeth that are the target of every caricaturist who portrays him. McNealy is, in fact, a skilled athlete who was captain of the golf team during his Harvard days and came within a swing of qualifying for the 1976 NCAA championship. Today, he plays for five amateur hockey teams in Silicon Valley and has the best golf handicap, 3.2, among 110 chief executives whose handicaps were listed by *Golf Digest* in its June 1998 issue.[1] In his public speeches, McNealy takes pains to project an everyman facade, dressing typically in baggy slacks and a sports coat, with his shirt open at the top and tieless. He paces on stage and delivers his lines in an offhand, almost mumbling manner.

McNealy's attention span is short—he makes up his mind quickly whether you're worth his time and dismisses you if you're not. He flits from subject to subject and resists being pinned down, preferring the all-encompassing, grandiose statement to the specifics, which he leaves to others. But there is much more to McNealy than meets the eye. He is a complex leader who can be charming, stubborn, inspiring, unpredictable, street-smart, and almost religiously devoted to a cause. His employees are fervently loyal, even as they shake their heads at his antics. "That's just Scott being Scott," is a frequent refrain inside Sun. McNealy was not the original leader nor visionary. He grew into those roles, as the company needed him to. To understand Sun today means understanding McNealy, as much as is possible with a man who zealously guards his private life and deliberately projects a somewhat misleading public image.

➤ Growing Up in the Rust Belt

McNealy was born on November 13, 1954, in Columbus, Indiana, the second oldest of four children—three boys and a girl—of Raymond William and Marmalee McNealy. The senior McNealy was a rising white-collar manager at American Motors who eventually became vice chairman of the auto manufacturer. The family moved around the Midwest during Scott's boyhood, settling in the Detroit area when he was in fifth grade. Scott was always interested in what his father did, friends and family members recount. As a boy, he would grab his dad's briefcase at night and look through the material inside. On Saturdays, he sometimes accompanied his father to the American Motors' plant. By the time he was a teenager, Scott was discussing American Motors' strategy with his father and joining him in golf foursomes with such industry notables as Lee Iacocca. At Sun, the memory of watching American Motors get buffeted by Japanese competition and lose market share instilled in McNealy a determination not to let that happen at his own company.

After the family moved to upscale Bloomfield Hills, Michigan, Scott attended a prestigious prep school, Cranbrook, where his unassuming manner, competitive spirit, and athletic abilities soon made him popular. Although he was never known for academic prowess, he achieved reasonably good grades without a lot of studying and scored an 800, the highest possible, on his SAT math test. In short, he excelled when he wanted to excel. "Our parents provided us with a very competitive environment," says Barry McNealy, Scott's younger brother by 18 months and a Sun global account manager in Detroit. "Our days were laced with sports. In the summers we raced sailboats, played tennis and golf, swam on teams, and played Little League baseball." The senior McNealy had attended Harvard, and urged his sons to go there as well. "Our parents expected that we would be contributors to the world," says Barry.

He sees elements of both parents in Scott. "My dad was never a politician. He was straightforward, never stepped sideways or backways," he says. Today, when Scott lists his pet peeves, one of them is that "he doesn't like to get in a dialogue when he asks a yes or no question." When Scott was out of college for about one year, the senior McNealy was ousted as a result of what Barry describes as a "political situation," no doubt fueling Scott's pronounced dislike of internal politics. Four years later, the McNealys got divorced, and Scott later moved Marmalee out to California, where she lives near him in Portola Valley, California. Marmalee is known for her outspoken, at times embarrassing, candor. "My mother is one of the most amazing people in the world," says Barry. "Scott has been an unbelievable son to her. They have a very special relationship." Marmalee accompanies Scott to many company functions, including his public appearances. "When he was working 80 hours a week and had no time yet for a wife, she was always a stable beacon," says Barry. "Eighty percent of the company has met my mother."

Before he could get into Stanford, McNealy worked as a foreman at a Rockwell International plant in Centralia, Illinois. Then, after Stanford, he was a trainee at FMC Corporation, which was building military vehicles in Silicon

Valley. From FMC, McNealy went to Onyx, and from there to Sun. "I love the factory. That's what business is all about. Making things," he told *Fortune* magazine in its October 13, 1997, cover story.[2] Similarly, he told the *New Yorker* magazine in a March 16, 1998, article, "My whole life, I just wanted to be a chief operating officer, and then someday run my own little forty-person tool-and-die shop."[3]

This attitude is a bit of McNealy myth making: *I'm just a guy who likes to work with his hands.* He also told the *New Yorker* that "I never wanted to be CEO," after watching the sacrifices his father and other auto executives, like Iacocca and Roger Smith, had made.[4] But McNealy has been an almost fanatically obsessed chief executive for a decade and a half, demanding long hours from himself, his executive staff, and employees. He loves being the CEO of Sun Microsystems; his official bio quotes him as saying he has "the best 24-hour-a-day job in the industry." In social situations, he loses interest in people who don't want to talk about Sun. Says Carol Bartz, herself a CEO and former Sun marketing executive: "If he wants to be, Scott can be charming, but most of the time he doesn't want to be. If you just want to drop him into the middle of people who don't know Sun and want to talk about the weather, he doesn't have the patience for that." McNealy also plays down his privileged, upper-class background, preferring to emphasize his links with the common man. Even though he owes a lot to his background, including his education and his early exposure to the management ethic, very few people with those advantages go on to found a great company.

➤ Nice Guy, Tough Guy

McNealy comes off as the quintessential, "aw shucks" kind of guy portrayed by Jimmy Stewart or Gary Cooper in the movies. He dresses informally; prefers beer to hard liquor; loves to eat at McDonald's; drives American-built cars; and co-owns a dog, Network, a large, muscular, black-tan-and-white Greater Swiss Mountain Dog that often appears in Sun's corporate ads. McNealy got married relatively late in life, in 1994, at the age of 39. "He was smart enough to understand that for the first dozen years of the company he was married to it and could not put the time into his family," says Barry. By all accounts, McNealy is devoted to his wife, Susan, and two young sons, Maverick and Dakota, and carefully shields them from the limelight. The McNealys live in the same house in Portola Valley, a wealthy, sylvan enclave of Silicon Valley, that Scott bought when he was a bachelor. "It's on a hillside with a nice view, but it's not some big mansion," says Doug Burgum, a friend of McNealy's since their Stanford days and now CEO of Great Plains Software in Fargo, North Dakota. "There's a guest room where he has his friends stay. Scott always remembers his friends."

One example of that is McNealy's golf outings, to which he invites his buddies down to Monterey to play. The first one was after Sun went public in 1986. About three dozen people attended, Burgum remembers. "Scott has a wonderful way of bringing together people from different backgrounds, junior high buddies and people from college and Sun executives. He probably has more good friends than anybody in his position." The golf outing "was run like a tournament," says Burgum. "Scott paid for everything. He was incredibly generous—plane tickets, picking you up at the airport. We all felt like celebrities. The golf tournaments are Scott's way of staying in touch," Burgum says. "Scott can meet with a head of state and also hang out with hockey players who may not know he's running a Fortune 500 company. There's nothing fake about him. He makes other people feel comfortable." That is, when he chooses to. McNealy's friendliness is self-limiting. He's most personable in settings in which he's with people like himself—competitive, hard-driving men who understand the language of sports and of business. A longtime Sun engineer says McNealy once told him, "The way to get promoted more quickly at Sun is to learn golf."

McNealy's friendliness masks a ruthless determination and sharp-edged business acuity. "He has the courage of his convictions, and is very quick to act on them," says Jon Feiber, a venture capitalist who was a Sun manager from 1983 to 1991. McNealy is willing to buck consensus views, even those of his own executive team, in favor of his own ideas. "He can be headstrong," says Feiber. "He's an awesome leader, but he may not be the best manager." Once McNealy makes up his mind, "he doesn't brook argument." ("Agree and commit, disagree and commit, or get out of the way," is one of those McNealy statements that has proliferated throughout Sun.) McNealy "disarms you with his low-key style," says Curt Wozniak, another friend from Stanford and a former Sun executive. "He has an incredible ability to motivate people to basically kill themselves because they're on a mission. He convinces you that you need to work 80 hours a week."

McNealy's combativeness and aggressiveness can be traced to his childhood, but those qualities have also been honed during many bruising battles with Sun competitors. "Sun has always had to fight hard to win," says Feiber. "It has succeeded in many respects because of Scott's force of will." The CEO lives and breathes Sun. The company's identity today is "completely intermixed with Scott," according to Feiber, and vice versa. "It's Sun first, McNealy second. He's not interested in Scott McNealy, rock star. He's interested in Sun, world beater." Feiber adds, "His personal life is private because it's none of your business, let's talk about Sun. What Scott wants to talk about is Sun, not Scott."

Although McNealy initially lacked the technical background of many high-tech CEOs, he is a quick study who has mastered the intricacies of business and technology. "Scott sees where the company is going to be years before anybody else does," says brother Barry. He adds, "When I came on board in 1995, HP was the darling of the world. Everybody in the field was 100 percent focused on HP. Scott never even mentioned them. He was saying it was Microsoft. Today we realize that." Wozniak adds that McNealy soaks up technical information and then reformulates it in a way that people can understand. "He's underrated from a technical perspective," Wozniak maintains. "Scott is able to take technology and synthesize it."

➤ King of the Sound Bite

McNealy is one of the better speakers among technology CEOs, although some would say that's faint praise. Technological brilliance doesn't necessarily translate into ability to communicate. McNealy, however, is able to describe technology in colorful, memorable, albeit simplistic phrases. It's not something that came naturally. "I knew Scott when he didn't know how to do one-liners," recalls Bartz. "He was a really bad interview in the old days. We worked on how to present himself." In a June 22, 1992, interview with *Computerworld,* McNealy recalled that he had to give his first public speech to a Sun user group two days after he took over as president of the company in 1984.[5] "I was petrified," he says. Like the other speakers who had filled the previous three hours, McNealy had prepared a slide show. "When I told them I had about 35 slides to talk them through, you could hear this audible groan." So he started clicking through the slides at lightning speed. "They loved it. They gave me a standing ovation," he says. "I accidentally learned a big, big lesson that day—that putting yourself in your audience's shoes is so important. They are coming here to listen to me, so I'm going to entertain them and tell jokes and be controversial."

If you watch a lot of them, McNealy's speeches begin to sound formulaic, but then so does Jerry Seinfeld's act. McNealy typically opens a speech with a "top ten" list in which he lampoons some obvious target. Lately, it has been Microsoft, but he has hit other competitors as well. He's called multinational Hewlett-Packard "the best printer company in the world," referred to a consortium of competitors as "big hat, no cattle," and dismissed IBM's product strategy as "security through obscurity." (This was before Sun and IBM became major allies.) In an April 17, 1998, address to San Francisco's Commonwealth Club, McNealy was in good form, promising to "cover subjects superficially but as controversially as possible." His list was "the top ten signs that you could be a monopolist," an obvious reference to Microsoft and Bill Gates, although he never mentioned their names. Some samples from the list: "Your house is bigger than the White House; Janet Reno has you on speed dial; Your idea of competition is Word 6.0 versus Word 6.1; You become a target for cream pies." McNealy then segued into his favorite topic, the lack of choice with Microsoft and how Sun would solve that by offering an alternative to the "fat hairball" that is Windows.

As can be seen from this example, subtlety, discretion, and tact are not McNealy's priorities. His speeches are in a style that approaches stream-of-consciousness, free-flowing from one topic to the next as it interests him. He often touches on the stupidity of government regulations on encryption, which prevent Sun from exporting some of its products; the need to allow more immigrants into the United States to fill the technology industry's workforce needs; and, of course, the desirability of enforcing antitrust laws. But all his public relations people admit there is no such thing as a scripted McNealy performance; he marches to his own inner voice.

Perhaps no one knows his speaking style better than Jeremy Barnish, director of corporate public relations for Sun and executive speechwriter for the last four years. A British immigrant, Barnish recalls the first thing McNealy ever said to him: "English and humor is an oxymoron. You're never going to write anything funny." Barnish has since proven McNealy wrong, but working with the CEO is definitely a collaborative process. To prepare for a speech, he and McNealy talk for 15 to 30 minutes. About two-thirds of the conversation is what jokes to tell. "Scott will take from 10 to 90 percent of my material," says Barnish. "I put the points on index cards." McNealy, who has a habit of arriving at a speech just on time, decides which points he'll use when he walks into the room and sizes up the audience. Barnish is forbidden to use the word *visionary* to describe McNealy. "Scott says, 'I'm just a guy telling them how to take advantage of what they've got already. It's like a politician with a stump speech.'"

➤ Going All Out for Sun

McNealy is willing to go to just about any lengths, short of exposing his family or his private life to public view, to make the case for Sun. At one event, he dropped down from the ceiling dressed as Batman. In another event, he did a takeoff on a Penn & Teller trick in which a person spits a bullet out of his mouth with a name on it. The next night, McNealy sprang out of Sun's largest server onto the stage. The bullet in his mouth read, "Bill Gates." His appearance at the Consumer Electronics Show at Las Vegas in January 1998 was one of his staff's favorites. After an introduction, the CEO skated through the crowd and onto the stage carrying a hockey stick. "Whoa, there's no brakes on these things," he says, careening around the stage. "We would have had the Starlight Express folks here [as Microsoft did], but I'm too cheap to spend money on them. So you've got me rolling around out here," he joked, to appreciative laughter.

Wearing gray pants and a dark blue sports jacket over a white shirt, McNealy gave the first part of his speech while standing, and at times rolling around, on his skates. "Why am I here? Sun technology is actually touching people everywhere and anywhere. When you think of computers, people think of something with a screen where you need a teen-ager to work it." He pulled out a StarTAC cellular phone from Motorola. "I'm going to boot my telephone," he said, and turned it on. Making one of his favorite points about how complicated the personal computer is, McNealy added, "When you turn the key in a car, you turn on 150 microprocessors, but you don't need to look at the manual to do it. We think computing ought to be some-thing you don't even know you do."

McNealy disagrees with the vision of computing of-fered by people like Compaq CEO Eckhard Pfeiffer, who sees a centralized computer in the home running func-tions from turning on the lights to playing on-demand movies on TV. "It doesn't strike me as a usable environ-ment," McNealy said. He suggested that parents can pun-ish a child who doesn't eat his lima beans by forcing him to troubleshoot this central computer for a week. "He'll in-hale his lima beans." McNealy then outlined his vision (only of course he didn't use that word) of the digital home, with specific-purpose appliances enabled by Sun's easy-to-use Java technology. "Java can be embedded in every device out there," he said, from smart cards to cell phones to TV settop boxes to washing machines.

This is vintage McNealy on several fronts: it feels spon-taneous; it's down-home and even slightly hokey; there's lit-tle techno-babble in it, yet Sun's view of computing is clearly laid out; and it appeals to the intended audience of consumer electronics representatives. "People are so tired of seeing boring speakers," McNealy told me in our single brief conversation. "I spent my entire educational life sit-ting in the audience watching the professors bore us to death. It is physically painful for me to watch somebody who's boring. I try to do my part to be as interesting as pos-sible while still delivering messages about Sun's value proposition."

■ MCNEALY VERSUS GATES

Like many leaders, McNealy is extremely effective when he's portraying Sun as the beleaguered, courageous under-dog taking on a powerful, bullying, identifiable opponent. This worked well in Sun's early years when the company was a small, feisty upstart. In a way, it was fortunate for

McNealy that the business objectives of Sun and Microsoft began to converge, because then he could target the Redmond, Washington, giant as the new enemy. And, what an enemy! Even though the annual sales figures of Sun and Microsoft are roughly comparable: $10.5 billion versus $16.7 billion, Microsoft's market capitalization of $435 billion smashes Sun's punier $43 billion.* The difference is the advantage of owning a monopoly, McNealy would say. Indeed, in response to a question posed at his Commonwealth Club speech, McNealy confesses that if he were running Microsoft, "I probably wouldn't do anything differently because the CEO is hired to maximize shareholder wealth, and [Gates is] doing exactly that by leveraging his monopoly."

In going up against the wily Gates, whose serene, upscale background is eerily similar to McNealy's (a prep school followed by Harvard, then founding a company, putting off marriage and children until later), the Sun CEO is in the battle of his life, which may account for some of the excesses of his prose. One difference between the two is that McNealy is a jock, although one with brains, while Gates is the ultimate nonathletic technology geek. Gates' golf handicap, according to *Golf Digest,* is a true duffer's 23.9.[6]

Most of the industry probably agrees with the sentiments behind McNealy's Microsoft bashing, even while they wince over the way he says them. "Somebody has to stand up and yell and scream and jump up and down about Microsoft," says ex–Sun manager Crawford Beveridge. "It's a big powerful ball rolling down the hill. Everyone stands around hoping somebody else will stop it. Thank God there is somebody." But when it comes to Microsoft, "Scott's moved past business into high religion," says a longtime McNealy acquaintance. "Scott says that to move people, you have to get wild and crazy, but he's a big guy now and it doesn't wear as well." Gates has not lashed out at McNealy, although he did concede in late 1998 that Sun is one of Microsoft's biggest threats. Steve Ballmer, Microsoft's second in command, has not been so circumspect. "Sun is just

---

* As of early 1999.

a very dumb company," he told the *New Yorker*.[7] "It makes me mad at McNealy that he takes part in that kind of corporate character aspersion."

McNealy's belligerence toward Microsoft has its defenders. "If Scott blinks at all, Microsoft will eat his lunch," says Feiber. "Anything other than absolute conviction and unbelievable maniacal desire to compete with Microsoft is going to lose. You're not going to beat Bill Gates by being conciliatory or compromising." Eric Schmidt, a former Sun executive who is now CEO of Novell, agrees: "The feeling within Sun is that they have beaten everyone but Microsoft and Intel, and that's the Waterloo," he says. "As long as you're winning, you can do what Scott does, which is speak out boldly."

➤ A Study in Contradiction

When it comes to Microsoft, McNealy displays a certain schizophrenia. His tactical shrewdness would suggest compromise, but that bumps up against his unyielding belief that the Redmond giant is the evil empire which must be defeated at all costs. Nowhere is this contradiction more evident than in his politics. McNealy is an acknowledged libertarian, and Sun has reportedly been a financial backer of the Cato Institute, the libertarian think tank in Washington. And yet, the Cato Institute issued a lengthy analysis attacking the government's antitrust lawsuit against Microsoft, while McNealy strongly supports it, maintaining that government intervention is the only way to combat a monopoly. "I'm not holding my breath waiting for Sun Microsystems to renew its support," Cato President Ed Crane told the *Wall Street Journal* in a June 9, 1998, article.[8] According to the same article, the Libertarian Party has called on the Justice Department to get its "bureaucratic Lilliputians" off Microsoft's back.

Libertarian economic theory holds that government intrusion will only impede the workings of the free market, lessening consumer choice and making monopolies more likely. If the free market is left to function on its own, the theory argues, monopolies won't last, because competitors will always find new ways to thwart them. Prominent Sun supporters, notably technology futurist George Gilder, have advanced similar arguments, like the view that Java could undermine the Microsoft monopoly by bypassing its dominant Windows operating system. Nonetheless, McNealy, as he did in the Senate hearing, continues to push for the government to take action against Microsoft.

Ruth Hennigar, who was general manager of the Java Products Group at Sun from 1995 to 1996, thinks McNealy's passion is misplaced. "I've yet to see anyone in the industry be as opportunistic as Bill [Gates] about directing his ship," she says. "Scott has a very successful company and he should focus on that, not on beating Bill." McNealy does recognize that. "We have never won one customer because we didn't like Microsoft," he told me. "We have only won because we have products that solve customer problems. That's the big dirty little secret. We build products that solve customer problems. How else could we have gotten to a $10 billion run rate with nary a bit of help from Microsoft or Intel?"

Other top executives have spoken out on the need for Sun to cooperate with Microsoft at least on a technology level. Under pressure from his executive team, McNealy has softened his public statements about Gates and Microsoft in recent months, but he'll never back down entirely. For one thing, it would be out of character. For another, he has anointed himself the anti-Microsoft guru and the press won't leave that alone. Although he professes to be sick of being asked about Microsoft, he has built a bonfire that can't be doused.

■ INSIDE MCNEALY'S WORLD

McNealy's public persona has taken precedence in recent years, as he's surrounded himself with capable internal managers and gone out to joust with Microsoft, but the

THE WIT AND WISDOM OF SCOTT MCNEALY

On Managing Sun:

"I want Sun to be controversial. If everyone believes in your strategy, you have zero chance of profit."

"Agree and commit, disagree and commit, or get out."

"The best decision is the right decision. The next best is the wrong decision. The worst decision is no decision."

"It's better to beg for forgiveness than ask for permission."

"Have lunch or be lunch."

"All the wood behind one arrow."

"Kick butt and have fun."

On His Competitors:

An industry consortium: "Big hat, no cattle."

IBM: "Security through obscurity."

Hewlett-Packard: "The best printer company in the world."

On Microsoft:

"Nobody should own the language of computing just like nobody should own English."

(continued)

THE WIT AND WISDOM OF SCOTT MCNEALY
(Continued)

"Probably the most dangerous and powerful industrialist of our age." (referring to Bill Gates)

"Ballmer and Butt-head." (referring to Microsoft's two top executives, Gates and Steve Ballmer)

"A giant hairball." (referring to Windows and Windows NT, Microsoft's operating systems)

"General and Motors." (referring to Microsoft and Intel)

On Computing:

"This is the computer of the future." (holding up a smart card)

"We're trying to drive universal webtone, so you just turn [the computing device] on, instead of having to look for a teen-ager somewhere to help you."

CEO remains very much the man in charge at Sun. "Scott doesn't get enough credit for being a great fiscal manager," says Bartz. "When I was there [at Sun], he was very focused on revenue per employee, keeping costs and inventory under control. He ran a very tight ship." McNealy tends to look at business the way a football coach looks at a game. "What's the game plan, what do we do in the first quarter, what contingencies do I have to put in place if something goes wrong?" He's a tactical rather than strategic thinker.

Inside the company, McNealy is the motivational cheerleader, firing up the troops with the desire to go out and kill the competition. "It's almost frightening the amount of frenzy he can get people into," says Beveridge, recalling when he witnessed a meeting between McNealy and the Sun salesforce. "Scott has the ability to get across what needs to be done. He can get carried away but he's good at that stuff. I suspect he yearns for the day when he could get back on that beer crate Friday night and talk to everyone in one room."

McNealy is no ivory-tower CEO. He gets out and interacts with customers, employees, and the media. At Sun, all of the executives make customer calls, and "Scott makes more sales calls than anyone," says brother Barry. "Scott has been at General Motors, Chrysler, and Ford." McNealy takes a red-eye flight into Detroit for a 7:00 A.M. breakfast meeting and keeps going all the way through dinner, then hops back on a plane, goes to the next city and repeats it. "In a week-long trip he'll see 40 customers," Barry says. "The pace that he keeps would kill anybody." McNealy even left the Senate hearing early to attend a customer meeting. Every salesperson is energized by making a call with the CEO. "What they don't understand is that he's got 40 of those that week and 600 all year," says Barry. McNealy has confided to his brother that the hardest thing about his job is that he always has to be in an up mood. "As the CEO, if they see you're down or you're overly tired, it's going to come across that the company's not doing well," says Barry. "He always has to be exuberant, positive, upbeat."

McNealy is older and wiser since he took over Sun at age 29 in 1984. He can still be cocky, competitive, brash, and impatient, but he's learned to pace himself and set a few limits. McNealy has learned to listen and to take advice from people he trusts, even to the point of bringing in a consultant in the mid-1990s to help him polish his leadership style. Yet McNealy's crowning achievement will always be what he's built at Sun—often in defiance of conventional wisdom. Novell CEO Eric Schmidt sums up by saying, "Scott's performance has been extraordinary. I find myself copying him more and more. He's inside my head. I ask myself, 'What would Scott do in this situation?' Having worked with him is much better than going to business school."

Chapter

3

Tooting Its Own Horn

Now that he was unquestionably the man in charge, in 1985 Scott McNealy could get down to business. Fortunately, as he was still a very young, very untried CEO, he had a lot of help from his executive team. To his credit, McNealy has never been afraid to surround himself with talented people, and in this period Bernie Lacroute, initially brought in to head engineering, became a strong second in command. Also on the team were Carol Bartz and Eric Schmidt, both of whom would later became CEOs of their own companies. From Apple Computer, Sun recruited Joe Graziano as its chief financial officer. On the technology side, Sun had Bill Joy, Andy Bechtolsheim, John Gage, and other brilliant engineers who joined the company from the most prestigious institutions of the day, like the universities and Xerox Corporation's famed Palo Alto Research Center (Xerox PARC).

Sun's success in the mid-1980s stemmed from technological advances coupled with innovative marketing and business tactics. It takes both of those to create a true powerhouse in the technology industry. If you lose sight of one or the other, you can be eaten alive. Apple produced the key breakthroughs that made the PC industry possible, but when it fumbled on execution, Microsoft swept by it. Because it has also styled itself as a Microsoft alternative, Sun is often compared with Apple. But one thing Sun has that Apple didn't is consistent leadership.

Under McNealy, Sun took a number of steps that showed how it was maturing beyond the start-up phase. It enlarged its network of independent software vendors (ISVs), who wrote applications that ran on Sun workstations, and expanded its market into such fields as automobile manufacturing and financial trading. But the most important step was developing a so-called standard that everyone in the industry would follow. "Standard" means that a critical mass of people in the industry, like ISVs and manufacturers, have agreed upon a particular set of software or hardware specifications. For example, when an ISV creates an application for Windows, it will work on every PC loaded with that operating system. The company that owns a technology standard assumes a much more influential role and can compel others to follow its lead. Up until this point, two-year-old Sun was dependent on standards developed by others, but now it would move to take more control of its destiny.

■ VERTICAL FOCUSING

Sun has always been an engineering-centric company whose products were considered the epitome of its value added. Even though McNealy himself was not a technologist, he continued to devote a tremendous amount of attention to products. But as a relatively small company whose competitors could throw more bodies into any particular deal, Sun learned the value of leveraging its true strengths by reaching out to partners, particularly as it sought to expand beyond its original market niche. This was evident in two related areas in which Sun, in the mid-1980s, enlisted third-party support: recruitment of independent software developers and entrance into new markets, such as financial services and automobile manufacturing.

The Sun workstation consisted of Bechtolsheim's hardware design and Joy's operating system, a refinement of Berkeley Unix called the SunOS. Together, these were considered the Sun platform; however, the platform was not of much use by itself. To be attractive to potential users, Sun needed applications. At first, it was selling engineering workstations to software developers who would write their own applications. As the company expanded into other markets, such as CAD/CAM or electronic design automation (EDA), it needed third-party software developers to write applications for these classes of end users. "It's the application that matters, because it positions Sun as a viable and appealing solution in different industry segments," noted Carol Broadbent, who was Sun's director of public relations from 1986 to 1990. But, getting third-party software developers to write for a platform can be something of a catch-22. Independent software vendors like volume platforms, so to get applications, you have to be big. But, to get big, you have to have applications.

In 1985, Sun started an aggressive marketing effort aimed at ISVs called Catalyst. Sun partnered with ISVs to develop programs for the markets it was targeting. For example, Sun would allow ISVs, which are generally small and cash-strapped companies, to share its booths at major trade shows. In exchange, the ISVs would demonstrate their programs on Sun workstations for visitors to the booths. Typically, ISVs would port their software to Sun from another platform—in other words, ISVs wrote the original program for someone else, but then reconfigured it so it would work on Sun's operating system. In some of these cases, Sun would advance porting fees to developers, who would repay Sun as they sold software to end users. Sun also would loan workstations to ISVs or offer developer discounts, all with the intent of building up its store of third-party applications. Catalyst eventually added a catalog of developers that became a potent tool for attracting ISVs in and of itself. If you were going to sell software into certain markets, you wanted to be listed in Catalyst. "There was a real FUD [fear, uncertainty, and doubt] factor to the Catalyst catalog," says Broadbent. "You had better be in there."

Meanwhile, on the sales side, Sun was proving adept at finding new markets for its workstations. Former creative services manager Carl Swirsding remembers that in the mid-1980s, financial traders on Wall Street each had a bunch of dumb terminals, linked to a mainframe, sitting on their desks to give them informational feeds, such as stock prices and various economic indicators. The Sun sales representative for the East Coast convinced the hapless corporate information manager who had to support all those that it could be done on one networked workstation per user. Instead of having to put 8 or 10 monitors on a trader's desk, "you put in a simple Ethernet cable and a Sun workstation, and everybody gets all the feeds [of information] simultaneously. You can put each feed in a window on the workstation," says Swirsding.

The hotshot stock and bond traders immediately saw the competitive advantage of using Sun workstations to get all the information in one place. Bear Stearns and Morgan Stanley were among the first to buy the machines; other Wall Street firms quickly followed. "Financial trader workstations were a sexy market segment that hadn't been targeted yet by anyone," recalls Broadbent. Sun swooped in and became the dominant vendor, and the segment remains a stronghold to this day. Sun's prowess in the financial trading market showed that "workstations can go mainstream. They're not just for engineers," she says. "Financial services illustrated where Sun was going and how Unix could compete."

Automobile manufacturing was another market dominated by separate, proprietary systems. This time it was the customers themselves, notably General Motors, who insisted that manufacturing automation computers from different vendors had to be able to work together. In late

1985, Sun jumped on board enthusiastically, appearing at the first AutoFact (for automated factory) trade show with networked workstations that could communicate with competitors' machines. Sun's sales and engineering team was elated when GM's network managers criticized larger vendors like IBM, Digital, and Hewlett-Packard for failing to offer the same advantage. Like financial trading, automobile manufacturing was another niche that the ambitious Sun was able to penetrate, because it was willing to break down existing barriers that its competitors would not breach.

■ SUN SETS THE STANDARD

The first standard to come out of Sun was the result of a technological triumph, followed by a marketing coup. In late 1984, a team of Sun engineers developed the Network File System (NFS), which allowed computers to share files with one another via a central network, rather than undertake the laborious process of copying files from one machine to the next. Bob Lyon, employee number 148 at Sun, headed the engineering team that came up with NFS. In January 1985, Sun showcased its new technology at the Uniforum trade show in Dallas. "We had it running on a Sun machine and several flavors of minicomputers," Lyon recalls. "Back then, what were networks good for? Sharing information, but all my information is in a file. So there was a huge need for a distributed file system." Apollo had one, but it ran only on its proprietary Domain operating system, which competed with Unix. Of critical importance to Sun and the industry, NFS ran on computers that used different operating systems, including Unix, IBM's and Microsoft's DOS, Apple's Macintosh, and Digital's VMS.

Lyon and the engineering team suggested a new strategy for making NFS a standard, which immediately won the support of Bill Joy. With new technology, says Lyon, "if you want to own the market, you have to develop the market, which means everyone needs to run it." Rather than keeping NFS solely for its own workstations, as Apollo had done, Sun chose to widely license the source code for the program to other vendors for a relatively nominal fee. The source code is akin to an architectural blueprint that tells developers how to build their own software, in this case NFS. Having the source code allowed licensees to integrate NFS within various technologies, not just from Sun, but also IBM, Digital, or Hewlett-Packard. This technique changed the rules on software standards and paved the way for the later success of Java.

The fear about sharing source code is that you lose control of your technology because competitors can license it and embed it into their own products. Sun overcame that fear. It became a leader by providing a standard that gave customers the presumption that because Sun had created the technology, Sun's machines would run NFS better than anyone else. Sun was founded and built on the belief in supporting an open system—that is, using technology readily available to others. "The stuff that we're building had to be open and shared," says Lyon. "What we found with NFS is that it's much better to be in the driver's seat on the evolution of a standard." One business strategy that will always work is "find a vacuum and fill it," he says, as NFS did. But Sun's strategy of making its technology easily adoptable meant that others could fill the vacuum, too. Sun's business strategists dealt with this as well. According to Lyon, "Sun's ultimate business was to sell its platform. You hook the customer with your technology [standard], and sell hardware in its wake. You land the fish by selling Sun equipment because [the standard] works so well with it, even though the standard also works with other vendors."

Sun had discovered what would become a key ingredient for the future establishment of software standards: anticipating the Internet culture in which technology like browsers is distributed freely. Companies that do this intend to profit by selling the underlying platform on which the browser runs or by selling related services. One problem, though, is that the technology's creator (i.e., Sun with NFS) has an inherent conflict of interest. Advances in the standard are driven by Sun's business needs, not necessarily what is optimum for the standard. In turn, competitors become resistant to the standard because it is tied to a rival's strategy. Lyon eventually cofounded another company, Legato Systems, to exploit shared technology to a greater degree than Sun could, or would. Similar resistance would emerge with Java.

In an interesting footnote, Apollo finally came up with an answer to NFS called Network Computing System (NCS), which enabled distributed network applications. Network Computing System was never able to displace NFS, but when Apollo was later absorbed by Hewlett-Packard, many Apollo engineers joined Microsoft and "some of the NCS technology got adopted there," Lyon says. However, the success of NFS indisputably established Sun as a force to be reckoned with. Never again would rivals dismiss the company, and they would be very wary of any future attempt by Sun to promulgate another standard.

■ THE NETWORK IS THE COMPUTER

Perhaps Sun's single most important promotional icon is its famous tagline, "The Network Is The Computer," which was stimulated in part by the success of NFS. Today, many people claim credit for coming up with the tagline, which was not considered any great accomplishment back in the mid-1980s. In fact, it was ahead of its time and, as a consequence, widely misunderstood by customers and even Sun employees. Dee Cravens, who joined Sun in late 1984 as director of marketing and communications, presided over the process that came up with "The Network Is The Computer." In his hiring interview with Lacroute and McNealy, he asked, "What do you want me to focus on?" Cravens recalls. "Scott said, 'I want you to focus on positioning this company because I plan on killing Digital and IBM.'" Cravens remembers thinking, "This guy is like 29 years old with a $100 million company. He's going to try to slay IBM and Digital and wants me to position the company so he can do that? But, what I was telling him was, 'Of course, I can do that.'"

When Cravens came on board, the tagline was "Open Systems For Open Minds." This phrase "was rapidly becoming our positioning," he says. "The concept of open systems played well with what we were trying to do. But 'for open minds' had negative connotations," he says. "Like if you don't use us, you have a closed mind. What we wanted to say was that no matter what system you're in, you could use a multitude of machines."

In early 1985, under pressure from Lacroute to figure out a better way to position Sun as a networking company, Cravens brought in a consultant, Doug Glen, to act as facilitator and called a meeting of marketing, sales, and engineering people involved in the distributed computing effort. "We had 30 people in the room and we were going through all these issues related to positioning," Cravens recalls. "One guy in the room named Jim Davis, who later went to work for Apple, was talking about the distributed computing concept (NFS) and having different computers able to communicate so the system is really transparent." Cravens replied that computers needed to be able to hand off information, freeing it from proprietary systems. At that moment, he turned to Glen and said, "Write these words on the board, 'The Network Is The Computer.'"

Of course, this being Sun, which encouraged independent thinking, there was no instant acceptance. Later that year, after thrashing over a lot of alternatives, Cravens' group presented "The Network Is The Computer" to Lacroute. "I wrote the words on the board and explained that it means the power of computing rests somewhere else and you have access through the network. Sun brings the ability to get at that information."

Lacroute cautiously bought into the new tagline, while McNealy was neutral. "There was a lot of blood in the hallways over it—there were people who loved it and people who hated it," says Cravens. "The engineering people loved it, the marketing people hated it because they said people wouldn't understand it." Cravens continued to put it in brochures. "At one point they killed it; then they brought it back," he says.

Cravens devised a plan to get McNealy to say yes or no to the controversial campaign. McNealy traditionally had a disdain for advertising because of its cost, preferring to position Sun via marketing and promotion that resulted in the company being mentioned in media articles about the industry. Cravens mocked up a three-page *Wall Street Journal* ad and took it into McNealy. The first page announced "the biggest merger" in American business history. The second page declared that this merger consisted of all the disparate computer systems running at corporations. The third page declared "The Network Is The Computer." McNealy picked up a pen and started correcting the copy. When he turned to the third page and saw "The Network Is The Computer," he said, "*That's* it." A press release announcing the tagline would quote McNealy this way: "We designed our architecture so that ultimately a user can get to all of his company's computer resources from his desktop system, without having to know the idiosyncrasies of every machine on the network. 'The Network Is The Computer' means all the systems work together like one big resource."

Not that the new tagline was home free. According to *Sunburst,* a mid-1980s study of outsider perceptions commissioned by Sun found only one customer able to identify the theme with Sun.[1] And, that customer got it backward, saying, "The Computer Is The Network." Still, the tagline stuck, in part because Sun was realizing that its success was inextricably linked to distributed computing via a network. Sums up former creative services director Swirsding: " 'The Network Is The Computer' was 10 years ahead of its time. People had no idea what it meant. This company was light years ahead of the entire industry in its thinking."

■ MISSED OPPORTUNITY

Sun wasn't always light years ahead in its thinking. It missed out on a technology that created another multibillion-dollar powerhouse: Cisco Systems. Cisco took the idea of distributed computing beyond file sharing and now dominates the increasingly important market that regulates how information flows between centralized computers (or servers) and individual machines (or clients). In 1984, in the same Stanford University computer center where Bechtolsheim built the first SUN, Leonard Bosack and Sandy Lerner, then husband and wife, figured out a way to let computer networks talk to each other by using a router. Acting, in effect, like an electronic postal service, router software breaks up electronic information into small pieces, or packets, and directs them to their destination via the Internet. The couple were actually using Sun machines to run their routers, having licensed the hardware from Bechtolsheim. In that time period, Sun might have seized on the same idea itself—as some within the company urged—but other priorities took precedence and the opportunity passed Sun by. Today, Cisco and Sun are the same size in revenue, but Cisco's $175 billion* market cap is four times Sun's value, reflecting Cisco's virtual ownership of an important market segment.

In the same year that Bosack and Lerner were developing their router at Stanford, Larry Garlick came to Sun from Xerox PARC. Garlick was typical of Sun's engineering recruits—the company has always been able to attract top talent because of its reputation for being on the leading edge of new technology and for letting its engineers tackle interesting projects. At Xerox PARC, Garlick had led the team that

---

* As of early 1999.

created the first internetwork router, and he brought some of those people with him to Sun. "I had at Sun people who could have created routing technology," he says. "We wanted to push our desktop architecture into routing. Every Sun workstation could be a router." This would have turned the Sun workstation into the platform for a new sector—routing.

But, this time, Sun's attitude and penchant for rule breaking got in the way. What Cisco did was not the kind of exciting shift to a new paradigm of computing that made the innovators and executives at Sun drool. In fact, routers are generally referred to as "plumbing" within the technology industry. You gotta have it, but nobody's eyes light up. Garlick says Sun met him about halfway when he asked for more investment to make the Sun workstation a routing platform. "They invested in high-speed network-ing," he says, "but not enough to get the whole job done." Garlick partly blames himself. "I wasn't good enough at selling my ideas. Routers seemed mundane. Sun wanted another NFS, something that changed the rules on every-thing, not a nuts and bolts type of technology." Cisco, he notes, "never changed the rules, but they created a faster-growing company than Sun." He believes Sun could have had its computer business and added routing on top of that. In other words, it could have been Cisco, too.

Khosla also feels that failure acutely. "The most stupid thing I feel personally that we did was to miss Cisco," he says. "After advertising 'The Network Is The Computer,' why hasn't *networking* been an area that Sun pursued? What is the road not taken?" Khosla says he, McNealy, and Bechtolsheim (who, ironically, is now at Cisco) have to share the blame for not honing in on what Cisco was doing. "At Stanford, Cisco was application software run-ning on Sun. We didn't see it."

► Desktop Obsession

Instead of targeting routers, Sun was trying to diversify its product line by making a play in the desktop computing market. This has been a dangerous obsession of the company for years. The fixation almost certainly caused Sun to miss the boat on routers and impacted its strategy for Java. Targeting desktop computing was one instance in which McNealy's vision went over the line into dogma, and hurt Sun.

Though workstations like Sun's sit on individual desktops, they are considered power computers for high-end users like engineers, software developers, and designers. Desktop computing refers to the personal computer, or PC—a low-end machine made by Apple, IBM, Compaq Computer, and others. It's a much higher-volume, though lower-margin, market than workstations. Sun has always wanted to break into the PC market, albeit with a Unix operating system rather than the desktop operating systems of the time—Macintosh, DOS, and later, Windows. McNealy, in essence, wanted to convert the desktop world to Unix. It was like a religious crusade.

Sun's most spectacular run at the desktop market came in the form of the computer Sun called the 386i. The *i* stood for "integrated," referring to the merging of a scaled-down version of Unix with some elements of DOS. Instead of the Motorola chip that the Sun workstations normally ran on, the 386i used the x86 Intel microprocessor line that was already becoming standard in the PC industry. To head the 386i effort, Sun hired Barry James Folsom, who had tried to develop an x86 line at Digital. Folsom joined Sun in 1985 as vice president and general manager of the East Coast Division in Massachusetts, where the 386i team was located. Recalls Crawford Beveridge: "Sun was ambivalent about the 386i. It wanted to move into the low end, but you needed a different channel, different product," he says. Further taking the steam out of the 386i development effort was the fact that it came early in the company's history, when sales of the Sun workstation series were just taking off.

Compounding the problem, Cravens recalls that Lacroute, to whom Folsom reported, couldn't get the

Massachusetts-based manager to return calls. "I remember Bernie [Lacroute] telling me, 'Get on a plane and go tell Barry James if he doesn't return my calls and do what I ask, it's a breach of contract.' " Cravens flew out to talk to Folsom. Folsom was a hard worker, putting in 15-hour days, says Cravens, but this didn't benefit the ill-fated 386i project. After Sun belatedly introduced the 386i in 1988, it wound up with more than 10,000 unsold machines in stock. The 386i was killed soon afterward when McNealy decided to consolidate Sun's efforts to one microprocessor (see Chapter 5).

In retrospect, it's easy to see how the combination of elements surrounding the 386i was a recipe for disaster. First of all, Sun didn't have enough bandwidth yet to manage a major project clear across the country. Without much supervision, Folsom and his team loaded up the 386i with enhancements that delayed its introduction and boosted the price. Second, the resellers who handled PCs didn't know Sun very well, because it mostly sold through direct original equipment manufacturer (OEM) channels. The resellers also didn't understand the Sun 386i's complicated operating system—a blend of Unix and DOS, and few agreed to stock the machine. Finally, there was little software available because ISVs didn't want to write applications for a product with so few customers. A decade later, Sun would again mount a serious effort to move into the desktop market—this time with a machine based on its Java technology.

■ POISED FOR THE FUTURE

Despite the failure of the 386i, as the 1980s wore on, Sun achieved significant milestones, the most important of which was that it overcame early leadership turmoil by naming the untried, brash McNealy as CEO. This turned out to be a fortuitous choice that, more than any other, made Sun what it is today. An intriguing footnote demonstrating how important McNealy had quickly become to the company was when Apple Computer made a bid to buy Sun in late 1985. The bid failed when McNealy declined to relinquish control. A December 16, 1985, article in the *San Jose Business Journal* suggested that the merger made sense in part because Apple would bring "proven leadership" in the person of President John Sculley, whereas Sun's management was "young and inexperienced."[2] Sometimes young and inexperienced does better than proven leadership, as history would demonstrate in this case.

On the technology front, Sun had introduced the Sun-3, which was a higher-performance workstation based on an upgraded Motorola processor. The Sun-3 had none of the problems of the Sun-2, and orders were pouring in. In addition, for the first time Sun created a standard of its own, NFS, and forced the big guys like Digital and Hewlett-Packard to incorporate Sun's technology into their offerings. On the financial front, Sun reached $210 million in revenue in fiscal 1986 and, in March of that year, completed an initial public offering (IPO) of its stock, raising $45 million. That doesn't seem like much today, but at the time, it was the largest IPO of a technology company in three years.

Sun's first annual report, published in 1986, had this to say: "Our rejection of proprietary systems in order to concentrate on our model of distributed computing, technology standards, and high quality is itself an innovation. And in a very real sense, this is Sun's proprietary product. That is why we are a world leader in heterogeneous computing and developing solutions for the future. We believe this leadership and innovation will power our growth for years to come." For once, an annual report was prescient. In the next two years, Sun would enter its hypergrowth period, when revenues would skyrocket to more than $1 billion.

Chapter

4

On Top of the World

In late 1985, Sun had launched the product that would cat-apult it into the billion-dollar club and blow away Apollo once and for all. This was the Sun-3 workstation series—an unabashed technological triumph whose launch intensi-fied traits that were to become the hallmark of Sun's cor-porate culture. Adding to the drama was that the Sun-3 had slipped its first deadline by a couple of months, and the second one—September 1985—seemed in doubt when both the engineering and marketing groups asked for more time. Engineering wanted to fix software flaws, while the marketing group had to redo its promotional material after the first package was vetoed by Bernie Lacroute, the executive vice president who oversaw engi-neering. In the past they might have gotten the extra de-velopment time, with Sun assuring customers that the wait would be worth it. But now, as the competition with Apollo was reaching a critical point, Lacroute and McNealy in-sisted that the Sun-3 would be introduced in September, spurning pleas from engineering and marketing. Apollo had already introduced its own machine based on the newly released Motorola MC68020 (a faster version than the chip Sun had been using in the Sun-2). McNealy and

Lacroute didn't want the Sun-3, which also incorporated the MC68020, to look like it was playing catch-up.

At the same time this competition was going on, Sun was adding employees daily, reaching more than 2,000 by the time it went public in 1986. With their insistence that the Sun-3 meet its deadlines, McNealy and Lacroute instilled in all these new employees a real sense of urgency and a knowledge of the company's objectives so that they each knew what they had to do and where the company was headed. One of McNealy's most notable traits is his ability to rally people around a cause. He demonstrated this early on with the Sun-3, saying, "Let's get it done so we can finish off Apollo."

In September, the Sun-3 was unveiled to a few hundred select customers and trade journalists at a Silicon Valley in-spot, Hyatt Rickey's, in Palo Alto. It was a typical launch where executives talked about the performance advantages and lower price—the Sun-3 cost about 15 percent less than Apollo's comparable product with similar performance. The new machine was an immediate success. In its first three months on the market, the Sun-3 accounted for one-third of sales in the quarter ended December 17, 1985. In the next quarter, the Sun-3 accounted for more than two-thirds of Sun's $57 million in revenue. Orders swamped the capacity of Sun's manufacturing facility in Mountain View, California, and it opened a new plant in nearby Milpitas. In fiscal 1987, Sun's revenues jumped 156 percent to $538 million, virtually all on the back of the Sun-3.

■ TOPPLING APOLLO

By 1987, Sun knew it had surpassed Apollo in revenue and market share. It took Sun just five years to overtake a larger, older rival. "In fiscal 1987, Sun's fifth full year of operation, we moved into a leadership position in our industry," crowed McNealy in the 1987 annual report. "Independent market data show Sun as the number-one supplier of technical workstations, measured by both revenue and number of units shipped." For the fiscal year ending June 30, 1987, Sun had earned $36.3 million in profit on $538 million in revenue, whereas Apollo netted $21 million profit on revenues of $553 million for calendar 1987. Comparing run rates in mid-1987, Sun was about $50 million ahead of Apollo in revenue, according to an article in the August 3, 1987 issue of *Computerworld.*[1] Financial ratios tell the story: Sun's profit margin was 6.7 percent, versus Apollo's measly 3.8 percent. The previous two years, 1985 and 1986, Apollo had posted $15.5 million in losses and reduced its workforce as it was forced to duplicate Sun's strategy: cutting prices and boosting performance. But, Apollo was chasing a moving target, and Sun moved even faster, further slashing the price of its low-end Sun-3 machine from $7,995 to $4,995.

McNealy was very aggressive in lowering prices, even beyond the recommendations of his sales managers. He "bet the company" more than once on drastic price cuts recalls Carl Swirsding, former head of creative services, while salespeople griped about their lower commissions and gross margins slipped. But McNealy was after more than fat profits and happy salespeople; it was volume and market share he wanted. Margins would follow. McNealy anticipated an important strategy that would become commonplace in the Internet era of the 1990s, used by companies such as Netscape, America Online, Microsoft, and Amazon.com. Do what you have to do to attract customers and lock in market share; then worry about profitability.

Out on the East Coast, Apollo couldn't figure out how to deal with Sun. Bob Tasker, now a senior vice president and analyst for the Yankee Group in Boston, was director of information technology at Apollo in the mid- to late 1980s. He remembers the slow, painful spiral that envelops a company that's losing market share and prestige to an upstart rival. In 1986, he says, managers were asked to cut their budgets by one-fourth because Apollo had missed its revenue growth targets. The original projection was for 40 percent revenue growth, then 33 percent, and then 25 percent. "Finally, they told us that it looks like revenue is going to be flat, so prepare a list of 10 percent of your staff that could be let go." Over a six- to nine-month period, "we went from a very positive, upbeat environment to 'oh-my-god'," he recalls. "It was boom times, and then all of a sudden people were talking about layoffs."

Another sign of the downward spiral was losing key people, notably Ed Zander, who joined Sun in October 1987 as vice president of corporate marketing after holding the same position at Apollo. "Zander was a big coup because we were stealing someone from Apollo," says Jonathan Lancaster, then in technical support for Sun. Apollo, he recalls, tried to downplay the loss of Zander by "putting out the word that they were sloughing off one of their duds." Some dud. Today, Zander is second in command to McNealy, while Apollo is a memory. In April 1989, Hewlett-Packard bought the company for $476 million and merged it into its own workstation line.

➤ R.I.P., Apollo

In retrospect, Apollo failed on several fronts: leadership, strategy, and culture. While Sun was taking a chance with the young, energetic McNealy as its CEO, Apollo replaced its founder/entrepreneur, William Poduska, in 1984 with John Vanderslice, who was supposed to take Apollo into the big leagues. Vanderslice "was an established East Coast corporate executive who had worked his way up through the ranks at General Electric and then had become the president of GTE Corporation," wrote Annalee Saxenian in *Regional Advantage: Culture and Competition in Silicon Valley and Route 128*.[2] "His background couldn't have been more different from those of the twenty-something graduate students and computer whizzes who had founded Sun Microsystems two years earlier."

Vanderslice's background with large companies was considered ideal for leading Apollo from a few hundred million dollars in revenues to a billion dollars and more. (That was exactly the rationale that some on Sun's board had in courting Paul Ely to become the CEO.) Vanderslice "was the right choice if you look in the rearview mirror, the wrong choice if you look out the windshield," says Tasker. "McNealy had by far the better vision. Apollo thought that people would buy their machines because their technology was the best, but people began buying cost efficiency. McNealy saw that, but Apollo missed it." In the early 1980s, Apollo had defined the new workstation market. "Apollo had built from scratch an absolutely elegant architecture. It was the most advanced operating environment commercially available," says Tasker. Sun, by contrast, kept design to a minimum by using existing technology like the Unix operating system and Motorola chip, so it was more efficient, using fewer people and maintaining lower inventory and faster response times than Apollo. Despite this, Apollo refused to change. "There was a holier-than-thou attitude [at Apollo]. The philosophy was that if it wasn't invented here, it can't be any good," Tasker says. This not-invented-here syndrome has tripped up many a proud technology company, and has even, on occasion, bedeviled Sun.

The cultures of the two companies symbolized a changing of the guard as well. Vanderslice would arrive at work in a limousine, Tasker recalls, wearing a tie and a three-piece suit. "He was a very straightlaced, stiff, traditional manager, a throwback to the '60s." Apollo's management structure emulated the hierarchal model of the Boston region's reigning minicomputer companies. Founder Poduska had come from Prime Computer, one of the leading minicomputer manufacturers, and brought his management team with him. Vanderslice did not represent a break with the past, but rather a continuation of it. On the West Coast, by contrast, McNealy would be photographed in newspapers wearing a T-shirt, shorts, and sandals. "I remember thinking that this characterized the differences in the two companies," says Tasker.

Jon Feiber, first an engineer and later vice president of networking at Sun between 1983 and 1991, succinctly sums up the Sun/Apollo difference. Sun was an opportunist that "loved to target a competitor and basically wanted to win at all costs," says Feiber, now a partner with Mohr Davidow Ventures in Menlo Park. "Apollo was a fairly staid East Coast company that got its butt kicked by a West Coast start-up with a take-no-prisoners attitude." He concedes that Apollo "had better technology, but Sun's technology was more malleable. That may have been more important than being better."

■ MOVING INTO OVERDRIVE

From 1986 through 1988, Sun enjoyed one of those hyper-growth periods that are legend in the high-tech industry. This is a magical time when triple-digit growth in sales is routine and new employees are added in droves. "In Sun's early days we were in a fool's paradise because we were so successful and everything was so easy," remembers James Gosling, a longtime Sun engineer who's now a vice president and Sun Fellow. "We had this great product and people just bought it." In blissful hypergrowth days like these, everything seems to be going right. Nothing is impossible. The company shoots for ever-higher goals. Work hours get longer and longer, but no one cares because they're on a rocket ship that goes straight up.

Sun had reached what Vinod Khosla called orbital velocity, although he wasn't there to see it. In only three years, revenues quintupled from $210 million in fiscal 1986 to $1.1 billion in fiscal 1988. The November 16, 1987, issue of the *San Jose Business Journal* described six Silicon Valley firms who were about to join the elite $1 billion club, that is, publicly traded firms with revenues above that figure.[3] There were only seven to that point, among them Apple, Intel, Hewlett-Packard, and National Semiconductor. While "some companies have taken decades to reach $1 billion in sales, others have just appeared on the scene," the article says. One of those is Sun Microsystems, "a brash newcomer riding a dizzying growth curve."

With tremendous growth comes the equally tremendous challenge of accommodating that growth from a resource and management perspective. During most of 1988, Sun added 100 new customers and 250 new employees every month, and doubled its salesforce. By the end of fiscal 1988, it had more than 7,000 employees, compared with 2,000 two years earlier. Sun also increased its worldwide square footage nearly 80 percent in 1988, to a point at which it was sprawled over 113 facilities domestically and 44 internationally. To this day, Sun is like many Silicon Valley companies that blew through a hypergrowth period in a tight commercial real estate market, with leased space wherever it could get it. Sun's official headquarters are in a single large building in Palo Alto, referred to as PAL-1, but most of the top executives sit in different locations, such as Menlo Park, Milpitas, Mountain View (the former headquarters), and Cupertino.

Marleen McDaniel, now CEO of Women.com in San Mateo, California, was employee number 62 when she joined Sun in early 1983 as a marketer. When she left in 1990, there were more than 10,000 employees. "The growth was part of the reason I left," she says. "I looked around one day and I didn't know anybody." On top of that, with all the hiring came a new breed of employee who looked upon working at Sun as a job, not a mission. McDaniel was spending 12 to 13 hours a day at the company, sometimes six or seven days a week. "I was young and unmarried and didn't think about it. I liked the people and I was learning things." Then, she says, Sun "started hiring people who came because it was successful, not because they wanted to make it successful. They were riding on its coattails and wouldn't take a risk. It was disappointing to me."

Carl Swirsding, who worked at Sun from 1983 to 1992, also remembers the hypergrowth period with mixed feelings—it was a great time to be there, but it irrevocably altered the company. With hundreds of new employees coming on board every month, "the whole atmosphere was turned upside down," he says. "Scott's advice was always to hire people more qualified than yourself because in a very short period they were going to be underqualified. Someone who comes in overqualified takes six months to get up to speed. Then they're productive for six months to a year. Then the company starts overwhelming them." Sun's hiring policy was not in anticipation of market growth, but rather, adding people as the growth made it essential. Consequently, "your need for resources always overwhelmed the company's ability to provide them," says Swirsding. "Just to be able to accomplish your objectives required working longer and longer hours. The incredibly rapid growth always put every employee, especially managers, in the awkward position of being under-resourced."

This lack of resources surfaced in other ways. The May 19, 1986, issue of *Electronic News* discussed how Sun was "facing a classic dilemma of fast growth—the costly and arduous task of keeping production, service and support operations on par with burgeoning sales."[4] The article goes on to describe missed delivery dates, quality control problems, spare parts shortages, strained production capacity, and poor customer support. Sun would later alleviate some of these problems when it opened its new manufacturing facility the following year in Milpitas and tripled production capacity.

➤ The Price of Success

In any business, a side effect of fast growth is creating a bigger target for competitors to shoot at. At $1 billion, Sun was a market-leading powerhouse that other companies were wary of. Once it had beaten Apollo, Sun no longer had any clearly defined enemy, which meant that its rabid drive to kill a single rival became more diffused. There were Hewlett-Packard, Digital, IBM, and even Apple, to a certain extent, but none of these competed directly in Sun's territory the way Apollo had. Hewlett-Packard was probably the closest, especially after it purchased Apollo, but Hewlett-Packard was a diversified company with multiple lines of business, many of which did not overlap with Sun. However, unlike Apollo, these companies did not make the mistake of underestimating Sun. In fact, they would later unite against Sun as it embarked on two major technology initiatives: one that sought to repeat its success with Network File System (NFS; see Chapter 3), and the second to create a new, improved Unix in partnership with AT&T.

To most people, the term "windows" in the computer industry has become synonymous with Microsoft's best-selling operating system of that name, but creating a windows interface was important for other vendors as well. Computer window systems allow users to display more than one screen of information simultaneously, and they were in widespread use in the 1980s. The problem was that every computer manufacturer, from Microsoft with its early version of Windows, to Apple with its Macintosh operating system, to the Unix vendors, had a different system. Sun had a product called SunWindows, which, as noted, was a big selling point for the financial market because it enabled traders to get simultaneous feeds of information from many sources on one computer. But SunWindows ran only on Sun workstations. Likewise, Digital, Hewlett-Packard, and other vendors had their own systems as well. This was an enormous hassle forcorporations that bought from multiple vendors, as well as for third-party software developers who had to recreate their products for each window variant.

The problem was similar to the one that Sun had solved so neatly with NFS. This time, a team of Sun engineers led by James Gosling created a product called the Network/extensible Window System (NeWS), which allowed any machine that had the software, whether it was from Sun, Hewlett-Packard, IBM, or whomever, to run windows. With NeWS, Sun followed the same strategy as NFS:

Sun would license NeWS to any vendor that wanted it, with the idea of turning the technology into an industry standard that everyone then had to use. Such a strategy would reinforce Sun's position as a technology leader and make its products more attractive to potential customers. The company formally launched NeWS at the 1987 spring Comdex trade show in Atlanta and followed with another presentation at the Unix Expo show in New York.

But a lot had changed in the two and a half years since the triumph with NFS—notably Sun itself. It was no longer a small, insignificant company that competitors could brush off, but a major vendor of computer systems and the market leader in an important segment—workstations. Not only that, its brashness did not endear it to competitors. With the exception of NFS and Java—two very important exceptions to be sure—Sun has not been successful at forging alliances with its peers. Only when its technology was so compelling, as with Java, has it been able to persuade others to jump on the Sun bandwagon. In most instances, Sun's cocksure, go-it-alone attitude paid off in focusing the company and fostering innovation, but had the adverse effect of alienating potential collaborators. And, NeWS was not a compelling enough technology to overcome that. A coalition led by Digital had developed an alternative called X Windows that was endorsed by most of the industry. "The NFS to Java era was very much a case of IBM, Hewlett-Packard, and Digital blocking Sun from creating any more standards," says former Sun engineer Larry Garlick. "The NeWS windowing system was one technology that got stymied as a result." Gosling, the "father" of NeWS, agrees. "What destroyed NeWS was NFS, because it was so successful. There was a really strong backlash to that from competitors," he says. "They mounted amazing opposition. And we didn't react as well as we should have." For once, Sun backed off and adopted the other standard, X Windows. McNealy's description, to Gosling, of what happened with NeWS is: "We were playing a game of chicken.

The other side blinked their headlights and we drove off the road."

NeWS was not a total loss for Sun. Technically, the idea at its core—independence from the underlying operating system—would be reborn in Java (another effort led by Gosling). The experience was a character builder as well. "We learned a lot about integrity, sticking to your guns, and dealing with adversity," says Gosling. "It was a big mistake not to stick with NeWS because, technologically, X Windows was a step backward. It really cost us because being forced to use it stifled some of our innovation." Going forward, Sun realized it had to be more stalwart in supporting its own standards and, at the same time, it had to work harder to convince other companies to endorse its standards. This meant cooperating with companies who are competitors in other arenas—an approach that has pervaded the technology industry and come to be called "co-opetition." Gosling says he and the engineering team wanted to be more collaborative with NeWS in getting other companies to contribute to it, but bureaucratic dissent overruled the effort. With the experience of NeWS behind it, Sun would be more savvy with Java. "It's almost like a Zen thing—you give away something so you end up getting more back," Gosling explains.

■ THE UNIX WARS

NeWS was but a skirmish—a prelude to an all-out war that Sun would fight over Unix itself. As we discussed, the Unix operating system was developed by AT&T's Bell Laboratories in the 1960s. It originally ran on centralized hardware like minicomputers, not on individual desktops until Sun popularized Unix for workstations. Thanks to AT&T's liberal licensing policies, Unix was widely available in colleges and research labs. The upshot was that a "priesthood" of Unix programmers had assembled who created their own unique culture. To be in this group was like being part of an exclusive fraternity made up of a group of young (and almost all male) engineering hotshots, all recently coming out of prestigious universities that had computer labs with access to Unix. Besides AT&T's own Unix, the Berkeley version that Joy brought to Sun had emerged as the other major strain. These two were the roots of numerous varieties of the popular operating system. "It was confusing to the marketplace—which one do I go to?" recalls Bernie Lacroute, who ran engineering at Sun. "If you can combine the two maybe we can start unifying that world." He and other executives at Sun agreed that it was a good idea to approach AT&T about that prospect, although Sun's engineers were not thrilled at having their independence compromised.

In October 1987, McNealy and Vittorio Cassoni, who had come from Olivetti to head AT&T's computer products division, signed off on a pact in which they agreed to work together on a merged version of their Unix systems. "We had the two best versions of Unix, and we both agreed that we should work together," says Sun cofounder Bill Joy. Under the terms of the deal, which was consummated in early 1988, AT&T could buy up to 20 percent of Sun, giving the smaller company access to much-needed capital to finance their expansion. Like Kodak, AT&T also got a seat on Sun's board, filled by Bob Kavner, who had succeeded Cassoni as president of AT&T computer products. "The idea was that we would collaborate on Unix and bring out one version that would leverage AT&T's brand credibility and Sun's market penetration," says Kavner, who left Sun's board in 1990.

Jim Moore, president of GeoPartners Research, consulted with AT&T and Sun on their Unix strategy in 1988. He remembers that effort had started with high hopes. Sun's scheme was to parlay Unix from a series of separate operating systems, each owned by a different company, into an open system that everyone in computing could use. This would enable Sun to fulfill McNealy's perpetual dream of moving out of the relatively narrow workstation niche into the larger market for general computer systems as well as realize Sun's founding vision of shared computing. AT&T was a plausible ally because of its long affiliation with Unix and its financial muscle. But what Sun and AT&T didn't count on was the reaction of the rest of the Unix world, notably Hewlett-Packard, Digital, and IBM. By developing a merged Unix operating system that could drive higher volumes at lower prices, "there was a sense that Sun and AT&T were willing to rip down the industry's pricing umbrella" to take control of Unix, Moore says.

A rival alliance coalesced, led by Hewlett-Packard, Sun's top rival in the workstation arena; Digital, which saw in Sun an increasing threat to its minicomputers and its burgeoning workstation business; and IBM, which was worried about AT&T's ambitions to add computers to its telecommunications stronghold. Calling itself the Open Software Foundation (OSF), this group eventually signed up 30-plus vendors and consultants in opposition to the notion that Sun and AT&T would control the ongoing development of Unix. In a classic comment, McNealy referred to OSF as "Oppose Sun Forever." In reaction to it, Sun and AT&T started Unix International, which counted among its supporters: Intel, Toshiba, Unisys, Motorola, Fujitsu, and about a dozen others.

"The announcement of our relationship galvanized our competitors. We gave them a reason to meet," says Kavner. "IBM, HP, and Digital in particular were against us because they had a common interest [with their own brands of Unix]." Shortly after OSF was founded in 1988, Kavner and AT&T's CEO, Bob Allen, received a call from IBM Chairman John Akers. "IBM said they wanted to meet with us [AT&T]," recalls Kavner. The IBM executives flew to AT&T's New Jersey headquarters in their helicopter and "essentially put an ultimatum on the table: you can join OSF, or we're going to try to undo your position in Unix." AT&T retorted: "We don't take ultimatums. We're going to do what we want."

Sun and AT&T convinced their coalition, Unix International, to agree to build products around their forthcoming version of Unix. OSF, by contrast, stole Sun's mantra and proclaimed itself the adherent of "open standards" that weren't controlled by any one company. While the two factions were bloodying each other's noses over the Unix turf, a bigger bully waited gleefully in the wings. Microsoft, already marching toward dominance in desktop computers, wanted to move up into the corporate world and was developing a higher-powered version of Windows, called Windows NT, to do so. And the "Unix wars" gave it the perfect opportunity. "From a rearview mirror standpoint, this [Unix battle] was a war over trivia, a war that gave Microsoft the opportunity to create a market for NT," says Kavner. This was a major turning point in the history of computing, because if the Unix world had banded together instead of fighting each other, it could have hamstrung Microsoft's push to expand. Instead, Microsoft threatens to engulf even the highest levels of computing, such as corporate networks, formerly the province of Unix.

➤ What Might Have Been

Sun and AT&T never had the opportunity to pick a marketing name or release their joint product. The relationship began to unravel due to cultural differences and disagreement on how to respond to the OSF threat. "Culturally there were real problems between the two companies," says Kavner. He and McNealy, who got along well, ended up having monthly meetings with the two development teams in which they devoted most of their time to dealing with "everyone's bitching about the other side." Lacroute characterizes AT&T as methodical, systematic, and bureaucratic. Its engineers were accustomed to doing what management wanted without asking questions. Sun's culture, by contrast, allowed "a tremendous amount of initiative on the part of the engineers, who had a mind of their own. If you told them to do something that was stupid, they would argue with you," he says. The cultural mismatch made it that much harder to tackle the difficult technical issues that were emerging. "The task was more formidable than anybody had envisioned, both at a technical and cultural level," says Lacroute.

Consultant Jim Moore was called in to straighten out the mess and found fiefdoms inside both companies who didn't want the Unix venture to succeed. At the same time, Sun was in hypergrowth and "had no planning, no processes," says Moore, and yet it tried to dictate strategy to AT&T. A unified Unix "was a hardware guy's fantasy," he maintains. It was an attempt to level the playing field on the operating system level—the software—while Sun would add value on the hardware side. The technology industry, however, was moving in the opposite direction, consolidating on hardware technology, such as Intel's microprocessor, and goosing software to add value. Microsoft took advantage of that trend, while Sun's attempt to drive the industry the other way failed. "Sun is at its best when it's leading a social movement in computing," says Moore. "You want to be involved with Sun, a part of the revolution." But if you don't get a critical mass to endorse it, such a strategy can also backfire, as with the Unix wars, which left Microsoft to claim the revolution as its own.

Neither Unix International nor OSF could rise above self-interest, and neither of their supposed Unix standards caught on. Kavner believes that if the Unix vendors had managed to put aside their differences and "all marched to the same tune, we could have dominated workstations and servers," the markets that today are still under increasing attack by Windows NT. Microsoft recruited the highly regarded Dave Cutler from Digital to lead its NT development in 1988, but it took five years before the product was launched in October 1993—years in which the Unix industry could have advanced its own standard. It didn't happen. Kavner says that he and John Young, the CEO of Hewlett-Packard, attempted to negotiate a rapprochement between Unix International and

OSF, but Sun and Digital were "the renegade voices. They were the two that didn't want to compromise. It was damn the torpedoes, we're going it alone." According to Bill Joy, OSF wanted to use a "technically inferior" version of the central piece of software in Unix, and "we couldn't afford to go backwards."

Lacroute blames the polarization on the fact that the various Unix vendors were such avid competitors that "nobody wanted to budge and give anybody else an advantage." Among Unix International and OSF, "you would always find someone who didn't want to cooperate," he says. "Certainly Sun was fairly active in that battle, but so was AT&T. One day Sun didn't want to agree to it, the next day AT&T didn't." At OSF, "Digital and HP were both very adamant" in their positions. He says the Unix vendors were not blind to the threat from Microsoft, but they just couldn't get past their own resentment of each other. "We all knew Cutler and what he was doing at Microsoft."

AT&T realized it wanted to sell computer systems under its own name, rather than depend on Sun, while Sun was increasingly balking at the bigger, slower company's demands. The two mutually "walked away" from their agreement, Lacroute says. In 1991, AT&T divested its stake in Sun and later wound up selling its Unix division to concentrate on hardware and services. Not everything was wasted, Lacroute maintains. Some of the new software code ended up in a next-generation operating system called Solaris, which Sun was developing to replace the Sun operating system.

■ SAVING OPEN SYSTEMS

Ironically, Sun could claim a certain moral victory out of the Unix wars. Though there was no unified Unix, there was a grudging acceptance of the idea of openness, which Sun had trumpeted as its raison d'etre. A unified Unix might have had everyone marching together, but it would have destroyed some of the customization and individualization that were the hallmarks of the Unix culture. "OSF ended up dulling the progress of a unified Unix," notes Moore. "But it legitimized openness, so [Sun competitors] hurt their own existing proprietary business models as well. By piling onto the Sun bandwagon, they caused openness to win but also kept Unix fragmented."

Several important lessons emerged during Sun's hypergrowth years that would prevail as the company matured and growth inevitably slowed. From NeWS and the Unix wars came the sense that Sun would have to carve out its own path, even when everyone else was going another way. The crystallization of industry opposition to Sun's initiatives reinforced the company's perception that its fate rested in its own hands. This had both benefits and repercussions. It differentiated Sun from among a host of computer system makers and enabled the management team and employees to focus the company's strategy. At the same time, it would leave Sun standing alone in many of its battles. As an article in the June 27, 1988, issue of *Forbes* magazine noted: "Even in a highly competitive industry, Sun is unusually friendless. Its one good buddy, AT&T, is not exactly helping: Its relationship with Sun has drawn the fire of some of the biggest guns in the computer industry."[5]

The Unix wars, coupled with Microsoft's looming presence, left Sun's executive team with a serious case of paranoia about what fragmentation could do to a technology. Within Sun, there was the conviction that Unix was by far the best operating system around, with greater flexibility, performance, and maturity than any other competing system, such as Windows NT. But the history of the technology industry has repeatedly demonstrated that the best product doesn't necessarily win when the strategy behind it is wrong. (Look at Macintosh versus Windows, Apollo versus Sun, or, in the consumer electronics arena, Betamax versus VHS.) After the Unix wars, Sun would never again allow its intellectual property to become subject to some kind of industry consensus, roiling technical progress in a political process. When the company rolled out Java six years later, it would use whatever means it took—including legal action—to resist any effort to lessen its control or fragment that technology.

Chapter

5

Hard Times

Like an adolescent wrestling with the challenges of impending adulthood, Sun toughed its way through troubled times in the late 1980s and early 1990s. The euphoria of becoming a billion-dollar company in just six years wore off as Sun confronted its first quarterly loss as a public company in 1989, difficult product transitions and consolidation on both the hardware and software fronts, a disastrous conversion of its internal information systems, leadership turnover, questions about the man at the top, and diminishing confidence among investors and employees. The joke inside Sun was that it was becoming the first DEC (Digital Equipment Corporation) of the 1990s, a reference to the East Coast minicomputer company that lost its way and was eventually acquired by Compaq Computer.

Those newspaper headlines that McNealy so prized turned dark, particularly when Sun reported its loss in June 1989. Suddenly, Sun was no longer a media darling or a daring start-up. In the fast-moving technology industry, it had become a tarnished star. "Sun Struggling with Own Success," said *PC Week* on June 19;[1] "Another Top Official Turns His Back on Sun," reported the *San Jose Mercury News* on June 16;[2] and "Hiccup for a Computer Superstar," wrote the *New York Times* on June 2, 1989.[3] The latter article opined that "Sun has grown so large, so quickly that some analysts have worried that it has grown to a size beyond its young founders' ability to manage. Until now Sun's executives have prided themselves on the company's decentralized management style, but some analysts have suggested that Sun might fall victim to problems related to uncontrolled growth."[4]

Like many a technology wunderkind, Sun found that skyrocketing growth has a way of covering up mistakes, until they multiply and can't be hidden any longer. The inevitable slowdown after hypergrowth tests a company's mettle and sets the stage for its future success. Many companies have foundered in this period of readjustment, like Apple, Netscape, and America Online, to name just a few. These downturns can destroy a company, pushing it into oblivion or into the arms of a competitor; or they can make it stronger. In Sun's case, the company became stronger, but at a high price, in the form of fleeing executives, cutbacks in technology, skepticism by the press and on Wall Street, and new burdens for McNealy.

Yet, there would still be triumphs during this period. Sun continued development of its own microprocessor design, SPARC, and a new operating system, Solaris. These would become the company's new crown jewels, joined eventually by Java. Without completely sacrificing its ebullient nonconformity, Sun also honed a new maturity that would help it move into the larger role of the corporate enterprise. In short, Sun grew up, to an extent, but it never lost its inner child in doing so. The creativity, the all-out effort, the sense of wonder, the willingness to take a dare—these would remain.

■ THE SPARC OF HOPE

The man who would become the father of SPARC couldn't believe his ears. Some small 300-person company, an obscure outfit by the name of Sun Microsystems, was wooing

him in early 1984 with what seemed like an insane pro-
posal. "My first thought was that these guys were a bunch of
looney tunes," recalls Anant Agrawal at the time of his first
interview at Sun in spring 1984. "They didn't know anything about chip design, but they were talking about designing a microprocessor to compete with Intel." Agrawal,
an engineer working for a start-up that was designing an
IBM mainframe clone, was skeptical; and the Friday interview at Sun concluded on an uncertain note. The next
morning, he got an urgent call from Vinod Khosla. "For an
hour I spoke with Vinod on the phone," says Agrawal. Finally, worn down by the Sun CEO's persistence, he agreed,
"I'll be there on Monday."

The story of SPARC is the story of what kept Sun going
in hard times—fearless creativity. Agrawal joined as employee number 335 in April 1984. The entire SPARC team
consisted of himself and one other engineer, Robert Garner. They were assisted by Bill Joy and David Patterson,
the Stanford University professor who acted as a consultant to Sun in its early years. "We were going to build
SPARC," says Agrawal. The task before this small group was
enormous. Microprocessor design is a tedious, multiyear
undertaking. First, the underlying architecture—the map
for how the components of the chip will be put together—
must be determined. Then that map is used to design the
chip. Finally, the chip has to be turned into a product in
collaboration with a foundry—a company that has a semiconductor fabrication plant (fab) and is willing to manufacture products for outsiders. Sun sensibly decided that
building a fab—a billion-dollar prospect—was not something it wanted to undertake.

At this time Sun was building its workstations using
chips from Motorola. It was also planning to launch an effort to develop an Intel-based PC, the 386i. Why, then, did it
need another chip? The answer had convinced Agrawal to
take a chance at Sun. "Andy, Bill, Scott and Vinod had concluded that if network computing truly takes off, the power
you need on the desktop will have to go up beyond Mo-

torola," he says. The demands of Sun's workstation market were already exceeding what Motorola could supply, while Intel's chips, aimed at the PC market, were not powerful enough for workstations, either. SPARC (which stood for *scalable processor architecture*) was based on a new technology developed at IBM but not yet commercialized. This was the RISC technology (or *reduced instruction set computer*) that greatly increased microprocessor speed, ease of design, and performance by limiting the instructions the chip had to follow. With RISC, more of the logic is carried out in software rather than hardwired into the chip, as with the Motorola and Intel designs. For Sun, going with RISC was another huge strategic decision in keeping with McNealy's risk-taking (pun intended) nature. If it failed, Sun would have wasted millions of research dollars and, worse, put itself onto a sidetrack to oblivion. In the fast-moving technology industry, it's hard to recover from such a resource-consuming detour.

In the first year, Agrawal and his team came up with an architecture they thought would work. But Sun had yet to find a fab. It looked like the answer would lie in Japan, where a lot of the semiconductor manufacturing capacity was located. In late 1985, Joy flew out to meet with Fujitsu. To this day, says Agrawal, people at Fujitsu remember when Bill Joy came to visit, wearing his funky, Berkeley-style clothes, while the Japanese were attired in Westernized suits and ties. The meeting was done on "a wing and a prayer," says Joy. Fujitsu's starstruck engineers "knew me because of Berkeley Unix, and they believed whatever I said." With Fujitsu on board, Agrawal began working with an engineer from the Japanese company to finish the SPARC design. Joy was heavily involved, too. "People think of Bill Joy as this software guy, but he's also a great chip designer," says Agrawal. During this time, "he was in my office every day with a new idea. They were brilliant ideas, but I had to get the product done. I finally had to say, 'Bill, leave me alone.' " It was a period of day-and-night effort for the small design team. Agrawal was only able to see his fiancee, who was attending college, by having her accompany him to Sun on weekends.

➤ Igniting Controversy

Spending precious research dollars on SPARC flamed some controversy within Sun. As word of the project spread, "you start developing antibodies [opposition]," says Agrawal. "There were people who said, 'Why are we doing SPARC when we're trying to grow the business on Motorola and nothing like this has been done before?' " Khosla adds that SPARC was a result of his decision to allocate 80 percent of R&D dollars to supporting the existing business line and 20 percent to speculative research—"stuff from the Bill Joys and Andy Bechtolsheims of the world." Other executives, like Bernie Lacroute, wanted to cancel SPARC, but its defenders, Khosla and board member John Doerr, convinced Lacroute and McNealy that SPARC was the key to Sun's future growth.

The SPARC project demonstrated how Sun's original business model was evolving. Rather than depending on technology developed elsewhere, as it had at first, Sun was realizing that the true powerhouses in the technology industry were those that owned their intellectual property. (Today, that early realization is confirmed by the fact that Microsoft and Intel have the highest profit margins in the industry, while the PC vendors that use Microsoft software with Intel chips find their margins diminishing.) To be sure, taking off-the-shelf parts and molding them into a workstation enabled Sun to jump-start its revenue. But, had it continued on that path, Sun would have become a commodity supplier of workstations, with low price as its primary selling point and its margins squeezed. By developing SPARC, Solaris, and Java, Sun was able to move to a more advantageous position in which it licensed valuable intellectual property to others while commanding higher prices for its own products.

After more than three years of work, SPARC was formally launched at a gala rollout at the Hayden Planetarium in New York City in July 1987. Lacroute drove the engineering team hard to fix some last-minute bugs before the launch. Agrawal remembers the planetarium was packed with analysts and trade press. "Bernie [Lacroute] and I were both very nervous," not quite sure all the bugs had been dealt with, he says. Then, as the launch proceeded without a hitch, "it was a great feeling to see this new architecture actually being used. I didn't realize how big this was going to be. It was still fun—we'd created a microprocessor and, look, it's working in a machine."

With SPARC, Sun tried to repeat its success with NFS and broadly license the new technology to other vendors, including chip manufacturers such as Fujitsu, Cypress Semiconductor, and Texas Instruments, and hardware vendors such as AT&T, Xerox, Unisys, and Toshiba. The intent was to encourage a market of SPARC-based machines, in effect Sun clones, that would all run the same software. "Sun will always try to play the open systems game," says Greg Xenakis, who was vice president of SPARC International, the trade association Sun formed to promote SPARC. Sun needed SPARC internally to boost the performance of its own machines, but it also wanted to make the chip design a standard by getting other companies to use it. This would have two main advantages. Higher volume results in lower costs for designing and manufacturing the chip. And, it also means that the all-important software developers community would write applications for the new chip.

This strategy was not very successful. "One place we didn't do well was proliferating SPARC in the larger market," admits Agrawal. The barrier was one that has continued to dog Sun. It wanted to own its intellectual property but make it a standard as well. It's difficult to do both, because a standard is driven by consensus, so that anyone using it can come up with an improvement. Sun has always had difficulty swallowing that. Recalls Xenakis: "We had all these chip manufacturers making SPARC chips but every time the licensees came out with something, Sun had first dibs on it." In addition, Sun undercut its clone makers by coming out with its own products at a lower price. "The clone manufacturers were fit to be tied," he says. Even though SPARC International was ostensibly an independent organization, with Sun just one of 11 executive members, Sun "was the 800-pound gorilla that dictated how the technology would be used," Xenakis says. "So it never took off. Most of the clones have gone away and Sun/SPARC are synonomous."

Meanwhile, cofounder Andy Bechtolsheim was leading an internal effort to develop a second-generation SPARC product that would offer high performance in a cost-effective workstation. Initially, Bechtolsheim, weary of the growing bureaucracy of a large company, had been prepared to leave Sun and found a start-up that would be funded by Khosla. This start-up would build the machine. As it happens, Sun wound up investing in the company, called UniSun, and later bought it back. Says Bechtolsheim: "This was my best time at Sun." He had free rein at UniSun. "I didn't have to talk to anyone about what to do and what not to do." He and his team of about 50 people only had to focus on delivering the product. This was the SPARCstation 1, a small, cheap, fast workstation that took the market by storm. The Yankee Group, a Boston consulting firm, called the SPARCstation the "SPARCintosh," in reference to its popularity. The product was announced in April 1989 at San Francisco's Moscone Center. When Hewlett-Packard chose the same time period to announce it had bought Apollo, many within Sun figured that was a competitor's effort to upstage the SPARCstation. It didn't work. Orders for the new machine began pouring in. The SPARCstation 1 was both the prelude to the future and the instrument of crisis.

■ THE LOSS QUARTER

Soon after the triumphant announcement of the SPARC-station 1, there were signs that Sun's fiscal fourth-quarter results were in jeopardy. Since going public three years earlier, Sun had had an uninterrupted string of profitable quarters, each one better than the last. But Sun had seriously underestimated demand for the SPARCstation 1 and overestimated demand for its existing systems based on a Motorola microprocessor. Internally, Sun was moving to a mainframe-based management information system (MIS), and a lot of the data it needed to forecast demand simply got lost. On June 1, 1989, a McNealy-authorized press release acknowledged that the fourth quarter would be "significantly below" the results of one year ago, and the company might even experience a "slight loss." In a bit of an understatement, the press release noted that the conversion to a new MIS system was "not without difficulties." As usual, "we were running on the edge," recalls Curt Wozniak, who was vice president of engineering and then vice president of marketing at Sun's hardware division from 1984 to 1994. "When we switched MIS systems internally, we couldn't take orders and we couldn't ship orders for a month. We didn't have enough of the new machines and we had too many of the old machines."

Compounding that were two major executive departures. Bernie Lacroute resigned as executive vice president, and Joe Graziano, the chief financial officer recruited from Apple in 1985, decided to return there. Carol Broadbent, a longtime public relations manager at Sun, recalls that both announcements really shook up the company. Graziano left on June 15, two weeks after the press release presaging a poor quarter. His departure hurt Sun's efforts to obtain lines of credit to tide it over the bad time. "The very next week Bernie resigned," she says. "He was running all the product divisions." Lacroute, older and more experienced than McNealy and the other Sun founders, had been an important counterweight to the Sun CEO in the eyes of employees and Wall Street. Ominous articles suggested that McNealy's hard-charging style was driving people away. Sun executives believed Lacroute had been forced out, or left before he could be blamed for the debacle. Lacroute attributes his departure to simple burnout. "I just got worn out," he recalls. "I never saw my family." He joined Kleiner Perkins, the venture capital firm where Khosla had earlier found refuge. As for Graziano, he was enticed back to Apple by John Sculley, wrestling with management turmoil of his own.

By July, Sun was forced to issue another press release. "We had to say it was even worse than we told you," recalls Broadbent. "That was our big fall from grace. We had been a rocket ship until that quarter." Everybody, she says, "was doing a duck and cover." Even McNealy heeded Broadbent's advice to maintain a low profile. The bottom line: Sun suffered a $20.3 million loss on $431 million in revenue for the quarter—its one and only loss as of early 1999. It also was the target of a class-action lawsuit by shareholders and settled out of court for $25 million. (If you'd put $100 into Sun at its 1986 public offering, it would have returned $255 in June 1987 but only $213 two years later.) For the full year, Sun's revenues were up 68 percent to $1.77 billion, but net income was down 8 percent to $61 million. "In the fourth quarter, which is typically our best, we found ourselves facing more than the usual number of hurdles, including a complex product transition and difficulties operating with a new management information system," McNealy wrote in the annual report. An additional problem was a decline in Sun's available cash from $128 million the previous year to just $54 million at the end of fiscal 1989. Sun's growth, said McNealy, created "a need for funding that far exceeds that of most companies."

➤ Turning Point

The quarterly loss and dwindling cash reserves, plus protracted negotiations with banks to obtain new lines of credit, sobered Sun up. If Sun had been a house, you'd have to say that most of the problems were cosmetic. There was no deep-rooted crack in the foundation that would bring the company down. Rather, it had slapped paint over patches on the walls for a little too long. McNealy had emphasized market share and growth over financial returns and profit margins. To win an important account, Sun would shave its margins to the bone. Sometimes, it didn't know exactly how close to the line it was running, or whether it had stepped over, because its accounting procedures had not kept pace with its growth. Like many technology start-ups, Sun had channeled its resources into products—making increasingly cooler products and selling those products at the expense of financial controls. One of the reasons for the switch to a mainframe computer was to improve financial accounting, though the glitches at first exacerbated the situation.

With the chief financial officer and the executive vice president gone, it was McNealy who stepped up to the plate. He, like Sun, had aged during the fourth quarter—externally and internally. McNealy's ability to continue as CEO without Lacroute and Graziano was questioned. "Scott was on thin ice," says Wozniak. "This was where he made a transformation. We had three and a half wheels off the road. He decided that was too many." Going forward, McNealy would put new processes in place, although the overriding strategy would remain aggressive. But underneath, there would be more attention paid to costs, not just growth. The manufacturing operation would attempt to perform forecasting methods, not just churn out product as fast as it could. Indicators like cash flow and inventory turns would be tracked. This was partially driven by the stringent covenants the banks put in place to make loans, but it also was a result of McNealy's realization of the need to alter Sun's course.

"Scott turned the focus to internal operational management," Wozniak says. Each vice president was assigned a process to oversee. "I worked on a new product introduction process, a schedule for developing and introducing products. What were the checklists? What steps would we take?" In the past, new product introductions had been driven by the need to match or outpace a competitor. Now there would be interim benchmarks and deadlines to meet. Cost containment was another target. Department managers had to assess each project on a return-on-investment (ROI) basis; controllers had to approve every expenditure. Carl Swirsding, who as head of creative services had been accustomed to doing glossy brochures and reports on demand, now told every department what each piece would cost and how it would be budgeted. Sun instituted a hiring freeze and a reduction through attrition. By September 1989, the workforce had been cut by about 200 people. It was a new experience for Sun after several years of nonstop growth.

"That 1989 experience taught Scott that if you spend time on internal stuff, like talking with the banks, you don't have enough time to do strategy and marketing and deal with customers," says Wozniak. "You have to be superb internally to be superb externally. He came through his trial by fire." The next quarter—the first fiscal quarter of 1990—Sun eked out a $5.2 million profit on record revenue of $538.5 million. Financially, it was back on track.

■ ALL THE WOOD BEHIND ONE ARROW

After "The Network Is The Computer," the most famous phrase to come out of Sun is, "All the wood behind one arrow." According to Sun lore, McNealy first used the phrase to describe a critical decision to consolidate Sun's products on one platform, its own SPARC chip. That eliminated the 386i, which used the Intel chip, and the highly successful series of workstations that ran on Motorola microprocessors. Today at Sun and throughout Silicon Valley, "all the wood behind one arrow" has become shorthand to describe almost any concentrated effort to launch a new product or eliminate noncore functions.

In late 1989, the decision was not obvious. Sun (as mentioned in Chapter 3) had devoted several years of effort to the 386i, and the Motorola-based architecture of the Sun-3 had gotten the company to the big leagues. Nonetheless, the financial problems of mid-1989 had shown that managing multiple product lines strung over three architectures was not in Sun's best interests. Besides, all three targeted the same customer—the "power" user. "Nobody needed three different machines for the same thing," says Bechtolsheim. "SPARC gave us performance and speed, which was what customers wanted. It became obvious as soon as the SPARC-station took off." Lacroute says his strategy was to use the 386i as a backup in case SPARC didn't take off. To him, Sun's mistake was to introduce the 386i to the market, rather than quietly killing it, once SPARC had proven that it offered better performance. "If SPARC had been screwed up, 386i might have been important. But something had to go," he says. "It was too costly to do all three." And, software developers weren't going to write applications for so many platforms.

After McNealy made the decision to consolidate on SPARC, on the next April Fool's Day in 1990, he came into his office to find a huge, 50-foot arrow extending through the office and out the internal window into the hallway. Sun had long been famous for its April Fool's Day pranks (see Chapter 6 for a discussion of its "work hard, play hard" culture), but this topped them all. When Agrawal, the father of SPARC, saw the arrow, "it felt like it was aimed straight at me," he recalls. In a way he was pleased; in a way he was terrified. "At the time, it was a really bold decision for Scott to come out and say, 'I'm not going to do Intel or Motorola'," Agrawal says. The company knew SPARC worked on a technological basis, but market acceptance was hardly proven. "We were going with no insurance policy," Agrawal says. If SPARC failed, there would be nothing to turn to in its place. "Scott had faith in the technology," he adds. "I had mixed feelings. I knew I had to get it right." Agrawal's design was now the mainstream at Sun, and everything was depending on it.

■ A PERFORMANCE GAP

During the early 1990s, Sun fumbled on execution. A follow-on to the first SPARC chip, called superSPARC, fell well short of expected performance levels. At the same time, Sun was asking its customers to move to its new operating system, Solaris, which contained elements of the improved Unix codeveloped with AT&T. But software transitions are notoriously tricky from a user perspective, and customers were resistant, especially when the software developers' community was slow to rewrite applications to take advantage of Solaris. Eric Schmidt, who spent 14 years at Sun in various executive roles before leaving in mid-1997 to become CEO of Novell, remembers the early 1990s as a time of "stagnation" in technology and in share price. "Sun was a very different company," he says, from the ebullient start-up and Apollo killer of the 1980s. Indeed, a headline in the December 31, 1990, issue of the *San Jose Business Journal* described how Sun was served a "dose of humility" as it continued its recovery from the loss quarter of 1989.[5]

Sun still had the will to try contrarian strategies. To induce customers to switch to Solaris, in early 1993 the company boosted prices in the range of $1,000 to $2,000 on its older machines, making them comparable in price to the newer models, which ran Solaris. That, of course, ran directly counter to the prevailing strategy, which was to cut prices drastically on old products once the newer version was available. But Sun felt it had to move customers to Solaris by making its new products more attractive. At the time, Sun claimed the price increases were made to offset higher production costs, but that hardly accounted for its decision not to raise prices on newer machines. "Clearly the intent [of the price increases] is to accelerate the migration to the new architecture and the new operating system," industry analyst Jeff Canin of Salomon Brothers told the *San Jose Business Journal* on February 22, 1993.[6] And it worked. By fiscal 1994, slightly more than a year after its launch, Solaris was the leading Unix operating system in revenue and shipments.

The move to Solaris was smooth compared with the recovery from superSPARC, which would take years. By this time, Sun had three foundries making versions of SPARC: Fujitsu, Cypress Semiconductor, and Texas Instruments. The latter was building superSPARC, but "our execution was terrible and superSPARC came out way below target performance and late by more than a year," recalls Chet Silvestri, who was president of Sun's microelectronics division from 1992 through March 1998. Sun was "dead last" behind RISC chips from Hewlett-Packard, Digital, and IBM/Motorola, which had just launched the PowerPC used by Apple. Silvestri came to Sun when Silicon Graphics acquired his company, MIPS Computer, which was making a chip that competed with SPARC. He wasn't sure whether Silicon Graphics would stand behind the RISC technology, so he came to Sun, whose commitment, by virtue of McNealy's "all the wood behind one arrow," couldn't be doubted. But Silvestri soon found himself with more than he had bargained for, in the midst of what he describes as "the doldrums" for Sun.

"What was clear was we had to cut our losses on super-SPARC and move to the next generation, which was ultra-SPARC," says Silvestri. Thanks to its wily sales team and a loyal customer base, Sun was able to increase revenue and profits, "but there was no real growth." Silvestri and Agrawal both credit Sun's software division, which oversaw Sun operating system and then Solaris, and its salesforce with keeping the company afloat. But Sun's triple-digit growth in revenues slowed abruptly to 11 percent between 1991 and 1992 and dipped even further to the single digits between 1993, when machines based on superSPARC were introduced, and 1994. Still, Sun was a substantial Fortune 500 company. Revenues totaled $4.69 billion in 1994, up 8.8 percent from $4.31 billion in fiscal 1993.

After the success of the original SPARC chip, Agrawal had gone off to work on another possible microprocessor design for Sun that wound up being cancelled. The company put him back to work on ultraSPARC, the development of which Silvestri had accelerated in a race to replace the disastrous superSPARC design. In late 1995,

Sun introduced ultraSPARC at the Microprocessor Forum, the premier industry conference on chip design. The launch occurred the same day that McNealy's wife, Susan, had their first baby, a son whom they named Maverick. The night before the ultraSPARC launch, Sun had a dry run for the employees. McNealy, his wife, and his mother, Marmalee, were all there, but McNealy had to pass up the actual event the next day when his wife went into labor.

After superSPARC, there had been doubt inside and outside the company that ultraSPARC would be any better. The crisis, Agrawal says, brought out the best in Sun. Disagreement dropped to a minimum as everyone concentrated on overcoming the difficulties. "We were all behind solving the problem—how do we get us out of trouble? It was never, 'should we have made this decision [to unify on SPARC]?' I've never seen so much teamwork in such a large company." The rumbling began again once the crisis was over and ultraSPARC's success was established. "When you're in a crisis, you don't doubt your strategy," he says. "Once you're through the crisis, you can ask whether you're on the correct course." UltraSPARC, paired with the Solaris operating system, powered Sun into the late 1990s. UltraSPARC leapfrogged the competition, zooming Sun from last to first on many benchmarks. It enabled the company to fill out its product line, moving from workstations to servers, high-powered machines that link computer networks together. Sums up Agrawal: "UltraSPARC turned Sun around. Scott told me on a business trip a couple of years later that it was the biggest turnaround in Sun's history. If we hadn't executed, Sun could have died."

■ THE PLANETS

McNealy had one more surprise up his sleeve for beleaguered Sun executives. This was a new organizational structure called "the planets," announced in early 1991. Instead of the largely functional structure that had prevailed until then, Sun would be split up into several smaller pieces, each handling a separate product line. The number of planets varied during the seven years they were in operation, from as many as 11 in the early days to a more manageable 6 or 7 during the mid- to late 1990s. The planets, or operating companies as they were formally known, operated as minibusinesses, each having its own profit-and-loss statement, salesforce, public relations staff, and so forth.

The push to get Solaris widely adopted was one spur for the reorganization. The first planet was SunSoft, whose primary focus would be Solaris and other software products. Next was Sun Microsystems Computer Company (SMCC), which was always the Jupiter among the planets, because it brought in the bulk of the revenue through sales of workstations and servers. Another motive for the reorganization was to keep Sun quick and nimble. McNealy had been impressed by what he saw at Sun's partners in Japan. He visited Toshiba and inquired, "Who's your top competitor?" only to be asked, "In what business?" Toshiba ran itself as a diversified portfolio with diverse competitors. McNealy intended the planets to be like the units within Toshiba—each concentrating on its own product line, business, competitors, and allies. For example, SunSoft would work to license that operating system to vendors other than Sun and get it ported, or altered to run on, platforms other than SPARC, even if that meant competing with Sun itself. Likewise, the SPARC Technology Business, later Sun Microelectronics (SME), attempted to license the chip to original equipment manufacturers who might create products that competed with SPARC/Solaris.

Crawford Beveridge, Sun's vice president of corporate resources until he left in 1991, remembers holing up with McNealy and other executives in late 1990 to talk about the notion of planets. "We had a big sales meeting in Hawaii in October," he recalls. "Everybody was having a great time out on the beach, while Scott and the staff were locked in a dark room doing the planets." The concerns, which turned out to be justified, were that the distribution channel and customers would be confused by separate salesforces and that SMCC would have the most clout because it brought in most of the business. Still, the planets did develop clear definition of product lines. "This was a transition the company had to make," Beveridge believes. "The organization was getting too complex and unfocused. Scott couldn't see how you could get SPARC products or Solaris to a much wider base if they were buried within the company."

Most of Sun's executives, however, resented the planets and the complications they caused, especially because McNealy pushed the bickering between the operating companies off on others. "Each planet had its own agenda," recalls Carol Bartz, who held various executive positions at Sun from 1983 to 1992, when she left to become CEO of Autodesk. "Working out how everything was going to interoperate was not Scott's strong suit. We had the 'rules of engagement' on how the planets were supposed to interact, but it wasn't practical. When issues would come up, Scott didn't want to deal with those. He wanted to focus on the next company or sale, not on an interplanetary battle." Adds Wozniak: "Conceptually the planet structure was beautiful, but when you got down to the next layer of detail, it was difficult to make it work. Scott didn't want to hear that. When you say something doesn't work, he says, 'I don't care. Make it work.' It never really got there."

Then too, the planets, like children squabbling for supremacy within a family, were always jealous of who was getting the most attention. First SunSoft was the golden child, then JavaSoft, which was formed in January 1996 to handle Java technology. "It's sort of like your dad saying, 'I like the last kid who's born,' " Bartz says. "Scott was always interested in where's the next excitement, not the nitty-gritty details of people fighting over budgets." The planets also diluted Sun's focus on the customer. "Before, if a customer wanted something, we'd do damn near anything," says Bartz. "Now if you were in SMCC and the problem was somewhere else, you had to go hat in hand to another planet and negotiate a change."

■ SUN RISES AGAIN

From mid-1989 through 1994, Sun was in one of those troughs that seem to be endemic to the hyperkinetic technology industry. Sun was lucky in a sense—its downturn was triggered by internal factors, including the move to a new MIS system and the failure of superSPARC, and could be fixed. This low period, even the highly disliked planet structure, did have its payoffs. For one thing, executives and employees learned what mettle their young CEO had, as McNealy took charge of the company after key resignations and put much-needed processes into place that would improve efficiency and increase individual accountability. The planets, though flawed, enabled the business lines within Sun to carve out new markets. "We had to move away from centralized management. That was not the way to run a new millennium company," says Ed Zander, who was president of two of the planets, SunSoft and SMCC, before becoming chief operating officer. "We got focused. Most of the success at Sun today was the result of focusing on key areas." JavaSoft nurtured the fledgling Java technology in a way that wouldn't have occurred within a centralized management structure, he believes.

McNealy came into his own during this period. He no longer had a strong right-hand man in Bernie Lacroute. (Ed Zander would later take on this role.) His chief financial officer had left him in a moment of crisis. He had to deal with demoralized employees, a skeptical press, and competitors who were only too glad to chortle, "We told you Sun was a flash in the pan." McNealy "hunkered down and weathered it," recalls Broadbent, who as public relations manager had to deal with the outpouring of press calls. On one especially bad day, "Scott came down and saw me through the glass and knew I was having a rough time," she says. McNealy came in and gave her a pep talk. "It's going to get better," he assured her. "Scott never shies away from trouble," Broadbent says. "He kept telling us, 'We're going to get through this; we'll be back.' "

Almost unnoticed amid the turmoil was the fact that Sun had moved upchannel, adding a new product line—servers—and a new level of customer—the corporate enterprise. This was not only a very forward-looking strategy, but it delivered the company from the immediate threat posed by Windows NT. NT was introduced in 1993 and was poised to gobble up chunks of Sun's traditional workstation market. In a speech to the New York Society of Security Analysts, McNealy asserted that Sun could no longer be pigeonholed as a workstation company. "Being in the engineering workstation market was good for getting us a high [price-earnings] multiple when we went public," McNealy said, according to an article in the October 20, 1994, issue of *Investor's Business Daily*.[7] "But we no longer position ourselves that way. We are taking on every aspect of computing in huge, dispersed workgroup environments. Not automating the architect, but the design floor; not automating the trader, but the entire trading floor."

One of the first markets in which Sun's servers would become popular was among companies emerging to offer Internet access, a niche Sun dominates to this day. Because Sun had fortuitously incorporated networking into its computers from day one, the company was well poised to leap aboard the Internet express as it gathered speed in the mid-1990s. The Unix operating system, not Windows NT, was the engine that powered the various servers that operated the Internet across the country, and Sun was the leader. "The Network Is The Computer" had finally come into its own.

Revenue for fiscal 1995, when Sun recovered its momentum on the back of Solaris paired with ultraSPARC, leaped by more than $1 billion, or 26 percent, to $5.9 billion. Net income was up an even more impressive 82 percent to $355.8 million. "Any way you look at it, fiscal 1995

THE SUN UNIVERSE OF PLANETS
IN APRIL 1994

Sun Microsystems Computer Company (*SMCC*) develops, manufactures, and markets workstations and servers; it also integrates and sells products from other Sun business units.

SunSoft develops and sells system software—specifically, Solaris—as well as network management and interoperability products that allow Solaris to link with other systems.

SPARC Technology Business (*later Sun Microelectronics*) sells SPARC processor and component designs.

SunExpress provides ordering and delivery of Sun products for end users and resellers.

Sun Microsystems Laboratories is the advanced research and development arm used by the other planets.

Sun Microsystems Federal sells to federal, state, and local governments.

SunService provides system support, education, integration, and other services to end users.

was a banner year for Sun—and for our stockholders," McNealy wrote in the annual report. The revenue gain of $1.2 billion was a single-year record. Reflecting his attention to operational management, he noted, "Key metrics of efficiency such as return on equity and return on assets finished at their highest levels in many years." Sun's core business, the cash cow that allowed it to invest in breakthroughs such as Java, was solid once more.

Chapter

Kick Butt and Have Fun

With its minimal level of defined processes and its predilection for chaos, Sun Microsystems can be a human resource person's nightmare. "Sun is different than any company I've ever been in," says Ken Alvares, who had 20 years' experience in the human resources field before joining Sun in 1992 as vice president of human resources and corporate executive officer. "We're a table-pounding, yelling, confrontational, maverick-like organization. We certainly don't describe ourselves as polite." This can be traced to McNealy, whose personality permeates Sun's culture. "Scott likes friction and confrontation. He encourages it," says Alvares. "He lets everybody battle it out, state their point of view." The result can be a cauldron of conflicting opinions, boiling up all over the place.

With McNealy in charge, you'd expect Sun to have an intense, mercurial culture, and it doesn't disappoint. "Kick butt and have fun!" is his internally directed sound bite. McNealy is scarcely seen these days by most employees, because Sun sprawls across a dozen different complexes in the San Francisco Bay Area alone, and the CEO is on the road a good deal of the time—but his presence is always felt. You can feel it in the large reproductions of

"Javaman" and other magazine covers featuring McNealy that hang in the lobbies of various Sun facilities to the posters of his sound bites that grace the hallways to the spartan cubicles in which most employees work. "Scott is totally intuitive and that's how he's driven this company," says Alvares. In McNealy's eyes, the cardinal sin is not acting, so everyone from executives to rank-and-file employees is expected to take their job and run with it. If that means stepping on toes, so be it.

The tension within Sun now is that, as the company has gotten bigger and expanded its customer base beyond engineers, it has been forced to curb some of the excesses of its freewheeling culture and install a certain amount of order via processes. At the same time, Sun has endeavored to retain enough of its youthful, unbridled enthusiasm, spirit of fun, sense of camaraderie and all of the other qualities that make it unique. For Sun to attract the kind of people it wants to have working for it—those who are brilliant and brash and don't wait for someone to tell them what to do—it has to allow some degree of the freedom of action and dislike of authority that marked its early days. But how much of that is too much? Molding its culture without destroying it is a continual challenge within Sun, as it is for many companies.

■ APRIL FOOL'S!

The most notorious manifestation of Sun's freewheeling culture has been its April Fool's Day jokes, which established its egalitarian, unorthodox mind-set from day one. Each April 1st, a group of employees, usually engineers, would stage an elaborate gag involving one of the executives. In 1985, the pranksters removed the entire contents of Eric Schmidt's office and set them up next to a pond between two of the buildings. The next year, they took a Volkswagen Beetle apart and reassembled it in Schmidt's office. In 1987, the team of jokesters picked on Bill Joy, parking his Ferrari on a platform just below the surface of one of the outdoor ponds, so that it looked like the car was resting in the middle of the water. Joy, embracing the spirit of the joke, got in a rubber dinghy to row out to his car. From there he used his cellular phone to call the American Automobile Association for help.

McNealy hasn't been exempt from the tricksters. There was the arrow through his office in 1990, described in the last chapter. One of the most memorable stunts occurred in 1988 when an enterprising group of engineers took out the wall between the offices of McNealy and his second in command, Bernie Lacroute, and turned both offices into a one-hole golf course, complete with a water hazard and a sand trap. "We did it all in one night," boasts a smiling Tom Lyon, who was an engineer at Sun for 12 years. The next morning, the team borrowed a golf cart from a nearby golf course to complete the illusion. When he came in, McNealy got in the cart and started driving around the building, "terrorizing everyone," Lyon says.

More recent jokes have included turning the office of one present-day executive, who's originally from Holland, into a Dutch landscape; taking all the parts out of another executive's prized sports car and putting in a computer and fax machine, so that it resembled an office; making an aviary out of an executive's office who was fond of birds; and covering an entire building with an exterminator's tent and putting a sign out front proclaiming the building to be "bug free."

Today the April Fool's jokes are waning as many members of the original core group that pulled off the gags have left. Ruben Pereida, a Sun engineer for more than 14 years, compares Sun in the old days with the "Wild Wild West," where just about anything could happen. "For a while," he admits, "it did get out of hand." But the tradition persists, although now the team that's going to do the joke is selected from employees who want to participate, and their target is also designated. Even the April Fool's gags have become subject to a process. Some employees see this as a sign of maturity, while others sigh for the good old days.

■ SUN WORSHIP

People who are drawn to Sun come as much because of the culture as the technology. Working on a hot technology is important, but there are hundreds of companies in Silicon Valley that can make that claim. Until Java came along and gave Sun the cachet of an Internet company, it was in danger of losing its reputation as a leading technology innovator (although its workstations and servers were respected for their technical excellence and beat out competitors in many benchmarks, such as floating-point calculations, used to compare classes of machines). Then, too, an established company like Sun has to compete not only against other seasoned companies like itself, but against the tantalizing lure of the start-up, which offers the possibility of going back to the beginning and playing the game all over again. One of Sun's shining lights, cofounder Andy Bechtolsheim, departed for that very reason. "I left Sun because I wanted the opportunity of starting a new business again," he says. "I wanted something different." (Ironically, his start-up company, Granite Systems, was eventually acquired by Cisco, where Bechtolsheim now works.)

As with most technology companies, the culture at Sun is heavily weighted toward engineers, although that influence tends to become diluted with growth and with the development of functional responsibilities, such as human resources, marketing, sales, public relations, and the like. In the early going, Sun was mostly engineers, drawn from universities to a company with kindred spirits, such as Bill Joy and Andy Bechtolsheim. The university/engineering method of getting things done is project-oriented, not hours-oriented. Engineers may work all night to debug the last bit of software or to solve a hardware problem like the monitors blowing up on the Sun-2. Sun retains that engineering insistence on meeting goals, whether it be in manufacturing, financial, or other areas. Another key tenet is employee empowerment—*you, the employee, do whatever it takes to solve a problem.* There is no rigid chain of command within Sun. Rather, there is the fluid formation and reformation of teams, which tackle various challenges as they come up. Engineers are also antiauthoritarian, prone to fierce argument over their own ideas and disdain for those who don't understand the concepts. "That's a brain-dead idea" is an oft-heard comment inside Sun.

Over the years, however, Sun's technical arrogance—"build it and they will come"—has been mitigated as the company broadened its product offerings and delivered more consistent financial results. "When I first joined Sun, every quarter was different. We needed more consistency for the market to trust us," says Lora Colflesh, vice president of human resources and corporate services. "Now we have that, and we've gone from arrogance to confidence. Confidence comes from having a consistent business." Thanks in the beginning to McNealy and Khosla and continuing with executives like Bernie Lacroute and Ed Zander, Sun's headstrong engineers have been balanced by pragmatic business needs.

That's a vital combination. Many innovative companies stumble when the tendency of engineers to invent technology for its own sake is not kept in check by management's need to dominate the market and create value for shareholders. Sun has been able to retain outstanding engineers by setting up a system of distinguished engineers and fellows, who can pretty much pick and choose what they want to work on. At the highest level, it has allowed Bill Joy to run his own little fiefdom—a small, hand-picked, advanced R&D team—in Aspen, Colorado. At the same time, Sun has strong personalities at the top, like President and Chief Operating Officer Ed Zander and Chief Financial Officer Mike Lehman, whose focus is on getting product out and meeting the expectations of customers and Wall Street. Add to that McNealy's ability to articulate a single, overriding goal—like killing Apollo or thwarting Microsoft. Although setting up the big enemy can seem like a melodramatic overgeneralization, it does compel engineers, administrators, and executives to look outside themselves and the company. "There's this hard-nosed attitude of who's the enemy and who's not," notes Alvares. "Some people within the company love it because it gives us a rallying cry. It gets people charged up. You work together better when you have a common enemy."

■ THE DARK SIDE

The Sun culture is for neither the thin-skinned nor the anal-retentive soul who prefers a carefully ordered existence. Witness Colflesh's experience. In 1993, when she called to express interest in working at Sun, the person who fielded her inquiry told her bluntly, "You'll never get hired here because you're not in the high-tech industry." Colflesh, who had spent 10 years in human resources management at TRW Incorporated, a Southern California defense contractor, was a bit taken aback, but she wanted to get out of the defense industry and sent in her resume to Sun anyway. "I wanted to prove them wrong," she says, exhibiting the persistence that is a prime requirement for working at Sun. She ultimately was hired as director of human resources for one of the then-planets, Sun Technology Enterprises, run by Eric Schmidt.

When she arrived for work, Colflesh personally went through another aspect of the Sun baptism-by-fire. Schmidt took her down the hall and told her, "Here's your office. Go to it." But there were three engineers sitting inside the office, hunched over their workstations and carrying on an animated discussion of a product design point. Obviously, they were there to stay. So Schmidt informed her, "Your first assignment is to find an office, get a phone, and get a workstation." Colflesh succeeded in her first assignment and, five years later, she's still at Sun, where she's endeavoring to make it a somewhat kinder, gentler place to work.

"Sun can drive people to distraction and burnout," she says. "It's an open environment where you can push back. That can be hard to take." The word "nurture" is never heard at Sun, and employees largely sink or swim on their own. "This is a place where we're so process-averse, you can pretty much do anything you want to do," says Alvares. "There are almost no constraints on doing things, no guideposts on how to get anything done. If you're a person who likes to come in and make an impact, this is the place. If you need some help getting started, there's almost no help. You have to go figure out what to do."

Another stumbling point for many employees is that Sun's headcount has never kept up with the amount of work to be done. Those who can't take the long hours and the never-ending tasks at hand sift themselves out. *Sunburst* recounts the recruitment, in 1988, of a highly regarded M.B.A. from a Fortune 500 company to do forecast analysis.[1] This new hire left after two days. "Never in his career had he seen so much work before him with so little staff to accomplish it," *Sunburst* said. He decided that "working in such a frantic place was tantamount to suicide." Concluded Zander, as he authorized a replacement: "This company is not for the faint of heart." Lack of resources is still a problem today, a decade later. In periodic employee quality surveys that seek to determine what inhibits people from doing their jobs well, "what we're finding is there's too much work to do and not enough resources," says Colflesh. "We need to hire more people faster. People are overwhelmed with the amount of work."

Colflesh—who now oversees benefits, employment, and employee services—is determined to make the adjustment to Sun a little easier for new hires than it was for her. "We weren't doing a very good job of assimilating new employees or helping them get started," she says. Now there's a new orientation program called "Arriving, Thriving, and

Surviving at Sun." The "Arriving" portion covers everything from employee benefits to learning how to use a Solaris workstation. The "Thriving" portion covers Sun's history and culture. "Surviving," in Colflesh's words, "is about what you can do *not* to self-destruct." It's about who an employee can call for needed resources or help in doing a job within the company. Besides that, Sun has inaugurated SunBalance, which allows employees to contact external resources for aid in handling work/family problems.

It's an uphill battle for Alvares and Colflesh to establish processes that would be considered essential in other companies. Human resources has to fight to win recognition from executives. Sun is in its adolescence, Alvares says, and consequently doesn't like rules. "We've got a mixture of teenager and adult in our blood. When you're a little bit of both, you don't want to be either. That conflict causes some paranoid behavior." For example, identifying the ultimate decision maker on a particular issue would seem a prerequisite for doing anything. Yet, at Sun, it's not clear. McNealy encourages his executive team to battle things out. Each issue has an assigned CXO who is supposed to be the final arbiter when there's a disagreement. Alvares is the CXO of titles and makes the call as to who gets elevated to vice president or director. But in times of change, when new issues pop up, "we're not sure who the CXO is," says Alvares. "If someone like Lehman disagrees with someone like Zander, what happens? The honest-to-god truth is we don't know."

The anarchic attitudes that hark back to the cadre of Unix engineers and recent university graduates who built Sun resist processes. "It's considered countercultural to put processes in place," sighs Alvares. "The word 'mandatory' doesn't exist at Sun. You can't put together a training program for all first-line managers. You have to sell everything you do." Still, processes are slowly being developed and maturity is lurking around the corner for the adolescent culture of Sun. As noted in the previous chapter, first to come were processes related to finances and manufacturing, to insure that Sun doesn't repeat the debacle of the loss quarter. Now, Alvares and Colflesh are working to establish processes that insure Sun doesn't lose talented people.

■ BEYOND ADOLESCENCE

First of all, sheer growth demands processes. When Colflesh joined Sun in 1993, it had 13,000 employees; now there are 27,000. To recruit and retain thousands of new hires every year, you don't want them all jousting for chairs, desks, and workstations. Secondly, Sun's customer mix is radically different today from the engineers who initially bought its workstations to design products. The original Sun was engineers selling to other engineers. Engineers like to fix their own problems and write their own software code. So once a sale is made, there's little hand-holding. By contrast, Sun's fastest-growing market today is sales of servers to the corporate enterprise. At this level, Sun must sell to a chief information officer or other executive-level person, and its machines will support networks of computers used by nontechnical people. So Sun must have customer support and services, and that means processes.

As Sun became a competitor in the enterprise, it ran up against companies such as IBM and Hewlett-Packard, which had highly developed infrastructures for customer support. "We had to change in every way you can think of," says Alvares. The salesforce was consolidated so that customers needed only one point of contact to the company. Salespeople take classes at the in-house Sun University that teach them how to handle a higher-level contact and how to communicate Sun's overall value added, not just the characteristics of one particular product. "We talked to engineering about talking to customers, responding to their needs," he says. Compensation programs were restructured to reward selling into the enterprise. Recruitment programs were tailored to attract people not only for their technical expertise, but for their understanding of the enterprise. Sun even, as Colflesh discovered, began hiring people from outside high tech, recognizing that expertise could come from elsewhere.

Another sign of that is a diversity training program, which used to be mandatory for managers but has become voluntary because "most people want to attend," says Colflesh. Although Sun reflects Silicon Valley's and McNealy's libertarian views and is resolutely against affirmative action quotas, its wide-open nature has made it easy for immigrants to join from the beginning. There is so much frenetic activity going on at Sun that someone with a different-sounding name or accent is hardly noticed. "I've never seen a more open company," says Masood Jabbar, a Pakistani immigrant who heads Sun's computer division. "You can question almost anything here. That creates an environment that's conducive to diversity and tolerance. I've never stayed at one place for 12 years except Sun because you're allowed to be who you are here. Very few companies our size allow you to be you." Of course, diversity brings benefits to Sun as well. "There's a receptivity to new ideas," says Jabbar. He points to an axiom attributed to Bill Joy: "Bet on the fact that innovation occurs. Bet on the fact that it occurs elsewhere." Sun doesn't have a problem with adopting good ideas from outside (except maybe when they come from Redmond). "This has become the premier place for innovation in Silicon Valley," brags Jabbar. "We don't have to think about affirmative action."

Sun has pushed its annual employee turnover rate down to a respectable 10 percent, compared with an average of 20 percent among the notoriously fickle denizens of Silicon Valley. But, several years ago, Sun's turnover rate was higher than that of its chief "people" competitors—large, well-regarded companies such as Hewlett-Packard, Cisco, Microsoft (which has a large presence in the Valley), and Oracle. Alvares remembers sitting in a management meeting where everyone agreed that "our single biggest problem,

and one that could kill us, is our inability to keep people."
They turned to him, a relatively new human resources director, and said, "How are you going to fix it?"

Alvares set out to find the answer. Exit interviews revealed that people were leaving Sun for four primary
reasons:

1. They either disagreed with or didn't understand the
   company's vision and, hence, didn't believe Sun
   could win.
2. They didn't get to work on enjoyable projects.
3. They either disagreed with, disliked, or disrespected
   management.
4. They could get more money and stock options somewhere else.

One thing Alvares concluded was that just throwing
more money at employees wasn't the answer. Sun's compensation package is at the 75th percentile in the Valley
(which means that its salaries are in the top 25 percent).
And, it has moved to broaden its stock option grants,
which initially went mostly to executives and star engineers, to include about one-third of all employees today.

More difficult were the challenges of getting people to
understand where Sun was going and why. Alvares enlisted
top executives, including the presidents of the planets, to
address these issues. The company instituted a series of
town hall meetings at which McNealy, Zander, and other
key leaders speak. It also started a program in which employees were encouraged to move around within their departments and develop new skills. For example, a financial
analyst might learn something about marketing or a salesperson something about customer support. Teams were
juggled to allow different people a shot at what was considered a hot technology, like Java for instance. Sun University developed courses for managers about dealing with
people, handling change, recruiting and hiring, and other
skills. Employees could take courses teaching them how to
communicate more effectively with their managers.

Colflesh is proud of the SunTeams program, in which teams from any division can win an award for solving a problem or coming up with a better way of doing something. For example, one complaint she used to field regularly was that employees didn't know who to contact with their human resources questions. Colflesh set up a team with members from all of Sun's divisions and established a customer council of employees. The result was SunDial, which provided a phone number and an e-mail address allowing Sun employees to obtain convenient access to human resources information. The solution won a SunTeams award. Other SunTeams have come up with methods to reduce cycle time and improve shipping time in manufacturing; and cut the number of hours it takes to close the financial books at the end of a quarter.

The road to adulthood is not an easy one. "Are we there yet?" Alvares asks. "Hell, no. We've got a long way to go." This company "will resist processes until we absolutely have to have them. We've got more systems in place now than six years ago, but not much." At some point in time, "we have to grow up," he says, or else lose people and customers to companies who already have grown up.

■ THE LIMITS OF CHANGE

As long as McNealy remains as the head of Sun, the culture will flow from him. Even as they cajole Sun toward adulthood, Alvares and Colflesh know that Sun's culture will retain elements of the CEO's boyish competitiveness and iconoclastic attitude. "The maverick image is part of the appeal of working here," says Colflesh. "This is a founder-based company and Scott is such a strong leader, he's very involved in H.R. decisions. I don't do anything without him saying, 'Yes, this is a good thing.'" Even though he's increasingly focused on representing Sun to the outside world, McNealy considers it part of his job to stay in touch with employees. When possible, he continues to give out the 5-, 10-, and 15-year service awards, bringing along his mother, his wife, and his kids. "People want to have their picture taken with him and shake his hand," says Colflesh. "He does really well in that setting." As for McNealy's bombastic statements about Microsoft or other competitors, "it's not in Scott to change," says Alvares. "The notion is that any press is good press and benefits the company." He adds, "Founders are wonderful visionaries. They have the uncanny ability to distort history in a way that confirms their present feelings."

But even McNealy has mellowed. No doubt being married and becoming the father of two young sons has changed his outlook. In the introduction to the current *Sun Employee Benefits and Services Resource Guide,* the CEO writes: "There's more to life than work. Maintaining the right balance between your career and other parts of your life is necessary for your happiness and well-being—and it's essential to Sun's continued growth." McNealy goes on to describe the broad range of Sun programs that help employees manage their time effectively, achieve a "healthy, active and secure life . . ." and, of course, have fun. Still, as the employees themselves will tell you, the hallmark of Sun is hard work and long hours.

Despite the contradictions and the difficulties, you'd have to say that Sun's culture is viable for people who crave challenge, excitement, expansive goals, and empowerment, and who don't mind confrontation and lack of supervision. Both at the executive and employee levels, Sun has managed to keep much of its key talent on board—witness Bill Joy, Anant Agrawal, and Masood Jabbar. As some of its stars depart, like Eric Schmidt, Andy Bechtolsheim, or Carol Bartz, they do so to step up onto a larger stage, running or starting a company. And, the company doesn't fall apart with the departure of this kind of talent. It regroups and goes on, with people like Zander and Lehman. Even McNealy is no longer indispensable. Sun, though it would be a considerably different place, has enough structure in place to go on without him.

"My definition of success [for Sun] is the same as everyone else here," says Alvares, "continue to gain market share and kick the hell out of the competition. People come here to change the world, not run a computer company." Then, he adds (warning: another car analogy is imminent): "We don't bring people in who can drive a car. We bring people in who can make the car."

The proof of Sun's culture may be Java, the breakthrough technology whose development will be described in the next chapter. Like the accident that led to penicillin being synthesized from a moldy petri dish left out too long, Sun's very chaos permits the unexpected discovery, and then the company has the inventiveness, market awareness, and determination to take that discovery and find a place for it. So it was with Java. "Java has given us renewed excitement and brand awareness," says Alvares. "My mother-in-law has heard of Java as something cool. She never knew before what Sun or Solaris was."

THE EMPLOYEE PERSPECTIVE

If you really want to know what it's like to work at a company, ask the employees. I spoke with a panel of five Sun employees, ranging from a financial analyst hired out of college to the veteran engineer Ruben Pereida, whose employee number is 506. Other participants in the September 1998 roundtable included: Beverley Bryant, who works with state and local governments on behalf of Sun's interests and has been with the company for about five years; John Cappelletti, a financial analyst with corporate resources who has been there for two years; Charlene Sul, a patent specialist for the past year and a half; and Steven Grigory, a product marketing manager with the workstation division who recently joined Sun from Apple Computer.

(continued)

THE EMPLOYEE PERSPECTIVE
(Continued)

They all agree that working at Sun means taking responsibility to shape your job. "Sun has a lot of processes but finding them is a challenge. You're very much on your own," says Grigory. People who aren't resourceful enough fade away, adds Bryant. "You have to look outside the box. If you can't adjust to new situations, you'll be out of here." At the same time, she never feels like she has to go through the chain of command to get something done. When she needs to put together a team, "I just grab people from different departments. We all do everything from copying to stapling to very high-level thinking." Cappelletti says that Sun gives you the rope. "You can either take the rope and be successful or you can hang yourself with it." There's no right way of doing something.

Although Sun's culture has changed over the years, one thing that has remained the same, says Pereida, is the workload. The others laugh knowingly. Grigory recalls that right after he was hired, he had to handle the launch of a new workstation for January 1998. Sixty-plus hours a week is typical, and no one leaves early because the rest of the team will jump down your throat. Sul notes, though, that there are breaks. "As soon as I finish something huge, the people I work for will say get out of here for the rest of the day."

Despite some of the negative press about Sun and its strategy, the employees aren't fazed. Says Bryant: "We're challenging ourselves to do the best we can. The press isn't seeing what I'm seeing." Sul, who handles intellectual property issues, works with internal inventors. "Maybe when those new ideas stop coming I will worry," she says, "but we're getting ideas every day."

(continued)

THE EMPLOYEE PERSPECTIVE
(Continued)

They're supportive of McNealy, even if they all don't agree with his stance on Microsoft. Bryant remembers watching the CEO speak during a town hall meeting in Colorado, scheduled to consider a new Sun campus. "They gave him a standing ovation, a thousand people in the heat," she says. Grigory calls McNealy the company's "best cheerleader." The Microsoft rhetoric is a way for him "to light up the crowd," he adds, although sometimes McNealy goes too far. For example, Sun employees are banned from using PowerPoint, a presentation program from Microsoft. "They make us use the Sun product," which no one else has, Grigory says. "We've got to interoperate [with Microsoft products]. That's what my customers want." He warns Sun not to go down the same path as Apple in losing focus on business objectives to concentrate on a religious crusade.

Chapter

7

What Is Java, Anyway?

More than anything else, Java has put Sun on the map of public consciousness. Your mother-in-law and that neighbor you meet in the shopping line have probably heard of Java as something cool and related to the Internet, even if they don't know and don't care what a Sun workstation is. Before the 1995 introduction of Java, Sun was known primarily inside Silicon Valley and to technical users within the business community. Though it had impressive products with its workstations and servers, Sun was an old technology company compared with the brash start-ups grabbing headlines in the mid-1990s. These were new companies like Netscape Communications Corporation and Yahoo!, created to exploit the alluring Internet, the technology world's latest frontier to be conquered. Netscape's browser enabled you to navigate this dizzying expanse of on-line information, graphics, and entertainment. Yahoo! provided the compass, a search engine, that pointed you in the right direction. Compared with them, Sun seemed a bit staid and conventional, a solid but unspectacular company churning out solid but unspectacular products for the already-charted country of corporate computing. As noted in Chapter 5, with the introduction of ultraSPARC,

Sun's products had leaped again to the top of their class, but it was a class that did not inflame the imagination of journalists, pundits, analysts, and other observers the way the Internet companies did.

Java elevated Sun, and to some extent its share price, to the ranks of Internet companies. You could argue, as Sun executives vehemently did, that Sun was already there. After all, its servers are used by the majority of Internet service providers, which operate powerful computers that allow individuals and corporations to link to the Net. When you boot up your own computer and activate your Internet browser, the machine that serves up your connection is probably from Sun, but there's nothing that leaps out at you and tells you that. Whereas, with Java, Sun has made a determined and generally successful effort to link its name with its new technology. It has developed trade shows related to Java and a memorable logo, a steaming mug of hot coffee, to designate the presence of the technology. Something like the "Intel Inside" campaign. And Java is stoked by such pundits as George Gilder, who proclaimed that Java makes operating systems like Microsoft's Windows "irrelevant." Sun CEO Scott McNealy has gleefully parlayed Java into a platform for headlines. Java is the weapon by which McNealy can simultaneously denounce Microsoft's control of the computer world and champion a supposedly freer, open model.

So just what is Java anyway? Thanks to Sun and the willing assistance of the trade press—which loves to elevate each new technology that comes along—Java has become a myriad of things. When it was born, it was a programming language, an alphabet and rules of grammar that enable software developers to write code for new programs. The difference between Java and older programming languages, like Basic, C, and C++, is that programs written in Java are not tied to any underlying operating system such as Windows or Macintosh or Solaris. Java programs can reside in one place—say the Internet—and be accessed and operated ("executed" in programmers' parlance) somewhere else, like your computer at home or work. McNealy, Gilder, and the rest of the missionaries have made this ability of Java's the centerpiece of a new "religion," encompassing the Internet and Netscape's Navigator browser, that promises to free us from the tyranny of Bill Gates. Thousands of software developers, small and large, are now writing programs in Java, creating a formidable community of allies for Sun. Meanwhile, Sun has developed a number of related technologies that are designed to promote use of Java in the business world and on consumer devices like smart cards and cellular phones.

To pierce through the cloud of hype surrounding Java and its various permutations, let's go back to the birth of the technology, which began life very precariously indeed.

■ THE SECRET PROJECT

In late 1990, one of Sun's star engineers, who had worked on the failed NeWS project (see Chapter 4), was getting restless. This was Patrick Naughton, then a 25-year-old, kick-ass programmer who personified the arrogant, frat-boy culture of Sun. He was sure he was God's gift to computing, and he didn't like being in limbo. "Having given up on the future of NeWS, I personally was deciding where I wanted to work next," he says. The NeWS group had been dispersed throughout various research initiatives at Sun, but the early 1990s was a dormant time for the company, especially if you were working on the software side. Sun kept Naughton occupied with what he describes as "busy work," so he did what most talented engineers in Silicon Valley do when they're not happy: he looked around for the coolest project going and hopped on board. In 1990 this was Next, the Steve Jobs–created company that was to be the next Apple Computer. Jobs, ousted from Apple in a political battle, was looking to step up from the world of personal computers to more powerful workstations. He had devised a product that potentially would compete with Sun and other workstation vendors: the computer itself was called Next, like the company, and the operating system, Nextstep.

After a personal meeting with Jobs, who hit it off with the young engineer, and a series of interviews at Next, "I was ready to get out of Sun," Naughton says. "My biggest worry was telling Scott McNealy," to whom he felt an intense loyalty. Naughton knew the Sun CEO better than most employees because he played in the same amateur hockey league three nights a week. One night after hockey practice, when the team was having dinner at a local hangout, Naughton blurted it out: He was leaving Sun. McNealy handled the situation adroitly. Rather than lash out, he gave Naughton the Sun sales pitch, accompanied by a list of reasons as to why Next would fail. (That prediction turned out to be accurate. Jobs abandoned the Next computer and turned his company into a software developer, which was eventually bought by Apple.) McNealy promised Naughton that Sun was going to get its act together and that he should hang on. The CEO told Naughton to pretend he was God and send him an e-mail with his suggestions as to what was wrong within the company and how to fix it.

McNealy's approach struck just the right chord with the ambitious Naughton. The result was a lengthy e-mail detailing Naughton's frustration with various projects at Sun, including the moribund NeWS. "At the time I was so frustrated by the directionless mass of dispassionate people in the group, that my own solution for them all was euthanasia," he says. Or, at least, "cancellation of the project." What Naughton envisioned in its place was a small, tightly knit group of people who would work quickly and without the bureaucracy and opposition that were beginning to retard other projects at Sun. McNealy forwarded the e-mail to a few other key people, who in turn sent it out to others. Naughton became the center of an intellectual backlash at

Sun by some of its brightest lights, who had been disappointed when the company chickened out on NeWS. James Gosling, the father of NeWS and Naughton's former boss, "saw the spark I started at the executive level of Sun and he started pouring gasoline on it as fast as he could," Naughton says. Bill Joy, now ensconced at his own skunkworks in Aspen, chipped in with a message of support. Gosling introduced Naughton to another internal refugee, Mike Sheridan, who had come when Sun bought his company, Folio, and then couldn't figure out what to do with it. "Mike had his share of Sun scars . . . James was clearly still crispy from getting burned on NeWS, and I was a flaming exit wound," says Naughton. "What a great team we would make!"

Gosling, Naughton, and Sheridan enlisted John Gage, now the chief scientist at Sun, as an ally in their quest to form a handpicked research group. Gage, an eccentric even in an eccentric company, saw this as an opportunity to return to the early, Wild West days of Sun. "Our feeling is if it's not technically interesting, we don't want to do it," he says. Gage concedes that Sun, as it grew, became more like other large companies, in which the mass of people are devoted to working on incremental improvements rather than breakthroughs. "But at the core of Sun is a group that wants to change things," he says. Gage recognized that the trio of Gosling, Naughton, and Sheridan were among that special group. So he turned them over to Wayne Rosing, who was getting ready to take charge of the newly created Sun Labs, an internal research arm. Over dinner with Gosling and Naughton, Rosing, who was older, more experienced, and more politically cautious than the two young engineers, was convinced by their passion. He bought into the idea of a project led by an elite group that would have the vague charter of designing a revolutionary new software product to fill the void left by NeWS. The project, funded by Sun Labs, was dubbed "Green," and the business plan was called "Behind the Green Door" (from one of the most popular pornographic movies of all time). What the name meant to the three team members was that their project would be kept secret from all but the top echelon at Sun and that they would be free to work without interference from the corporate "antibodies" that usually sprang up to nay-say a nascent technology.

➤ The Green Team at Work

In mid-January 1991, the Green Project trio, plus Sun Labs' Wayne Rosing, and Sun's resident hardware genius and cofounder, Andy Bechtolsheim, flew up to Aspen to stay at Bill Joy's house for a week and try to determine what Green was going to do. It is just this sort of unstructured, informal brainstorming that often gets squashed in large bureaucracies with precisely defined processes, but which is essential to stimulating innovation. Not every engineer at Sun, of course, got to go off and do his or her own project, but prove yourself a brilliant programmer or designer and you were rewarded with increasing degrees of autonomy. This group in Aspen was searching for the holy grail of the technology industry, a product that will take computing to the next level, driving what's referred to as a paradigm shift. Only a handful of products have done this, including Intel's microprocessor, which made the personal computer possible; Apple's Macintosh, the first user-friendly computer operating system; and Netscape's browser, which made surfing the Internet accessible. That January, the half-dozen engineers at Bill Joy's house talked about the future of computing, why products fail, and what they could build that wouldn't.

The next stage of brainstorming came after the core trio returned to California and attended an off-site meeting of Sun vice presidents and directors. "The three of us were sitting in a hot tub talking about the idea that there was no common way for [consumer] devices to talk to each other," Sheridan recalls. This was followed by a trip to a Japanese-owned plant where microprocessors were running things like air conditioners and elevators. Out of those two events, plus the earlier meeting at Joy's house, came the final idea: a portable consumer device (hardware) with an operating system (software) that could interact with any other system out there. While a couple of other engineers were recruited to work on the hardware design, Gosling was assigned to a key component: writing a universal programming language to create applications for the device. Without applications, hardware is inert and useless. "My part of the project was to go off and deal with the language problem," says Gosling. "I started writing stuff and needed a name. I was looking out the window one day and named it 'Oak.'" Oak was a small piece of the overall project at the time, but it would later, torturously, branch off and become Java.

For more than a year, the Green team, having moved off-site to a location alongside start-up companies and venture capitalists on Silicon Valley's famed Sand Hill Road, worked to perfect the technology: a small consumer device, an operating system, and applications written in Oak to run on it. Other key team members were Ed Frank, Chris Warth, Craig Forrest, and Jon Payne. In September 1992, the group delivered a working prototype of a machine called the Star7, a six-by-four-by-four-inch machine that could run a variety of applications, including a shared message board, wireless paging, a television program guide, and VCR programming. As an example of the kind of offbeat, childish humor that permeated the Green team, Naughton started calling the Star7 box "Yoppo." Yoppo is a drug used by South American tribes as a rite of passage into manhood; its signature is that it causes a green discharge from the nose. On that uplifting note, the Green Project was officially ended; it was time for the next step, devising a compelling reason to make people pay for this thing. "The Green Project created Oak as a by-product," says Naughton. "Its use was totally obscure." No one as yet had a clue as to what to do with any of it.

➤ Beyond the Green Door

At first, Sun's interest was in commercializing the entire Green Project, including the hardware and software. To do this, it took the controversial step—at least to Sun executives who were already reeling with the decentralization of the planets—of forming a separate company to undertake the task. FirstPerson Incorporated, entirely funded by Sun, was treated as a start-up, and lodged in its own headquarters. In an ironic footnote to history, FirstPerson set up in Digital Equipment's old Western Research Lab in Palo Alto, where a few years previously, the Open Software Foundation had been formed to oppose Sun/AT&T's Unix venture. Sheridan had by this time moved on. "I left Green after we finished the prototype," he says. "I was so burned out from working for two and a half years at a pace you couldn't sustain." As he was leaving, "what I worried about was packaging this so people could understand it better than NeWS. I didn't want to see us blow this opportunity." The opportunity was in the hands of Rosing, Gosling, and Naughton, who formed the base of FirstPerson. They hired more people, including a few from Jobs' company Next, which had just cancelled development of its workstation, and started work on a new business plan.

Making this transition—from research to commercialization—is where most projects fail. Gosling, who worked as an IBM researcher before joining Sun, estimates that less than 5 percent of IBM's research projects became actual products. At Sun, that ratio was expected to be higher, because the smaller company didn't have the resources of an IBM. According to participants in these endeavors, Sun had spent about $1.5 million on the Green Project, and would pour another $16 million or so into FirstPerson. Because the company was struggling at the time, those sums were not negligible. In the meantime, team members were desperately searching for a consumer niche for the Green products, so that those millions wouldn't go to waste. Because Sun had never created consumer products, Green was a real learning process. "We were going around to customers in the consumer industry asking them what they were working on, what they wanted," says Gosling. "We were trying to figure out what the issues were."

In March 1993, a few months after FirstPerson got up and running, Time Warner Incorporated kicked off the kind of fervor that would later surround the Internet with its announcement of an interactive television trial to take place in Orlando, Florida. Interactive TV was the hyped technology of its time. People would be able to shop via their television set, order video on demand, cast their ballots, suggest how popular soap operas should turn out, and so forth. Time Warner CEO Gerald Levin proclaimed that the Full Service Network (FSN), as the Orlando experiment was called, "will change the way people use television." The much-anticipated battle for this huge new market would come down to the cable companies, like Time Warner, and the phone companies, both of which owned potential conduits (respectively, fiber-optic cable and copper telephone lines) into the networked home of the future. The FirstPerson team seized upon interactive television as the answer to their technology in search of a need and bid eagerly for the FSN deal, which had an April 1994 deadline to be operational.

"Everyone was interested in the Time Warner trial—it was supposed to be the next great wave of the future," recalls Gosling. What the cable company lacked, though, was the technology to deliver its FSN. It needed a settop box with an operating system powerful enough to handle such tasks as video on demand, in which thousands, perhaps millions, of people might simultaneously request the same movie on their TV. The box also had to be small enough to fit on the top of a TV and relatively simple to use and program. The FirstPerson technology seemed to fit the bill perfectly. Other competitors included Microsoft and, surprisingly, Silicon Graphics Incorporated (SGI), which at the time was just down the street from Sun in Mountain View. SGI prided itself on its powerful, graphics-intensive workstations, but it had not developed any settop box technology, according to Sun's team. (SGI declined to be interviewed for this book.) "SGI got into it having no technology," says Gosling. However, SGI founder Jim Clark, who would one day leave the company to start

Netscape, didn't want to miss this attractive new market. According to Gosling, he promised Time Warner that it could own the settop box that SGI would develop to run the FSN, and walked off with the contract. "We thought we had the deal," says Gosling, "and we were in shock when it went to SGI."

He believes now that it was a control issue. Time Warner and the phone companies were old-line companies with centralized hierarchies, and they wanted to run interactive TV in the same way. Sun, on the other hand, envisioned a much looser network that individuals could access via their settop boxes. "We were pitching something very much like today's World Wide Web," says Gosling, "and companies like Time Warner wanted something they could control." SGI, he says, fed this control-oriented version by "giving [Time Warner] all the ownership of the intellectual property, which Sun wasn't willing to do." (Time Warner ultimately killed the FSN in 1997—the cost of the SGI settop box, around $3,000, was out of reach for consumers.) The same control issue foiled another prospective deal for FirstPerson's technology—this one with 3DO Company, which had sprung up to compete with Sega and Nintendo in the video game arena. 3DO wanted a settop box that would enable users to play its games on the television set, but it also wanted exclusive rights to the technology, and McNealy wouldn't budge. Sums up Rosing: "What we had was a technology in search of a market. Each time we tried to make a connection with a customer it didn't work. We kept coming up empty-handed."

➤ FirstPerson Upended

FirstPerson languished in the months following its failure to land any settop box deals. With cancellation imminent, internal strife was rampant among the strong-willed, opinionated team members. Naughton and Rosing fought openly over a new business plan, with Rosing denouncing the younger man as a "cowboy" for suggesting that the technology should be repositioned to the Internet. At a

July 1993 off-site meeting, Naughton remembers propos-
ing the "crazy" idea of posting the Oak source code on the
Internet, so anyone could use it. Rosing says it was impossible to write a business plan because there was no sustainable market among the alternatives then available:
settop boxes and low-bandwidth PC networks that didn't
have enough firepower to deliver rich consumer content.
Naughton decided "he didn't want to work for me any
longer, and he agitated to get me out," says Rosing. Besides
those problems, Sun itself was in trouble. Its second-
generation SPARC chip, superSPARC, had been a disaster
(see Chapter 5), and the company was taking hits to its
share price and its bottom line. The upshot: Oak and its related technology "were hanging by a thread," says Rosing.

For Gosling, it was a period of deep discouragement.
He had lost out on NeWS, his cherished technology of the
1980s, and now, it seemed, Oak was about to meet the same
fate. "I had just sunk several years of my life in doing this
technology, which was well on its way to a wastebasket," he
says. "I was pretty pissed off." The technology appeared to
be dying not because of any inherent technical problems,
but because of internal spats and a misreading of the market. "When we decided to focus on settop boxes and the
cable and telco industries, we didn't understand how
really broken they were," he says. "Given the way that
things had gone with NeWS, I was convinced the same
thing was going to happen again."

But he wasn't ready to give up, not even after FirstPerson
was dissolved and much of the team laid off. It was here that
McNealy's loyalty and commitment to Gosling, a trusted,
star programmer, played a role in keeping Oak alive. "Scott
was gung ho to keep Gosling," says Rosing. In early 1994,
McNealy, Rosing, and Gosling had dinner together one
night to talk things over. They went to a Japanese restau-
rant, in itself a sign of McNealy's devotion to Gosling, because the CEO hated Japanese food. Recalls Rosing: "James
told us he wanted out of the company. He was complaining
about the antibodies killing his ideas." Rosing championed

the Oak technology, saying it was worth pursuing, and Mc-Nealy agreed. Soon after, he redistributed the elements of FirstPerson technology within Sun, placing Oak under one planet, the Sun Microsystems Computer Company, while the hardware was allowed to quietly disappear.

Rosing and Naughton continued to butt heads over Java until Rosing, fed up with all the infighting, retired in mid-1994. Naughton kept pushing for a new business plan, unveiled in February 1994, which called for Oak to be used to build interactive applications for the Internet. Eventually, he, too, wearied of the seemingly endless battle and departed from Sun in October of that year, moving to Seattle to join Starwave, an Internet content creator that's now part of InfoSeek. Gosling was left to carry on the fight for Oak. "I did a fair amount of wheedling to keep it alive, as did Bill Joy," he says. And Eric Schmidt, who had just been named Sun's chief technology officer, also became a champion of the project. Out of that hot potato period in mid- to late 1994 came consensus around the critical idea to graft Oak onto the Internet and also a name change.

"We were this small ragtag group of survivors from an atom bomb blasting," says Gosling. "We wanted to make sure our technology saw the light of day." Although Bill Joy is widely credited with leading the charge to the Internet, Gosling says the repositioning came as a result of lengthy conversations between various people inside Sun, including himself, Naughton, Joy, Gage, and Schmidt. "At about that time the Internet was turning into the kind of public network that we had been trying to get the phone companies and cable companies to build," says Gosling. "We picked up our toys and applied it to what people were doing on the Net." At another off-site meeting (this time sans hot tub), "we were having this free-flowing conversation that went on for a couple of days. Bill [Joy] was certainly incredibly important in it." Adds Joy: "We helped convince [the powers at Sun] that the Internet is real. So let's just do something [with Oak] for the Internet and ship it."

Oak had one more hurdle to pass, an internal review

within Sun. Thanks to the planet structure and the individualized charter that Sun had handed to its engineering teams, the company wound up with several different, potentially competitive, programming languages. "All the wood behind one arrow," not to mention common sense, seemed to suggest that the company converge on one of them. Arthur van Hoff, an engineer with the Oak development team, remembers sitting in a conference room on a hot summer day in 1994 to discuss the various languages. "All the development teams got together and we had a long, open discussion," he says. "We each had half an hour to blow our own horn." Oak/Java emerged as the winner because it seemed to have widespread potential in more arenas, including the Internet. This being Sun, the other projects remained in limbo, not quite dead, while Java got the lion's share of the attention and resources. "Nothing ever dies at Sun," says Sheridan. "It just loses its champion."

In roughly the same time frame, the trademark lawyers at Sun had determined that Oak would not do as a name for the product because it was being used in too many other places. Gosling and Kim Polese (who later founded Marimba), the product marketing manager for Oak, tapped a naming consultant and convened a meeting to come up with a new name. What was left of the Oak team "came in for the afternoon and it was basically a food fight," says Gosling. "We wound up with this list of eight or ten names." The one that ranked the highest was "Silk." Gosling shudders at that. "I hated the name because it gave me the creeps—it reminds me of spiders." His own favorite was "Lyric." Java, he recalls, was in the middle of the list, fourth or fifth. "We told the lawyers to pick the name that was clear [of trademark problems]," Gosling says, "and that was Java."

■ JAVA TAKES OFF

Even as Sun was putting its internal resources behind Java and getting ready to release the first publicly available version of the language, Java remained an unknown quantity both inside and outside of the company. Consequently, it was still an endangered species. Such is the noise created by the endless succession of the latest and greatest technology products that many simply get lost in the crowd, fail to garner significant sales, and fade away. In the technology world, where new products are introduced almost daily, a product doesn't really exist until it's got mind share—before that, it's like a tree falling in the forest with no one hearing it. Mind share refers to the groundswell of attention by important newspapers, analysts, industry commentators, and others. As McNealy says, "There's no such thing as bad press." Polese, who would soon leave Sun with three other members of the Java team to form an Internet start-up company called Marimba, orchestrated the mind-share campaign for Java, ably aided by Joy, Gosling, and other team members. This campaign, for a product that had only recently found a mission and was barely out of the development stage, has to rank as one of the most effective launches in the history of hype.

One of the first things Polese did was to convince the *San Jose Mercury News* to do an article about Java in March 1995.[1] The day the story was supposed to come out, she paged through the business section and found nothing. Disappointed, she dropped the newspaper and then gasped. There it was, on the front page of the *Mercury News,* not the business section at all: "Why Sun Thinks Hot Java Will Give You a Lift." As the newspaper of record in Silicon Valley, the *Mercury News* wields a lot of clout, and when it covered Sun at all, it was usually skeptical. "This [Java piece] was the first positive article in the *Mercury News* on anything Sun had ever done," says Gosling, with perhaps a touch of hyperbole. Polese was soon besieged with e-mails and phone calls. "People had had no awareness of this thing," she says. "Now everyone wanted to know."

The *Mercury News* story was quickly followed by Java presentations at Sun's annual developers conference in May 1995. The conference was really supposed to be devoted to Sun's mainstay operating system, Solaris, "but it got taken over by Java," says Gosling. "It was clear that we had the momentum going." The whole Java team was in the audience when Marc Andreessen, the baby-faced hero of the Internet who had invented the browser and brought it to Netscape, walked up on stage and announced, to thunderous applause and cheers, that Netscape was going to incorporate Java in future versions of its Navigator. "I remember thinking, 'This is the turning point,' " says van Hoff. Inside Sun, the question changed from, "What is Java?" to "How can we use Java?"

Next came an August 28, 1995, article by the provocative technology guru George Gilder in *Forbes ASAP,* a bimonthly publication of *Forbes* magazine devoted to technology.[2] Gilder is one of the most influential thinkers on the impact of technology, on the strength of such books as *Microcosm,* which describes the microprocessor and its reach, and numerous magazine articles. So when he declared in "The Coming Software Shift" that Netscape's browser and Sun's Java programming language were the twin technologies that could topple the Microsoft/Intel hegemony in personal computers, people sat up and took note. "To the extent that Java or a similar language prevails, software becomes truly open for the first time," Gilder wrote. "The Microsoft desktop becomes a commodity; the Intel microprocessor becomes peripheral."

Next, the *New York Times'* respected technology columnist, John Markoff, jumped on the bandwagon.[3] In the September 24, 1995, issue of the newspaper, Markoff proclaimed that Java could become the "next big thing in computing." He had a compelling metaphor to explain what Java was all about: "Currently, the Web . . . is a fairly static medium," he wrote. "A computer user connected to the Internet can visit Web sites, but doing so is similar to watching the world through a storefront window. Java essentially removes the glass from the window. It can serve simultaneously as a universal translator—enabling programs to move fluidly between incompatible operating systems—and as a go-fer. With the help of a browser like

Netscape, it can run across the Web and the rest of the Internet to fetch programs from the powerful computers that run Web sites and bring the programs and the information they generate . . . back to a user's home computer."

This is the kind of press that Sun had long dreamed of and had not achieved since its early days. The embrace of Java by important opinion makers gave the company the buzz as a leading-edge innovator once again. But, it also presented Sun with a new challenge: it had to deliver on all of the buzz. And, this was a challenge that McNealy and company relished, after making it through the dark years of diminishing growth, uncertain product acceptance, and relegation to technology backwaters.

■ THE JAVA TRIP

Naughton was right in entitling his own memoir of the development of Java *The Long Strange Trip to Java*. In a less chaotic company than Sun, Java might not have survived. Its existence owes much to Sun's tolerance of individualism and its empowerment of selected stars. "In one sense, Java was totally accidental," says Gosling. "And yet it wasn't." It wasn't because McNealy encourages people to experiment and take a chance. This includes funding advanced development and research without defining the outcome. Sun is not content with incremental improvements to its existing products; it still wants to change the rules and move to the next level. To do that means closing your eyes and rolling the dice without knowing whether you'll hit it big or crap out.

Java did need a ton of luck to keep it alive. "It was on the block an incredible number of times," says Gosling. He cites a folk theorem within Sun that states that the value of a project is related to the number of times it's cancelled. The more it's cancelled, like Java, the more valuable it is. "Projects get done because people feel passionately about them and they go to the mat and fight," he says. "There are people at Sun Labs who are still going off and being wild and crazy." He describes one engineer who stalked into his office recently with "something really cool"—a program that allowed Web page formatting in multiple styles. Gosling told him to keep working on it and figure out where it fits within Sun. "The problem with all of these things, you've got to find a home for them," he says. These new ideas that pop up constantly in an environment like Sun's face three fates: getting snuffed out, being integrated into an existing product, or becoming the start of a new business. In an established company such as Sun, the first two are more likely scenarios than the third option.

In a start-up, every innovation can become a new business, but once a company has left the start-up phase and has real customers to whom it must deliver real products, innovation is bedeviled by continual friction. A start-up can concentrate solely on developing what it believes is the best product for a particular market, but an installed base of customers has demands that must be satisfied. Customers almost never want breakthroughs; they just want what they've already got to run without crashing. A standing joke within the technology industry goes like this: "How could God create the world in six days? He didn't have an installed base."

As the emergence of Java demonstrates, Sun has succeeded in fostering innovation even while it enlarged the customer base for its existing products. But this kind of breakthrough innovation is a messy process that doesn't lend itself to rules and centralized control. Sometimes, you just have to have faith in talented people and let them take the bit in their teeth and go. Most of the time the results won't see the light of day, or, as with NeWS, they'll run into market or competitive resistance and disappear. But even failure can be a prelude for success. Without NeWS, there might not have been Java. "The learning process that James [Gosling] went through on NeWS crystallized his thinking on Oak," says Rosing. "Java is a definite descendant of NeWS." It's clear that what really made Java possible was the people—rebels and malcontents like Gosling, Naughton, and Sheridan—and the fact that they were able to reach enough of a detente with the bureaucracy to do something great.

Chapter

8

Java Boils Over

In four years, Java had made the transition from orphan to prodigy. Now Sun had to find ways to market and commercialize the technology. In this endeavor, Sun had to become a new type of company. Java's appeal was to a customer base where the company was little known. Before Java, Sun had made its living as a hardware company. It was hardware that defined the company and brought in the billions in revenue. "Without Java, Sun would have been a commodity supplier of servers and workstations," says Kim Polese, the Java product manager. But with Java, Sun had to expand its knowledge base from the corporate world to the consumer world, which played by vastly different rules, and develop a web of relationships with vendors who served consumers.

It was clear to Sun executives that Java was a compelling innovation, but now it was time for the technology to become a real business. As a programming language, Java was not much use unless Sun could enlist software developers to write appealing applications with it. These would be a different group of developers than the ones who created applications for Solaris, which were high-end functions aimed at corporate users. Java applications were aimed at general PC users. They had to be fun, lightweight, and available over the

Internet. "Sun had to start from ground zero and do all of this," says Polese. Unlike Microsoft, which had a formidable structure of thousands of programmers to create applications for Windows, Sun had never played in this particular sandbox. But the company reached back to its origins and made Java an open standard by giving developers (via the Internet) detailed specifications on the language that enabled them not only to use it, but to customize it. That was something Microsoft had never done with Windows. "Java was made an open standard that everybody could contribute to," says Polese. "This way, the future success of Java doesn't rest solely on Sun."

Java's other appeal is that it supposedly is a "write once, run anywhere," language—to quote Sun's mantra. In theory, a programmer could develop an application in Java that could run on Windows, on Macintosh, on Solaris, or anything else, without needing to go through a tedious rewrite to make it compatible with each separate operating system. Although Java is not quite the universal programming language that Sun claims, it is closer than anything else. These qualities of openness and near universality, coupled with a genuine fear of Microsoft in the development community and the hype generated by Sun's successful product launch, enabled Java to find adherents in droves. "Java before 1994 was known and programmed by 25 people, all within Sun," recalls William R. "Burt" Sutherland, who took over Sun Labs after Wayne Rosing left. "By spring 1995, there was an explosion. Very quickly there were thousands, then tens of thousands of programmers. It took off because we put it on the Internet and it met an unfilled need for a universal language."

■ CONTROLLING AN OPEN STANDARD

In regard to its control of Java, Sun could have taken one of two existing roads. It might have turned Java over to an industry standards body like the International Standards Organization (ISO) or the Institute of Electrical and Electronics Engineers (IEEE). The evolution of Java would then have been determined by a rather slow-moving, consensus-driven committee of industry representatives. The advantage of this is that it decouples a technology from a single company, providing a democratic, open approach that presumably guarantees that changes to Java benefit the majority of users. The disadvantage is that standards bodies can become very political, as happened with the two competing sides in the Unix wars, and then development of the technology is stymied or fragmented. The other road Sun could have taken was to emulate Microsoft and retain complete control of Java. That is, Sun would not publicly release any of the so-called application programming interfaces (APIs) needed to create Java programs and would have dictated any changes to Java itself, as Microsoft does with Windows.

Sun chose a hybrid course: It posts drafts of changes it wants to make to Java on the Internet and invites feedback from the developers community. It has also licensed Java broadly to companies that want to incorporate the technology into their own products, including such power-houses as IBM, Oracle, Netscape, and even Microsoft (see the section of this chapter entitled "Playing with Fire" for more on the Microsoft license). These licensees can themselves come up with improvements to Java, which must, however, be approved by Sun. The idea of this hybrid approach is that Sun can trumpet an open standard while maintaining some control over how quickly and by what means Java advances. At the same time, Java licensees theoretically have enough input to keep Sun from making changes to Java that only benefit Sun—as an example, Sun could decide to make Java compatible with Solaris and not with competing operating systems. In late 1997, the ISO endorsed this hybrid approach by designating Sun as the official keeper of the Java flame; that is, when changes to Java are proposed, Sun is the only one that can submit them to the ISO for designation as a standard.

All this may seem rather esoteric, but the notion of an

open standard gives Sun, which is an insignificant player in the software world, expanded clout to keep Java from splitting into opposing camps like Unix. In several public speeches in 1998, McNealy explained why Sun was pursuing this course with Java. "There are three strategies for developing a standard," he says. "One way is to go to a committee, like Unix did, which moves at the speed of Congress. If you've got to wait for consensus the war is over, because somebody [in the committee] is always against everything." The second strategy is Microsoft's. "It's like they own where the brake pedal on your car goes and they don't tell you where they're putting the brake pedal on the next model." The third strategy is to put the standard in the hands of a for-profit company (i.e., Sun) that wants to move "at the speed of the Internet" in advancing the standard. "The Microsoft model is unilateral in a dark smoky room," he says. "The Java model means we have last call," but other companies can make recommendations, which Sun may accept or reject. Sun has accepted a few changes from other companies, notably IBM, McNealy says. "A standard to me means a high volume of users agree on the specification for how it operates," he says. " 'Open' is the process by which they reach agreement." (An alternative that McNealy doesn't cite is to give away the software, called shareware in the industry. A Unix variant called Linux, written in 1991 by Finnish graduate student Linus Torvalds, has achieved significant popularity this way; its source code can be downloaded free from the Internet. Sun announced in late 1998 that it would support Linux by developing a version on ultraSPARC.)

Sun is trying to have it both ways, remarks Geoffrey Moore, a high-tech marketing consultant and president of The Chasm Group in San Mateo. "They're working hard to keep control of Java but still make it open." Deep down, he suggests, there are those within Sun who would like to have the type of control over Java that Microsoft has over Windows, but Sun has positioned itself as an alternative to Microsoft's closed world. "People don't want another Microsoft," says Moore, because of the fear the Redmond giant inspires. Sun is walking a tightrope by retaining enough control over Java so that it doesn't splinter, yet allowing enough input and influence from outsiders so that Java becomes an open standard.

Java software developers generally applaud Sun's efforts to make the new technology as open as possible. "Sun has taken an extremely valuable asset over which it had total control and offered it as an open standard," says Rick Ross, president of the New York–based Java Lobby, an independent forum of 17,000 Java developers and other interested parties. He agrees with McNealy that the traditional standards development process, vetted by committee, "moves too slowly to meet the needs in today's high-tech world," pointing out that previous computer languages, such as C and C++, took almost a decade to be fully adopted. Under the auspices of the ISO, "Sun is acting as the steward of an open development process where they will make the decisions after a multistep program for evolution of the program," Ross notes. "Scott doesn't just wake up and say, 'We're going to change Java'."

■ A NEW PLANET

After Java's introduction in mid-1995, Bill Joy and a few others within Sun were determining the business strategy in an ad hoc fashion, rather like Sun in its start-up phase. "We were running a little bit out of control in making things happen," Joy concedes. "Making the connections [with allies]. Making the programming language ubiquitous" through the open-standard process cited above. But for Sun to turn Java into a real business, it had to make the technology into something more than a programming language. Nobody ever made much money solely from a programming language, which is like having an alphabet or language without any books or documents based on it. (Esperanto, anyone?) If Java was going to become the third jewel in Sun's crown, along with SPARC and Solaris, it would take more than offering the language over the Internet to any self-styled techie who wanted to play with it. It would take strategic focus around Java as a platform for computing. Sun realized that, and in January 1996, it formed a new planet, JavaSoft, to handle Java and the development of related technologies, and recruited Alan Baratz to run it.

The entrance of a new planet in the Sun orbit boosted the level of internal conflict. After McNealy, Baratz is probably the second most controversial executive at Sun. In his early forties, the tall, dark-haired Baratz has all the requisite hubris that it takes to work at Sun. He also has a regal manner that contrasts with McNealy's "common touch." Baratz spent 15 years in the high-tech industry, first at IBM, where he wound up as director of strategic development, and then as head of one of the first Internet-based, on-line services, Delphi, which was part of media mogul Rupert Murdoch's News Corporation before being spun out as an independent unit. Analysts questioned Sun's choice. Baratz "seems to be a mismatch," says Evan Quinn, former director of Java research for International Data Corporation in Framingham, Massachusetts. Baratz has neither the technical background in software products nor does he generate the sense of trust that would rally people to the Java cause. Delphi was never particularly successful, so Baratz's "track record for running a strategic organization is not positive," Quinn adds.

An engineer by training, with advanced degrees from the Massachusetts Institute of Technology, Baratz has made the transition into management and obviously relishes the trappings of power. As head of JavaSoft, he had his throne. The new operating company soon overshadowed its more venerable siblings within Sun, at least as far as media and analyst attention. In particular, SunSoft, which oversaw Sun's Solaris operating system, was envious of all the attention focused on this upstart. "I detected tension between SunSoft and JavaSoft," says David Folger, a Java analyst with the Meta Group in Burlingame, California. "It was obvious to me that neither one wanted to give in to the other's position," when their views on how to develop a piece of technology clashed. SunSoft didn't want to be relegated to incremental product improvements, while JavaSoft paraded its grand ideas of changing the world. Baratz's Java *uber alles* point of view didn't help, either.

Internal conflict aside, JavaSoft did move forward with additions that would enrich Java and make it useful to more than just engineers writing software code. In one vital step, Sun has introduced an environment that can run Java applications on any computer regardless of operating system. This is the Java Virtual Machine (JVM)—a computer, if you will, that runs in software, not hardware. The JVM sits on top of whatever computer you have on your desk and allows you to run all those new applications that programmers are developing in Java. It's the combination of Java the programming language and the JVM that positions Java as an alternative to Windows or, for that matter, any other desktop operating system.

JavaSoft got started with about 50 people on board. "We were setting up a new operating company to focus on this new thing: evolve a technology, deliver a technology, market and sell it, support the developers," says Baratz. Over the next two and a half years, JavaSoft grew to almost 1,000 people. "We've grown from a handful of people to a rather significant organization," he says. "We now have the critical mass we need to drive Java's development."

➤ Java Heats Up

The first half of 1996 saw momentum and support building for Java, culminating in the first Java developers' conference, called JavaOne, in May 1996. Only a year after the official launch of Java, 6,000 people gathered in San Francisco to toast Java as the center of a computing movement that would give developers and users unprecedented freedom in writing new applications for the Internet and corporate networks. Sun's adage, "The Network Is The Computer," had new meaning in the Internet era. Riding the burst of enthusiasm, Corel Corporation, an Ottawa,

Ontario–based competitor of Microsoft, announced that it would develop an office suite of productivity applications written entirely in Java. This was throwing a gauntlet in the face of a giant, for the Microsoft Office suite, including word processing, a spreadsheet, and other business applications, dominated the corporate market to the same extent as Windows. In August 1996, Kleiner Perkins Caufield & Byers of Menlo Park, one of the premier Silicon Valley venture capital firms, stoked the Java fire when it formed a $100 million fund to invest in companies that were developing Java-based software. Among the backers were Sun, of course, but also such technology and telecommunications powerhouses as Cisco, Compaq Computer, IBM, Tele-Communications Incorporated (TCI), and US West.

"Java has re-empowered the development community," says Ross, who adds that he had never bought a product from Sun and had no interest in them until Java. "I believe in my own ability to influence events as an individual," he says, expressing the sentiments of many software developers. The people who write applications—as opposed to more complex operating system software—generally work in small operations and adhere to a code of fierce independence. The large companies that own operating systems, including Microsoft and Sun, must woo the application developers to make their operating systems successful. The operating system is a skeleton; the applications are the muscles and tendons that enable a computer to do interesting things, like surfing the Internet or crunching numbers. In the case of Java, its applications operate through the Internet or an internal company network, and range from clever graphics tricks on Web sites to dissemination of corporate employment opportunities. "Java has reignited the spirit that you can change the world," adds Ross. "It has tremendous potential. We want to see this run in our households, our telephones, our cars. Java is a common denominator, a general-purpose language that connects all of them. It is our best hope for a great range of innovative possibilities."

Corel's embrace of Java was touted as a leading example

of the technology's potential to change the competitive landscape. Corel stuck a toe in the water in 1995 and did test applications written in Java. "Before you knew it we were writing a whole office suite. You can use Java to write real stuff," says Paul Skillen, Corel's vice president of software products. "It opens up new abilities and new applications that take advantage of the technology." Corel was so excited that it tripled the number of people it had working on Java to 150. "We were a poster child for Sun at the time," says Skillen. "What Java offered was platform independence. And it has increased developer productivity. Our programmers get more done" because Java is a sleeker, newer language than older alternatives. Java is less likely to result in memory problems or bugs and it can also handle multiple tasks. Lastly and perhaps most important, adds Skillen, "it's the soul of the whole Internet revolution."

Java did more than reenergize the development community. It also reenergized Sun. "Java started with three people and has now permeated every nook and cranny of Sun," says Ron Rappaport, an industry analyst with Zona Research in Redwood City, California. He met with a hardware group at Sun whose purpose was to discuss workstations and servers. "In the middle of the presentation is three slides on Java and where it's going," Rappaport recalls. "The evangelism of Java has swept through Sun. Java has been seen as a floor wax, car repair, everything is shipping with the word Java on it," the analyst jokes. Java has positioned Sun as an Internet leader and in that way boosted sales of the company's other products. "If you're a big corporation, you want a technology vendor on the leading edge technologically," says Meta analyst Folger. "Java gives Sun that edge."

■ PLAYING WITH FIRE

Whether Sun liked it or not, Microsoft still controlled about 85 percent of the computer desktops of the world through its Windows operating system. If Sun didn't want to be confined to the remaining 15 percent, it had to dance with the devil. It decided it had to license Java to Microsoft, even though the two companies were and are bitter competitors. This sort of deal making is typical of the technology industry, because its products rarely, if ever, stand alone. Instead, the products require technical hooks to enable them to operate properly with other technologies that corporations and individuals choose to buy. As an example, even though Apple was almost destroyed by Microsoft, it is also dependent on the Redmond company to supply the majority of the productivity applications that run on the Macintosh. In an equally double-edged paradox, Sun had to allow Java to operate on Windows for its claim that Java was an industry standard to have any validity. Whoever heard of a standard that didn't apply to 85 percent of the world? Likewise, Microsoft, the ruler of the individual computer desktop, was frantically trying to reposition itself to the wired world of the Internet in 1995 and 1996. That meant it had an overriding reason to embrace the Java technology created by one of its severest critics.

"In late 1995 we had a lot of work to do to establish our credibility in the Internet space," says Charles Fitzgerald, the group program manager for Microsoft's Internet Client and Collaboration Division. Sun, he acknowledges, "did a good job of tying Java to the Internet market." In negotiating the contract with Sun to license Java, which took from December 1995 until March 1996, "both companies tried to structure a deal that allowed us to get what we wanted," Fitzgerald says. Microsoft got access to a hot Internet technology, while Sun got access to Microsoft's huge distribution channel and customer base, not to mention the validity of having its new technology endorsed by the software industry leader.

Baratz, who joined Sun as the Microsoft negotiations were just getting started, vehemently defends the contract, even though it would later explode in a messy, time-consuming lawsuit in which Sun alleged that Microsoft breached their agreement (see Chapter 10). "Under the assumption that Microsoft is going to behave like a law-abiding corporate citizen, licensing to them was and is the right thing to do," insists Baratz. "We had to assume that Microsoft would not breach the contract and would not co-opt the technology." On that basis, licensing to Microsoft gave a huge boost to Java's credibility. "I would do it again in a second, if I believed Microsoft would not breach it," he says. Mike Morris, Sun's vice president and general counsel, is equally adamant. "We went into this agreement with our eyes open," he says. "We wrote the agreement as tightly as we could. Were we naive because we thought Microsoft would follow the contract?"

Some of Sun's allies think so. Eric Hahn, formerly Netscape's chief technology officer, says that the Internet company, whose early endorsement of Java the previous year had been critical to Java's success, argued against licensing to Microsoft. "They were giving Java to our worst competitor," he says. Microsoft's incorporation of its browser, Internet Explorer, into Windows threatened to puncture Netscape's hold on the browser market. Adds Hahn: "Netscape was paranoid about Microsoft's Java agenda. We told Sun they were in for trouble if they licensed it to Microsoft. There were early signs about Microsoft's mixed agenda." Hahn believes that, with the lawsuit, "Sun is trying to put more protections in via the courts when they should have written a stronger contract to begin with."

No matter what they stood to gain, in retrospect, says Fitzgerald, "both companies would probably say they'd just as soon not have done that deal." Baratz agrees—it's about the only thing the two agree on.

■ THE JAVA ALLIANCE

Although it may have rued the Microsoft agreement, Sun has effectively used Java as the base of a strong alliance with several other technology powerhouses. As noted, Sun has long had the reputation for being a maverick company, making its own way in the world without regard for what others may think. Its defiant stance in such situations as the Unix wars and McNealy's acerbic comments about competitors—like his description of an industry consortium as "Big Hat, No Cattle"—have not won Sun a lot of friends. But with Java, Sun had the chance and the compulsion to turn this around. In the first place, it needed strong allies to help make the new technology ubiquitous. Unlike most of the major software companies, such as Microsoft, Sun was not devoted solely to that field of endeavor. It had a hardware business and a microprocessor business. In doing it all, from chip design to hardware development to software, Sun has only one real counterpart, which is IBM, almost eight times Sun's size. So, Sun was stretched pretty thin even before Java; and McNealy, Zander, Baratz, Joy, and other decision makers had the sense to recognize that Sun couldn't carry the Java banner alone. In Java's adaptability and versatility, Sun had the ideal tool to reach out and repair some of the bridges that it had torn down over the years—and build a few new ones.

Sun reached out to Oracle, Netscape, IBM, and Apple. In December 1996, these companies formed what some analysts dubbed the SONIA alliance to promulgate Java as a standard development environment for Internet applications. Besides that, the alliance was obviously meant as an anti-Microsoft force, with each member involved in competition with the software giant on one or more important fronts. "The enemy of my enemy is my friend" seemed to be the prevailing sentiment, because there were also deep competitive divisions among the SONIA companies, especially between IBM and Sun. The SONIA alliance personified the complexity of relationships in the technology industry, where co-opetition has become the rule. That is, you compete for business one day in one setting, and cooperate on the next. Each member of the alliance had something different to gain.

Java solved a huge problem for Big Blue, as the world's

largest computer company is nicknamed: it provided a common language that enabled all of IBM's various products, ranging from mainframes to personal computers, to communicate with each other. "We were excited because we saw Java as a way to tie together all kinds of computing platforms," says David Gee, IBM's worldwide program director for enterprise Java marketing. IBM has thrown 2,600 programmers into its Java effort, by far more than any other company, including Sun." As the world becomes more and more connected, there's a growing need to standardize on a platform that's widely adopted and runs in different places. For us the answer is Java," says Gee. The fact that Sun developed Java rather than IBM, for whom the technology was of much greater use, just goes to show that innovation can't be channeled on demand. Although IBM didn't come up with Java, "we saw its potential very early on and jumped on the bandwagon," says Gee, rather than succumbing to the not-invented-here syndrome that had once plagued the company. "We no longer build an ocean somewhere else when we don't need to," he says.

At Oracle, CEO Larry Ellison had long tired of playing second fiddle to Bill Gates. Oracle, based in Redwood City, is the leading vendor of relational database software, which is used by major corporations to store their treasure troves of internal information and make it accessible to qualified users. Ellison is the second richest software CEO (a distant second to Bill Gates,) and he has long looked for ways to trump Microsoft. He found one in the Java alliance. Gary Bloom, executive vice president of Oracle's system products division, put it a shade more diplomatically for this book: "The primary aim [of the alliance] was to provide alternatives in the marketplace to the pure Windows and Windows NT model of computing," he says. "That takes several kinds of technologies: network capability, from Sun and IBM; database software from Oracle; and advanced browser technology from Netscape."

Sun had actually dallied with buying Apple earlier in 1996, which would have provided it with a ready entree into the consumer market, but backed off when McNealy blanched at the price. In retrospect, that was probably for the best. Sun had enough on its plate without tackling the myriad of problems facing Apple, whose Macintosh was rapidly losing market share to PCs running Windows. In late 1996, Apple was scrambling to survive under its designated turnaround CEO, Gil Amelio, and seized on Java and its ability to reconnect the isolated Macintosh with the rest of the computing world as possible salvation. (The following year, Apple would oust Amelio and restore Steve Jobs as CEO. Jobs then cut a deal with Microsoft and pulled Apple out of the formal Java alliance, although Apple continues to use the Java technology.)

Netscape, the smallest alliance partner and the one whose immediate existence was most threatened by Microsoft's entry into the browser market, was in the "Java jihad early on," says Hahn, who left Netscape in mid-1998 to become a private investor. As a software company, Netscape was concerned about Sun's ability to support Java in the Internet world, where Sun was an unknown quantity. "We thought Java was important but we weren't convinced Sun would be a great technology supplier, or be responsive and fast enough," says Hahn. "Depending on Sun scared some parties within Netscape, so we created a shadow Java organization within Netscape." In Hahn's opinion, Netscape's willingness to package Java with its Internet browser, then the overwhelming leader in that marketplace, did more than any of Sun's moves to popularize the technology.

■ JAVA SLIPS

Even while the Java alliance was coalescing, it was evident that demand for Java technology was building so rapidly that Sun couldn't keep up with it. "The biggest problem with Java has been its own success," proclaims John Mitchell, president of Non Incorporated, a Java consulting company in Moraga, California. When Sun released Java

1.0 in 1995, "it wasn't very well designed," he says. (Remember that with software, it's generally not until the third incarnation that a new program runs very well.) "Java took off so fast that Sun didn't have time to clean it up and make it industrial strength. There hasn't been enough time for the language to settle out." Sun/JavaSoft was trying to promote Java in so many places that the company didn't wait until it had a mature product.

You can get very good cross-platform performance with Java," Mitchell allows, "but it's not ideal. Java is the 80 percent solution. For 80 percent of what most people want to do, it works very well." For the other 20 percent who want to do more complex things, Java doesn't work as well. But with all the hype, expectations were higher than 80 percent. "Java was so over-touted that you get a backlash whenever there are problems," Mitchell notes.

Corel found out about Java's limitations when it was forced to abandon its highly publicized effort to write its office suite in the language. The Java suite was slower and had fewer features than alternatives already on the market, in part because the new language was still in its infancy and in part because of the common denominator problem previously cited. Concedes Corel's Skillen: "We made some mistakes, and the 'Java poster child' died." In retrospect, he says, Corel gained valuable experience in developing the Java office suite, but should have kept the effort quiet until it paid off. "The big downside for us is that it was a very public experience," he says, "and we're still paying for the failure." However, Corel remains committed to Java. "What we learned [from the failure] is that too many Java applications are just rewritten old applications," Skillen adds. Corel's new approach is to use Java to break up programs into smaller pieces and allow people to download whatever piece they need rather than install an entire memory-hogging program on their own computer.

Another problem that retarded Java's progress was dissension within Sun. JavaSoft wanted to promulgate the technology as a broad-based standard by getting as many other companies and developers to use it as possible. But SunSoft wanted Java to run seamlessly with Sun's existing technology, like Solaris, in an effort to boost sales to the corporate market. "Is the goal to maximize sales and profits or push Java?" asks Mitchell. "They couldn't decide." Janpieter Scheerder, then president of SunSoft, concedes there was stress. "What SunSoft has done is deliver [product] day after day," he says. "Meanwhile, JavaSoft is the little sister with cute ponytails." SunSoft's goal was to "make Java better by building Java applications on Solaris," he maintains, while JavaSoft's goal "is to provide ubiquity."

The stress was complicated by the fact that many of the early Java applications were aimed at consumers, a market that Sun knew next to nothing about. "The Sun of two years ago [1996] was far less familiar with how to make consumer software successful," says Ross. Accustomed to dealing with corporate information systems experts who bought the best products based on technical specifications, "Sun expected the market to recognize a technically superior product and buy it. That's not what makes a consumer buy. The consumer cares about what it does for them." In 1996, Sun had not yet formed a cogent message about just what Java could do for people. So far the technology was mostly used to dress up static Web sites with moving graphical elements. JavaSoft was grappling with how to make Java more appealing to consumers and companies that made products for consumers, eyeing such niches as smart cards, cell phones, and settop boxes. SunSoft was plunging forward with new Java-based technologies for the corporate market. The strategy was murky, and as we'll see in Chapter 10, about to come under serious attack by Microsoft.

■ RIDING THE JAVA ROLLER COASTER

Java took Sun back to those thrilling days when it was a brand-new company with a whole world waiting to be conquered. Once Sun executives discovered Java's purpose and tied it to the Internet, the media machine went into full gear and Java was embraced by everyone from Microsoft to IBM to George Gilder as the programming language for the wired era. Sun's strategy for Java at first was defined by the Internet: give it away and they will come. So Sun, at Joy's urging, posted it on the Internet and programmers by the thousands downloaded Java and used it. As Java became popular, Sun licensed the technology to large companies who wanted to use it in multiple settings for fees estimated at as much as $30 million apiece, but were more likely lower. Sun had a hit, but it didn't quite know what to do with that hit. It's like that uneasy feeling that Dr. Franken-stein must have had when the monster opened his eyes for the first time. Once Java became public, all the analysts who followed Sun demanded to know, "Where's the beef? What's the strategy? Where's the revenue from Java?"

To be sure, Java has brought a lot of intangible benefits to Sun: mind share, identification once again as a technol-ogy innovator, the centerpiece of a potent alliance, and a new weapon to do battle with Microsoft. The question is, are those benefits critical enough to justify hanging on to the technology when revenues are so far not substantial? Sun has not really answered that, except to say, *wait and see. There are big things coming.*

"Java represents the emotion, the drive, the energy of Sun," says analyst Rappaport. "Sun has made it a life mis-sion, but there comes a point where you can't let religion get in the face of the bottom line. The reality is that Sun has to sell servers and workstations." Baratz responds that Sun has derived licensing fees and royalties from Java, al-though he acknowledges that revenue isn't very significant to a $10 billion company. And, because they're one-time fees, licensing revenues eventually dwindle. Beyond that, says Baratz, "we're building new services and applications on the Java platform," such as teaming up with credit card companies to embed Java in new smart cards or auto-mobile manufacturers to offer Java applications that help drivers navigate (see Chapter 11). None of this, however, will yield meaningful revenues for several years.

Because the technology exploded as rapidly as it did, Sun initially drove Java like a start-up. That meant moving so quickly that mistakes were bound to happen. Sun is now in the process of correcting those mistakes and moving Java from a start-up mode into a position as a stable, reliable technology with multiple uses. It has made a lot of promises that have yet to be kept, but, for all its miscues, Sun has in Java an exciting technology that offers breakthrough potential. At the same time, the heightened awareness surrounding Java has placed Sun squarely in the gunsights of Microsoft. For all of McNealy's nose thumbing, Sun was negligible to Microsoft when it was merely one of a number of vendors of workstations and servers. Though Microsoft is moving into that arena, it never acknowledged Sun as a primary competitor—until Java. Java upped the stakes significantly, pushing McNealy and Gates into the same center ring.

Chapter

9

At War
with the Evil Empire

During their early years, Microsoft and Sun grew into separate giants with kingdoms at opposite ends of the earth. Microsoft's DOS and Windows operating systems and its applications suites ran the vast majority of personal computers bought for the home or the workplace. Microsoft was king of the individual desktop, where people toiled away without much regard for what the rest of the world was doing. With its workstations, Sun targeted a higher level of user, such as an engineer or a financial trader, who did complicated tasks like writing software or figuring out hedge formulas, which required a more potent machine than the PC. As it evolved the workstation into a server, which linked together corporate networks, Sun moved into enterprise computing. Its servers were the repository of mission-critical applications and information stores that were accessed by thousands of users throughout a corporation.

Until the early 1990s, there was little, if any, overlap between the markets where Microsoft and Sun operated. To be sure, Sun made an abortive try at Microsoft's turf, the desktop, with its ill-fated 386i, but that was eventually buried, and Sun went back to its core competency. But then each company developed a technology that increasingly encroached on the other's territory. With Microsoft, it was the introduction of Windows NT in mid-1993, an upgraded operating system designed for corporate networks. Having saturated the desktop arena, Microsoft needed new markets to assure the heady growth its shareholders were accustomed to, and moving up into the corporate environment seemed like the way to go. NT was squarely aimed at Unix workstation vendors, including Sun. Sun's countermove to NT was Java, introduced in 1995. With Java, Sun mounted another effort to develop a desktop computing environment intended to loosen Microsoft's choke hold there. So Microsoft was moving up, and Sun was moving down, and a clash was inevitable.

Scott McNealy, of course, has been targeting Microsoft and Bill Gates as Sun's biggest enemy for several years now, but Gates has only recently returned the favor. In a September 7, 1998, speech in Paris to the European Information Technology forum run by International Data Corporation (IDC), Gates acknowledged that two companies, IBM and Sun, were likely to provide the toughest competition for Microsoft in the future. IBM because it's so big and has so many resources. (And it's Sun's closest ally.) Gates also said: "Sun has got a lot of the messages that people out there are thinking about." John Gantz, IDC's senior vice president, said Microsoft had beaten other competitors like Novell and Netscape, and was now training its guns on IBM and Sun. A prospect that has to shake up even the pugnacious McNealy.

■ NT THREATENS UNIX

Windows NT as an operating system offered three key advantages over the various flavors of Unix: it was cheaper, it was interoperable with the predominant desktop operating system, and it was unified. So, developers that chose NT need not write their applications for multiple platforms, like versions of Unix from Sun, Hewlett-Packard, Digital, and IBM, but could concentrate on a single operating system. For computer vendors, NT allowed them to slash prices on workstations and interact more easily with Windows on the desktop. Corporations could get cheaper workstations that gave away some functionality to Unix but not enough to make a difference to large numbers of users.

NT has made dramatic inroads into the Unix market. In 1996, Unix vendors sold 708,438 workstations, compared with 133,397 units running NT, according to Dataquest, a market research firm in San Jose. By 1997, Windows NT had more than doubled to 386,213 units, whereas Unix had declined to 630,281. In 1998, Windows NT units totaled 750,972, whereas Unix sales remained flat at 617,447. Computer vendors who sold NT units included those who had moved up from the PC world, such as Compaq and Dell, as well as Unix workstation vendors who decided to hedge their bets. By 1998, virtually every major Unix vendor— except Sun—was also selling NT. Hewlett-Packard was particularly avid. In 1998, it sold 307,710 NT machines, making it the leader in that segment; Compaq (by virtue of its takeover of Digital) was second at 143,257. Meanwhile, Hewlett-Packard sold only 92,422 Unix machines last year, down from 105,908 in 1997 and 141,233 in 1996, according to Dataquest. In 1998, Sun widened its lead as the number one Unix workstation vendor, selling 322,623 units, 52 percent of the total. That actually represented an increase over the 277,281 machines Sun sold in 1997; it was the only major Unix vendor to boost its unit sales.

McNealy's decision to stick with Sun's Solaris/SPARC technology and not to license NT as an option for customers was a controversial one. Some analysts criticized it as an example of McNealy's hatred of Microsoft interfering with his business acumen; others felt that Sun now presents the only clear alternative in the marketplace. Although Unix operating systems such as Solaris are still ahead of NT in terms of their technical capabilities, "more and more of the high-end workstation use can be done on NT," says Greg Blatnik, vice president of Zona Research in Redwood City. The all-important software developers community, the people who write the applications that make operating systems useful, "want to develop for the dominant platform, NT," says Blatnik, "so the application space isn't there for Unix workstations." However, because its competitors are blurring their message to customers by offering both NT and Unix, Sun's Solaris may become the only surviving Unix in workstations. "Sun has an overwhelming share of the [Unix workstation] market," says Jack Gold, program director for Meta Group in Waltham, Massachusetts. "Their competition is NT—HP, Digital and IBM are all moving there. Sun is the lone holdout." He expects that within a few years, "Sun will have the Unix market to itself."

Microsoft's stance, not surprisingly, is that Unix will fade and NT will triumph. "NT is in the process of relegating Unix to an important footnote in computer science history," asserts Ed Muth, group product manager of Microsoft's Desktop and Business Services Division. Sun "is a very worthy competitor," he allows, "but they're just wrong in terms of the basic sweep of history." He says Sun shareholders should be asking McNealy why he doesn't add to the value of their shares by collaborating with Microsoft on NT. "No other competitor company in the world denies its shareholders the benefits of Windows NT," Muth says. "If Sun would like to be a really big company, one would think they'd do NT."

McNealy has stated on numerous occasions that doing NT means that Sun would lose control of its intellectual property and become merely an "automobile dealer" reselling Microsoft and Intel technology. (NT runs on Intel microprocessors.) "NT is Solaris '93. They're about five years behind," he says. COO Ed Zander emphasizes that Sun is not going to "pay taxes" to Microsoft and Intel to license their intellectual property. "Compaq, HP, and IBM have to pay exorbitant profits to Intel and Microsoft," he says. "We own our intellectual property." With Solaris/SPARC, Sun has gross margins in the 20 percent range, he says. "Would we rather have margins in the 20s or have the kind of miserable financial performance nearly every other computer company is now announcing?" Sun's unflinching attitude is best summed up in an advertising campaign it ran in late 1998, asking why any company would want to run important corporate programs on Windows NT. "Isn't there enough suffering in the world already?" the ads asked, next to a picture of actress Sally Struthers, who regularly appears on TV to appeal for donations to Save the Children. Funny, but not in particularly good taste.

Masood Jabbar, president of Sun's Computer Systems division, which manufactures the workstations that compete with NT machines, says he's wavered himself on the question of whether to join the masses and provide customers with a choice of NT or Solaris. Jabbar says McNealy's decisions "often border on reckless," and the NT issue "seemed like one of those times." Sun's customers "have been demanding that we provide them with a total solution [NT as well as Solaris]," he says. "There isn't anybody left who hasn't done that except us. I've often debated it, but now I say, thank God we didn't. Doing just Solaris differentiates us and keeps us focused." The companies that have moved to NT are struggling, because they depend on Microsoft to update the technology, and Microsoft is often late in releasing its upgrades. "That's what happens when you lose control of your destiny," says Jabbar.

■ THE DARWIN SOLUTION

Sun should appreciate what the NT vendors have done, because it's what Sun itself did a decade ago to competitors like Digital and Apollo. When Sun first began selling its workstation, it undercut competitors' prices by offering a ready-made solution with a standard operating system. That's exactly what NT is now doing to the Unix world. Technical workstations that sold for $40,000 to $50,000 a few years ago have fallen into the $10,000 to $15,000 range today. In January 1998, Sun introduced its entry-level Darwin line of workstations, selling for under $3,000 (without a monitor), an unheard-of price in this market just a year or two ago. By forcing pricing down to these levels, NT has reinvigorated demand for workstations, says Peter ffoulkes, principal analyst at Dataquest's workgroup computing program. "In the last decade, the workstation market has been very stable, growing about 9 to 10 percent annually. There's now more growth in the market because the entry-price level is going down." But lower prices create a challenge for Unix vendors, who are accustomed to commanding high margins to cover the cost of maintaining their individual operating systems.

Sun's strategy has been twofold: it has moved down-market and up-market. With Darwin, Sun has a workstation that's price-competitive with NT machines, although Sun gives away considerable profit margin. That's demonstrated by the fact that Sun sold 52 percent of Unix machines in 1998, but they represented only 39 percent of Unix dollar volume. To offset the trend toward lower prices and declining growth in its traditional stronghold, Sun has developed a thriving business in high-cost, high-margin servers, competing with IBM and Hewlett-Packard in offering these mission-critical machines. NT's technical performance still lags Unix, and that gap remains important at the server level, where customers demand the best, most stable operating system. NT servers are making inroads, but so far primarily at the low end, such as workgroup and departmental servers. Says analyst ffoulkes: "Servers will follow the same trend [as workstations], but at some considerable time behind." Sun, he predicts, will remain the top Unix workstation vendor and compete strongly in servers. Steve Milunovich, managing director with Merrill Lynch in New York, says Darwin is a defensive strategy to keep Sun as a player in workstations. However, Sun's growth will come from servers, where its business is increasing 30 percent annually.

One key customer of both Microsoft and Sun sees NT winning the workstation market, but trailing behind Unix in servers. Dennis Walsh, chief technology officer for General Motors' Information Systems and Services division, says the carmaker, like other companies, is moving to replace Unix with NT at the low end. "We only have a few hundred NT workstations today but there's going to be thousands," he says. "In the long term, the problem with Unix is there are too many versions." He believes that if Solaris does become the only Unix, "it would be much stronger competition to NT." At the server level, "it will be at least five years before NT moves up," Walsh says, and even longer at the very high end where corporations need the robustness of Unix.

Microsoft's Muth says NT is knocking off the desktop workstation market by sectors. For example, in mechanical and architectural computer-aided design (CAD), "it's mostly NT," he says, while Unix is strong in chip design, special effects, and software engineering. "The more exotic the application area, the more long-lived Unix will be." Nonetheless, he says, "the workstation battle is over. If you go to an engineering department that still has Unix workstations, everybody also has a PC. With Windows NT they can have one device. One management environment. The writing is on the wall for every Unix-centric workstation market." Darwin "won't even be a footnote." With servers, Muth acknowledges, NT has a long way to go. "We have harvested the low-hanging fruit," he says. "The pace of change is glacial." Ultimately, though, NT will overcome resistance because of the powerful advantage of unity. "You want an architecture that runs from the client [desktop] to the corporate data center," Muth says. "Ideally, you'd like to have the same system services, security model, on the desktop and the server. The marketplace has decided on the desktop. What server is most synergistic? That's NT."

Jabbar counters that Darwin is winning back market share in desktop workstations, although it's mostly from other Unix vendors. "In the desktop Unix space we have 50 percent market share," he says. "We're number one in 12 of the top 17 [vertical] markets." In Sun's fiscal fourth quarter, ended June 30, 1998, "we had the all-time best desktop quarter we've ever had in the history of this company." Jabbar agrees with Muth on one observation: the workstation market is a series of niches. Sun's higher-level workstations remain popular in segments such as oil and gas exploration, financial trading, and multimedia, where "our competitors drank the Kool-Aid [NT]."

In servers, Sun is continuing to find new customers, Jabbar says. For example, at the low-end workgroup server market, where NT has been predominant, "we were nobody two years ago," he says, and Compaq and Dell were the market leaders. "Lately we've entered that market and last year we grew 80 percent," he says. "Compaq has started running ads against us." At the top of the line, Sun's e10,000 server, "which brings mainframe discipline into a Unix box," is aimed at the corporate data center (where vital informational databases reside) and high-end services like Internet providers. "In the last 18 months we've sold over 750 of these babies for $1 million to several million dollars apiece," Jabbar brags. Unix, at least in Sun's Solaris incarnation, is not going quietly into footnote status.

■ THE CRAY COUP

The e10,000 class of servers, now the glory of Sun's booming server business, came about because of a stroke of serendipitous genius on Sun's part and a stroke of stupidity on the part of a competitor. In 1996, Silicon Graphics Incorporated (SGI), which was the leader in the sexy, high-profile market for workstations that did entertainment special effects (a la *Jurassic Park*), decided to shore up its product line by purchasing supercomputer manufacturer Cray Research. Supercomputers are very costly, very powerful computers used in rarefied situations that require colossal performance, like tracking spy satellites or predicting the weather. The federal government is, in fact, the main buyer for the segment. But as other classes of computers became more capable of doing some of this work, the supercomputer market was being cannibalized from the low end in much the same way that NT was creeping into the Unix space. Cray was already struggling with declining market share when SGI bought it. That ill-advised acquisition, plus SGI's failure to diversify into broader markets beyond entertainment, have left the onetime media darling in a tough turnaround situation.

Meanwhile, Sun, which has traditionally not made many acquisitions, was eagerly eyeing one line of Cray's business. Cray had licensed Solaris and SPARC from Sun to develop a new product—a high-end server—that would provide customers with a less costly alternative to the supercomputer. Jabbar remembers holding a couple of secret meetings with his former boss, Phil Samper, who had left Sun to become president of Cray, in early 1996 to discuss possible purchase of the company. "We changed our names and met at the Airport Hilton," says Jabbar. "He asked if we were interested in buying the whole enchilada. We weren't. I asked Phil if he would sell us the business systems division," which made the Solaris/SPARC product. "He wasn't interested in breaking up Cray." So the matter ended.

Then, when SGI bought Cray a few months later, its executives contacted Sun about selling the business systems division, because they weren't interested in continuing a product built on a rival system. Sun was delighted to oblige. The deal would fill out its product line and also snatch a potentially valuable piece of business from a competitor. Jabbar remembers the server hadn't been a big seller for Cray, because customers were reluctant to buy a high-level product from a company with such an uncertain future. Sun, of course, was in a perfect position to exploit the e10,000 line, because it was based on Solaris/SPARC. "We had a weekend meeting with SGI and made the deal," says Jabbar. "It was one of our best. The beauty was that we took over this team of a couple of hundred people who fit right in." The product team is based in San Diego, with a manufacturing plant in Oregon. Sun kept virtually all of the team members in these locations and even met the development schedules that Cray itself had set out. "I've never seen an acquisition take place where every schedule was met," says Jabbar. "We launched the product on Cray's original schedule even while we integrated the team inside Sun." Chet Silvestri, an ex-Sun executive who has also worked at SGI, crows that Sun snatched the crown jewel of Cray out of the deal. "We didn't have a server as big as what Cray had designed [with Solaris/SPARC]," he says. "It was a tremendous coup. The rest of Cray was dwindling away."

At the time, Sun and SGI faced similar challenges. Each was trying to break out of niche workstation markets and into more general business computing. Both companies saw Microsoft's Windows NT squeezing them out of the low end and both decided they needed to move into higher-end markets in which NT was not yet a threat because of its lower performance. But, while SGI shot up into the stratosphere with the purchase of Cray, whose products were so specialized they offered little room for growth, Sun chose a path into the newer, potentially fast-growing segment of network servers. The result was a $1 billion line of business that is still expanding.

■ CONCEDING TO THE REAL WORLD

Even executives within Sun agree that the company's anti-Microsoft campaign went too far and resisted the need to coexist with NT. McNealy's speeches trashing Microsoft were at odds with what customers wanted, which was to run disparate systems seamlessly. Sun was so keen on presenting itself as the undefiled alternative to Microsoft that it ignored the fact that its customers had to live in both worlds. It was very slow to develop links between NT and its own systems, or to enable its workstations to run Microsoft applications, which dominate the business community. "Sun acts like they're the last crusader," says John Olstik, a senior analyst with Forrester Research in Boston, "but the reality is that customers have both Unix and NT, and want solutions that interoperate. Every time Scott gets up on his bully pulpit, customers are worried." Thomas Jahn, chief information officer of Menlo Park–based Raychem Corporation, a customer of Sun and Microsoft, seconds that. "It's dumb to spend the energy criticizing a competitor. That does not add any value to the customer," he says. "The customer cannot be held hostage in the war between Sun and Microsoft."

Even though it champions open systems, in reality Sun has sometimes failed to capitalize on its customers' need for integration with a competitor's technology. Bob Lyon, the engineer who led the development team that produced Sun's early technological triumph, the Network File System (NFS), left Sun when it wouldn't fully exploit NFS's ability to connect different systems. In 1988, he cofounded another company, Legato Systems of Palo Alto, which licensed NFS and builds software that allows corporate customers to share data across NT, Unix, Windows, Macintosh, and other operating systems. Here's another opportunity that Sun failed to seize because of its go-it-alone approach. Legato today is a $143 million company with a 75 percent annual growth rate and a $2 billion market cap.

Under prodding from Zander, who is more pragmatic than McNealy, there's now a recognition within Sun that business customers want to use Microsoft and Sun technologies together. Says Zander: "You can't deny the fact that there's tens of millions of Microsoft desktops. Our customers need a reassurance that we're not this radical corporation that forces you to pick between Microsoft and Sun. Microsoft is a legacy environment. We can embrace and extend that environment." Jabbar admits that Sun was late in embracing Microsoft, but now plans to accelerate release of products that make interoperability easier. "I have a huge customer base and it's my job to make sure I protect their investment," he says. "Our Windows and NT connectivity has evolved as customers expressed their needs. We didn't want to be an island."

At a September 1998 show in New York, Sun unveiled a broad series of initiatives designed to enable its technology to work with Microsoft's. The elaborate fanfare surrounding the show, Sun's own Enterprise Computing Forum, was no doubt intended to camouflage the fact that Sun was pretty slow in getting to this particular party. One new technology will let Sun workstations run Microsoft applications such as word processing, which means that engineers who use Solaris won't have to have two machines on their desks: a workstation and a PC. Sun also introduced software that allows Solaris servers to plug into Windows NT environments and operate network services such as authentication and file and print sharing. "Solaris can be dropped into an NT environment and the user will not see a difference," says Jabbar.

Better late than never, say analysts and customers, who were pleased by the announcements and the sense that cooler heads, like Zander, are tempering McNealy's single-mindedness. "The trick for Sun is to avoid getting branded as anti-Windows," says analyst Bret Rekas. "The anti-Microsoft rhetoric can't get in the way of the fact that Sun is selling boxes and connectivity." He doesn't believe Sun distorts its image of being the only pure Unix vendor by adding links to Windows and NT. "They can say to customers, 'we'll never do a Windows box, but we'll connect you.' "

■ THE NETWORK COMPUTER

Sun subscribes to the theory that the best defense is a good offense. With Microsoft's NT carving out pieces of Sun's market, Sun attempted to turn the tables by using Java as the centerpiece of a movement to dislodge Microsoft's hold on the desktop. The weapon of choice: the so-called network computer (NC), a smaller, easier-to-manage desktop machine that could bypass Windows by using Java technology as its operating system. The idea was that an NC user could, via a network, download applications as needed from a more powerful server. This would eliminate the requirement to have a memory-hogging operating system like Windows and applications sitting on the desktop. Instead, applications could reside on the server as shared resources, lowering the costs of maintenance. As noted in Chapter 3, Sun had been down this road before with the 386i, but this time executives were confident they had a better shot. They had Java, which George Gilder had annointed as the beginning of the end for Microsoft, and they had the enthusiastic collaboration of the other Java Alliance members: Netscape, Oracle, and IBM. Oracle CEO Larry Ellison was, in fact, the most avid campaigner for the NC, proclaiming in September 1995 that "the PC is a ridiculous device." He also predicted that consumer and business NCs would outsell PCs by the year 2000.

Sun, Oracle, and IBM all scrambled to develop versions of the NC, but so far, except for limited success on IBM's part, the device has never caught on. The reasons range from poor execution and late delivery, notably by Sun and Oracle; squabbling within the Java Alliance (see the next section); and a savvy response from Microsoft and PC vendors, who essentially turned low-end PCs into NCs. Instead of buying NCs, potential big-name customers like Federal Express and Saab Automobile switched to the stripped-down PCs. General Motors' Walsh says the automaker is testing NCs but hasn't bought anything yet. "It's not a big issue with us to replace desktops with NCs," he says, citing the maturity and familiarity of the PC compared with the new entrant. Mark Biser, manager of technical support for Volvo, takes a similar wait-and-see attitude on the NC. "I don't ever see it as being an across-the-board solution. With the price of the PC dropping as fast as it is today, there would be a lot of resistance from the end user to give that up in favor of an NC." As for the cost of maintenance being lower with an NC, Biser says the devices are too late to market to take advantage of that. "We've already invested heavily in desktop management solutions, which allow us to upgrade the PC's functionality from the server," he says. "We don't need another device to manage."

Charles Fitzgerald, a group program manager for Microsoft, challenges Sun: "Show me a product." The NC, he jokes, "equals not cheap, not compatible, not coming." He believes the NC is at best a replacement for old-style dumb terminals, which originally connected to mainframe computers, performed limited functions, and didn't offer any processing power of their own. To take on PCs, "NCs have to be competitive in price, performance, and functionality with what's already there, but they're not." Industry analysts largely agree with him. "The NC is an immature product, and it's tough to use that to compete with PCs that have fallen below $1,000 in price," says Forrester's Olstik. The NC has also stalled because Sun and its allies were late in getting out real product. Sun's JavaStation, for example, was more than a year behind schedule, finally coming out in the spring of 1998 compared with an announced ship date of February 1997. "IBM is the best NC company," says Milunovich, of Merrill Lynch. "I doubt that it will be a big business for Sun. It certainly won't replace the desktop PC."

Distracted over problems in its mainstay database market, Oracle has since backed away from the NC, turning a subsidiary that was supposed to produce the hardware into a software arm. "NCs are not a failure," insists Gary Bloom, executive vice president of Oracle. It's just that PCs stole the turf by adding a browser and cutting prices, thereby becoming NCs themselves. IBM and Sun remain committed to the NC, although they're busily redefining expectations. Howie Hunger, director of channels and marketing for IBM's Network Computer Division, says it is the largest supplier of NCs with more than 100,000 units sold, mostly to customers in finance, travel, transportation, and distribution. IBM is also collaborating with Sun to beef up the JavaOS for Business, the Java-based operating system that was supposed to power NCs. Because the JavaOS wasn't ready, IBM has used other systems on its NCs and plans to ship Java only on high-end devices, beginning in 1999.

Jabbar admits Sun made some mistakes with the NC, notably in treating it solely as a replacement for the desktop PC. "We absolutely believe there's a huge market for a fixed-function device that's easy to administer over the network," he says. "There have been certain setbacks because we were probably a little ahead of our time." The Java-Station will have a narrower use than originally envisioned, he says, becoming a device for performing defined functions, like taking airline reservations. Jabbar has established a separate business unit to handle the JavaStation. "I believe in it and I know Scott believes in it."

Don't write off the NC yet. The idea behind it—that computing should be portable and easy to use in different environments (and not dependent on a single company)—persists. What happened was that "the world focused on the NC as a $500 hardware device," Jabbar says, "and it was Larry Ellison who put that stake in the ground." The NC should be approached as software that enables computing anywhere by accessing a server, rather than as hardware. "It's a computing environment that you move around to wherever you need it," he says. "That's a very powerful concept, but it takes time to get established" (see Chapter 11).

■ RIFTS IN THE JAVA ALLIANCE

The difficulties in launching the NC exposed some rifts in the Java Alliance, which was held together more by mutual distaste for Microsoft than anything else. Although Sun had envisioned the NC as a shining demonstration of Java's ability to defeat Microsoft on its home turf, such was not the case. Oracle, as noted, is no longer actively pursuing the NC. IBM, in actually managing to sell some of the devices, has established that there is a modest market, but not one driven by religious dislike of Microsoft nor enthusiasm for Java, as Sun had hoped. "The NC is not Java, contrary to Sun's belief," says IBM's Hunger. "We have been approaching customers asking them to tell us what they want rather than demanding they use Java. You don't need Java to do network computing."

IBM and Sun remain close, especially in their continuing collaboration on the JavaOS, but Sun and Netscape came to a decided parting over developing a Java-based browser for use in the NC. Right after it released Java, Sun had created its own browser, called Hot Java, but that was proving inadequate, in Netscape's opinion. "Hot Java doesn't cut it," says Brian Bennett, who, as Netscape's director of OEM and strategic sales, manages the Sun relationship. Ten of the top 25 Web sites "didn't even render on Hot Java," he says. But for the JavaStation to live up to the notion of being a network computer, it had to be able to access the Internet. No existing browser would work, because none was written in Java. So in early 1996, Netscape agreed to develop a pure Java browser, called the Javagator. Eric Hahn, Netscape's former chief technology officer, says Sun had a twofold purpose: "They wanted a Java browser for the JavaStation and they wanted a browser to compete with [Microsoft's] Explorer." Again, Microsoft on the brain.

Within Netscape, skepticism about Sun's motives started to build, reaching a climax when Sun licensed Java to Microsoft. By 1997, "we basically concluded that Netscape could no longer view Java as the jihad," says Hahn. "We recognized that our path on Java was diverging from Sun's and we began to back off on our development of a Java browser." Even while Netscape was working on the Javagator, Sun continued to pursue Hot Java, says Hahn, using it as a threat whenever Netscape grew restive. By the end of 1997, Netscape was wrestling with its own financial problems and could no longer afford to devote people and money to a development effort it didn't really believe in any more. The Javagator was cancelled and "Java was no longer considered a top-tier development agenda within Netscape," Hahn says.

Sun's Alan Baratz says the company is now retooling Hot Java to run on any operating system where there is a Java Virtual Machine. "We still need a Java-based browser because we have devices like the JavaStation that only support Java programs," he says. Netscape, in the meantime, has withdrawn from "doing anything with Sun on the NC," according to Bennett. There continue to be points of contention as to what obligations the two alliance partners have to each other. "We're going to end up settling those," he says. "Both of us agree that we don't want to go to court." (Netscape later announced it would merge with America Online.)

■ ON THE FRONT LINES

Right now, Sun is waging a three-front war with Microsoft. The first front has seen Microsoft launching an attack against Sun's stronghold of enterprise computing, with Sun retaliating by lobbing a few missiles into Microsoft's home base, the desktop. The second front, which I'll describe in the next chapter, is being waged in the courts, while the third front (see Chapter 11) takes both companies into new territory. As far as the first front, Sun has more than held its own in its traditional corporate market, with workstation sales relatively steady and server revenues growing rapidly. In 1998, when many computer vendors were struggling, Sun consistently reported better sales and profits than Wall Street expected and a faster growth rate than any vendor except high-flying Dell Computer.

Sun's advantage is the ability to tell a coherent story while competitors are delivering mixed messages. IBM, Hewlett-Packard, and Silicon Graphics, for example, are selling their own Unix platform as well as NT, which means they're affected by Microsoft's notorious delays in getting out NT upgrades. Compaq, busily digesting its acquisition of Digital Equipment, is trying to figure out what its play in the Unix world is. Meanwhile, Sun goes merrily on with its cry, "Unix [as in Solaris] today, tomorrow, and forever." By the middle of 1998, Sun had surpassed Hewlett-Packard as the number one Unix vendor in terms of revenue and was the leader in Unix servers for the first time.

But Sun's foray into Microsoft's territory, the desktop, where it sought to make inroads with the NC, met with decisive defeat. Sun's overanticipated, underperforming JavaStation never met expectations. Indeed, the biggest user is probably Sun itself, and that's because McNealy insists that employees have a JavaStation rather than a PC on their desks. IBM, with its much greater range of products than Sun, may yet make a success of its NC line, but not in the grandiose way originally envisioned by proponents. The NC did succeed in awakening the PC world, namely Microsoft and hardware vendors such as Compaq, Dell, and Gateway, to the fact that there was a market for cheaper, trimmer PCs than the $2,000 fully loaded model. They have moved to fill the gap, in the process blocking the NC's attempt to colonize the corporate desktop market. The washout of the NC also exposed a rift within the alliance of Sun, IBM, Netscape, and Oracle. Each has gone its separate way with regard to the NC. If Sun is winning with Unix, it's losing with the NC. Net result: Sun's experience in the first front of the war with Microsoft so far can be considered a draw.

Chapter

10

The War Escalates

Sun was on the defensive against Microsoft's Windows NT, but with Java it could take the offensive, a position the combative McNealy much preferred. Java had the ability to hurt Microsoft where it lives: by substituting an Internet-based network for a monolithic operating system, namely Windows. Microsoft knew it had to do something about Java. "Bill Gates' body language when you talk about Java is very telling; when you mention it, it looks like you've poked him in the stomach," says Patricia Seybold, president of the consulting firm, Patricia Seybold Group, in Boston. Seybold, who advises large, early-adopter companies on technology choices, says those companies see a role for Java, not as the desktop operating system for the network computer, but dishing up applications and information from the server, thereby bypassing Windows. "My customer base is very torn," she adds. "They like Microsoft for making it easier with one-stop shopping, but they also don't want to be locked in. Java is getting more attention because it's positioned as the Microsoft alternative."

Java may be the Microsoft alternative, but Microsoft is still one of the largest Java developers. As pointed out in Chapter 8, Sun decided it had to license Java to Microsoft or miss out on 85 percent of the installed base in desktop computers. Over the objections of its ally Netscape, Sun entered into a contract with Microsoft that was probably doomed from the start, and has now wound up in the courts. "Everybody knew before that agreement was signed how it was going to end up," says Tom Kucharvy, president of Summit Strategies in Boston. "If Sun had refused to license to Microsoft, Microsoft would have said, 'how can they call it cross-platform?' It was obvious that Microsoft was going to take [Java] in its own direction. The lawsuit was inevitable." Sun should have known that Microsoft would play hardball, pushing the contract to its limits. For its part, Microsoft had ulterior motives in seeking to align itself with Java so that its Windows development community reaped the benefits. Sun seemed to believe that Microsoft would deliver a Java-based technology for Windows that did not diverge from Sun's. Wishful thinking!

Sun's determination to protect Java from fragmentation stems from its long experience with Unix, which would have been a far more potent competitor to Windows NT as one unified operating system. Remembering the Unix wars, Sun executives were determined to avoid the same fate with Java, which they advertised as a run anywhere program compatible with all operating systems. First Microsoft delivered a Java version allegedly incompatible with Sun's, so Sun sued. Then came another unpleasant shock. Hewlett-Packard Company had launched a move to create a Java-like competitor in the market for embedded systems (software that runs largely unseen in devices like printers and fax machines). So Sun faced another threat to its control of Java.

Overlapping Sun's Java lawsuit was the Department of Justice antitrust action against Microsoft. In late 1998, both court cases were ongoing, one in San Jose and the other in Washington, D.C. Some of the evidence in the Java suit seemed applicable to the government's contention that Microsoft was taking unfair advantage of its monopoly position in desktop systems by seeking to destroy any alternatives, such as Sun's Java or Netscape's browser. That, at least, was a point that McNealy kept pounding home. In enlisting the courts in its war against Microsoft, Sun was as usual embarking on a risky course of action that could backfire. By seeking judicial restrictions on Microsoft, Sun might be opening the door to increased government scrutiny of the rest of the technology industry—something McNealy, for one, would abhor.

■ THE JAVA SUIT

In October 1997, about a year and a half after signing the Java licensing contract with Microsoft, Sun's executives had seen enough of Microsoft's alleged violations. Sun filed a lawsuit charging that Microsoft had breached the Java licensing contract by passing off its own corrupted version of Java as the real thing. "For me lawsuits hold about as much appeal a root canal," said McNealy, in an October 5, 1998, opinion piece he wrote in the *Wall Street Journal,* entitled "Why We're Suing Microsoft."[1] Sun "didn't grow from zero to nearly $10 billion in 16 years by suing our customers, or our competitors for that matter," he said, but added that Microsoft "has not abided by the [Java] agreement" that it signed in March 1996. "We owe it to our shareholders, our other customers, and our partners to ensure that this contract is honored."

The suit, filed in U.S. District Court in San Jose, also accused Microsoft of trademark infringement, false advertising, unfair competition, and interference. "Microsoft signed a contract to distribute Sun's Java technology . . . in a manner that conforms to our specifications and passes our compatibility tests," McNealy wrote in the *Journal* article.[2] Instead, Microsoft claimed "they had a right to change the formula to suit their needs." He compared the situation with McDonald's deciding that its customers wanted a sweeter Coke, "so the fast-food giant unilaterally changed the formula, distributing a new concoction at its 10,000 or so outlets." Microsoft, charged McNealy, wanted to flood the market with a "polluted version of Java technology" and "subvert the growth of a new software industry that's not dependent on the Windows operating system." Specifically, Sun in the lawsuit claimed that Microsoft was shipping an altered version of Java, customized to run with Windows, on version 4.0 of its Internet Explorer browser. Developers who used Microsoft's Java to create new programs would find they were only compatible with Windows, instead of living up to the "run anywhere" promise of Java.

Microsoft promptly countersued, alleging that Sun failed to live up to its own obligations under the Java contract. The suit also said Sun had repeatedly made false statements about the compatibility and desirability of Microsoft's products. In an October 21, 1998, letter to the *Wall Street Journal,* responding to McNealy's piece, Paul Maritz, a group vice president of Microsoft, said Sun wanted to "kill Windows" with Java and when that failed in the marketplace, "it has chosen to litigate rather than innovate."[3] Maritz said the special licensing agreement that Microsoft signed with Sun "provides [us] the right to improve and enhance the Java technology for Windows in ways that best serve our customers." Sun, he added, "is now trying to break the deal by asking the court to let it change the rules of the game. . . ."

Sun tried to resolve the issues with senior Microsoft officials for six months before throwing up its hands and filing suit, according to General Counsel Mike Morris. "The only basis on which they were willing to deal with us was to realign the license agreement in a way that advantaged Microsoft and disadvantaged all the other licensees." Every one of the 150 or so licensees has adhered to the contract, he says, except Microsoft. "If Sun permitted Microsoft to breach that agreement, what does that say to the other licensees?" Consequently, after Microsoft released Internet Explorer, "we looked at the code and it was in breach. We felt we had no choice but to go to court." Despite all the rhetoric swirling around Microsoft, Sun didn't want to sue, he insists. "Analysts who say this is part of a jihad are simply crazy. They don't know what we went through trying to avoid a lawsuit. If Microsoft came to us and said they'll abide by the agreement, we would withdraw the lawsuit. We're not a stupid company."

Sun CFO Mike Lehman, who oversees corporate legal affairs, asserts that Microsoft altered Java in an unacceptable way. "They didn't use all the letters of the alphabet and they added some of their own, to make sure Java would run only in the Windows environment. They are not creating a better Java. They are creating something else, trying to change it to their advantage." He adds, "There's a very conscious pattern on their part of insuring that Java would not succeed" the way Sun intended it. Indeed, in its lawsuit against Microsoft (see the section later in this chapter), the Justice Department cited internal company documents that stated that Microsoft's objective was to "kill cross-platform Java by growing the polluted Java market." According to the government, e-mail messages by Microsoft officials suggested the company needed to "steal the Java language" and to "fundamentally blunt Java momentum" to protect Windows. The government produced e-mail from Bill Gates criticizing IBM for working with Sun on Java. "The Java religion coming out of the [IBM] software group is a big problem," Gates wrote in an October 1997 message, which also referred to IBM as "rabid Java backers."

Charles Fitzgerald, Microsoft's group program manager for Java products, says all those comments were taken out of context. To some extent, Microsoft got spooked by statements from "the George Gilders of the world" that Java and the advent of Internet-based computing was going to undermine Windows. "Our natural response was to say how do we go out and win this thing." Microsoft believes in Java, he adds, "but we're not sure every application should be optimized for cross-platform performance." In a front-page story on February 1, 1999, the *Wall Street Journal* detailed the internecine warfare within Microsoft over what to do about Java.[4] According to that article, two factions inside Microsoft were competing in early 1997: one urged the company to embrace Java and cross-platform computing, the other wanted to bolster Windows by adding an Internet browser and a version of Java that would run well on Windows, but not on other operating systems. In March 1997, the article says, Bill Gates rejected the views of the pro-Java contingent within Microsoft and "decided to protect Windows at all costs."

■ JAVA DEVELOPERS OF THE WORLD, UNITE!

Fitzgerald has a point when he says that Sun's one-size-fits-all software doesn't fit everyone's needs. Microsoft's implementation of Java has performed better than standard Java in certain benchmark tests. Java developers like John Mitchell, of Moraga, California, admit to being frustrated with Sun's approach in advancing Java. "Java is still immature," he says, "and Sun and JavaSoft have been feeling their way about what to do." Nonetheless, Mitchell supports Sun on the Java lawsuit. "My worst frustrations with JavaSoft and Java as a technology are better than all but the smallest problems with Microsoft. Microsoft has the callousness of a monopoly." He says Microsoft made changes in Java to flex its muscle and splinter the market.

While Microsoft and Sun lawyers debated the technical details on which the suit will be resolved, most Java developers sided with Sun. "Microsoft's goal has been exposed—to undermine Java" says Rick Ross, president of the Java Lobby, which represents Java developers. As a developer, Ross says Microsoft's attitude toward Java has changed from embracing the product to actively campaigning against it. In March 1996, when Microsoft signed the contract, "they were telling us that Microsoft loves Java, and we began to make decisions based on that. Then they changed their course, and now we [as developers] have to throw away all our work."

To some observers, Sun's lawsuit seemed like an attempt to rewrite a leaky contract by going to court and capitalizing on the already bitter war of words with Microsoft. "Sun had to sue because the agreement appeared to be so vague," says John Zukowski, who trains Java developers at the MageLang Institute in San Mateo. "Microsoft is using that vagueness to make a version of Java that runs only on its platforms." Zukowski faults both Sun and Microsoft. "As soon as Microsoft signed on the dotted line, it seemed like it was their intention to split Java," he says. But Sun was caught off guard when it probably shouldn't have been. After all, McNealy had been complaining about the "evil empire" for several years. "Sun needs Java on the Windows platform," says Zukowski, "but they just didn't expect Microsoft to change Java as quickly or as extensively as they did." A few developers suggest leaving it up to the marketplace to decide. "The best judge and jury is the consumer [developer]," says Paul Ambrose, CEO of WebLogic in San Francisco. "If Microsoft is not including things the consumer wants, let the consumer rap Microsoft or not buy the product." As for the lawsuit, "any potential gain Sun might get from reining Microsoft in is far outweighed by the negative impression Sun gives."

What it comes down to is that Microsoft wants the benefits of Java as a programming language, but refuses to recognize Java as anything beyond that. That approach minimizes Java's threat to Windows. Sun, however, sees Java as far more than a language. To Sun, it is a platform that can be the launching point for a whole series of products that doesn't depend on Windows. However, regardless of the lawsuit's outcome, that division was likely to persist. Even if Microsoft is permanently enjoined from using the name Java, it has established an alternative. "Whatever they call it, everyone will know it's an implementation of Java optimized for Windows," says analyst Kucharvy.

■ A SUN VICTORY

In November 1998, more than a year after the suit was filed, U.S. District Judge Ronald M. Whyte issued a prelim-

inary injunction siding largely with Sun, according to
company press announcements. He ruled that Microsoft
must rewrite its current version of Windows and its
browser, Internet Explorer, to comply with pure Java specifications. Microsoft was given 90 days to alter its software,
or delete Java entirely, but wasn't ordered to recall any
products. The decision was a significant victory for Sun,
which could now expect to prevail in a full trial that was
slated to proceed in 1999, and came at an awkward time
for Microsoft, embroiled in the antitrust lawsuit described
later in this chapter. Microsoft's Fitzgerald says the company wasn't happy about the timing of the decision, coming just as witnesses in the antitrust case were testifying
about Java. However, he adds, "Sun is trying to portray it as
evidence that Microsoft might have been up to something,
but the ruling is very narrow and clearly related to the
contract dispute."

Microsoft will comply with the injunction by adding
Sun's mechanisms for doing platform-specific applications,
but it will retain its own Windows-customized mechanisms.
"Sun's mechanism is not a very good one," Fitzgerald says.
"We'll give developers a choice between ours and Sun's." At
the trial expected in the second half of 1999, Microsoft will
continue to argue that the contract allows it to make
changes in Java needed to make it more compatible with
Windows. "We think we signed an agreement that doesn't
require us to support Sun's mechanisms," he says, "and
we're still confident that we're going to prevail." He believes
that Sun's preliminary victory, while symbolically "a big
one," doesn't mean much in the technical sense. "They're
forcing us to add another way to build Windows applications in Java, but it's hard to see that anybody will use it."

Another option for Microsoft would be to develop a so-
called clean-room implementation of Java, meaning it
would build its own version of the programming language
that did not rely on any of Sun's technology. In that case,
however, it could not be called Java. "We could do that [a
clean-room implementation]," says Fitzgerald. "To the degree that Sun is just a pain in the ass to deal with, we're

going to look for further options." He accuses Sun of being focused on demonizing Microsoft rather than delivering the best technology. "To the extent that Sun wants to inflict mediocre applications on Windows developers and use Java as a weapon against us, at some point we might say that [supporting Java] is more trouble than it's worth."

In a telephone conference call with the press right after Whyte's ruling, Java President Alan Baratz tried to downplay Sun's understandable euphoria. "We are not asking Microsoft to remove any enhancements that they might have added that do not interfere with Sun's public interfaces to the Java technology," he said. "This is an opportunity for Microsoft to rejoin the Java community and support this evolving industry standard." He did not expect Microsoft to drop Java from its products entirely. "Microsoft will not back away from the Java technology," he predicted, "because of the importance of the technology with the industry and the pressure on them by the developer community and by their customers."

The Java ruling, preliminary though it was, seemed to presage a final victory for Sun and a damage award against Microsoft in the upcoming trial. It also added fuel to the already hotly burning fire that is the Sun-Microsoft rivalry. Coupled with the huge America Online-Netscape-Sun deal announced a few days later, there could be no doubt that Sun was emerging as the chief corporate obstacle to Microsoft's control of the technology world. "Really all this [Java] ruling does is ensure that the balance doesn't tip to Microsoft," said Baratz. "It's basically generating a level playing field for all the competitors."

■ THE HP WAY

Hewlett-Packard, which has been a close ally of Microsoft in promoting Windows NT, seemed to be playing in the Redmond camp on Java as well. In March 1998, Hewlett-

Packard announced that it would develop its own version of embedded Java, just as Sun was getting ready to enjoy all the hoopla surrounding its annual JavaOne conference in San Francisco. Sun executives considered Hewlett-Packard's timing a low blow. From Microsoft they might have expected trouble. But from Hewlett-Packard, a far more gentlemanly competitor despite its longtime association with Microsoft, Sun had not anticipated such defiance. Microsoft, incidentally, was the first to publicly support Hewlett-Packard's move. Later in the year, a dozen other companies, none as significant as Microsoft or Hewlett-Packard, would follow suit.

Hewlett-Packard has been a leader in the embedded systems arena for years, with such products as printers, medical devices, and scientific instruments. "Suddenly Sun told us they want to define the [Java] standard for this market," says Philippe Lamy, director of marketing for Hewlett-Packard's Enterprise Systems Group. "They have no understanding of that market, or its needs. What Sun wanted to do with embedded Java did not fit that industry. We would have to teach Sun what to put in there." Besides being unresponsive to the demands of the embedded market, Sun wanted too much in royalties. "The pricing structure was not fair," Lamy says, for a product that would merely be a piece of a larger technology. Again, Hewlett-Packard knew what its market would bear and Sun did not.

Baratz was noticeably testy in responding to a barrage of questions about Hewlett-Packard at Sun's 1998 JavaOne conference, which was supposed to be a forum celebrating Java's success. Instead, during a press conference at Java-One, reporters honed in on a competitor's move. Baratz at first tried to downplay the significance, saying that Sun and Hewlett-Packard were continuing to negotiate. Finally, he cut off questions about Hewlett-Packard altogether. Said Baratz: "We've just devoted far more time to what HP has done than the impact it will have in the marketplace. We've made many announcements about how Java is maturing and being deployed that are far more interesting to talk about. From this point on Java is going to continue down the same path we outlined two years ago. If you have the major embedded device and semiconductor companies going down one path [standard Java] and a few companies down the other, Java will survive."

Lamy says that another concern is control over Java's evolution, which Hewlett-Packard would like to see placed in the hands of a third-party standards body, instead of Sun. Hewlett-Packard, remember, was on the opposing side to Sun in the Unix wars and has been the target of Mc-Nealy's sharp insults on more than one occasion. "HP does not trust Sun," says analyst Kucharvy. Hewlett-Packard is balking, at least when it comes to embedded Java. "To give Sun control over such a potentially valuable product is hard for HP to swallow," Kucharvy says. Sun is still adamant about avoiding the consensus-building model for evolving Java, which Baratz maintains is too slow and unwieldy.

Already in court with Microsoft near the end of 1998, Sun was attempting to smooth things over with Hewlett-Packard. Neither company expected the dispute to escalate into a lawsuit, because what Hewlett-Packard was apparently doing was allowed by the contract. That is, it was rebuilding one selected piece of Java technology from the ground up, a clean-room implementation that was legal. Hewlett-Packard intends to call its version Chai. Sun analyst Bret Rekas did not consider the move too much of a threat to Sun's Java strategy. "Ultimately, developers will decide Java's fate, not Microsoft or HP," he says. "It's not in the developers' interest to have a factured Java, so consequently they're more inclined to work with Sun."

In a personal interview in late 1998, Baratz expressed similar sentiments. He told me that Sun is confident it can compete against Java variants in the marketplace. One of the core values of Java, he notes, is its ubiquity. "Java delivers value that no other technology can," he says, which is why software developers, business customers, and scores of others "are committed to preserving the integrity of the

Java platform. No one company, no one entity can stop this tide."

■ THE GOVERNMENT WEIGHS IN

In its Java spat with Microsoft, Sun played the role of the injured party. When the federal government decided to take on Microsoft, Sun played the role of the cheerleader. In May 1998, the U.S. Department of Justice filed a historic lawsuit accusing Microsoft of using its Windows monopoly to crush competition in the technology industry, especially in compelling computer makers to buy Microsoft's Internet Explorer rather than Netscape's competing Navigator browser. A separate lawsuit filed by 19 states contained similar allegations. Joel Klein, assistant attorney general for antitrust, said Microsoft launched a "barrage of illegal, anticompetitive practices . . . to destroy its rivals." Although Netscape was the primary rival named in the lawsuit, it also described Microsoft's treatment of Java as an example of the company's predatory practices. "The plan was not simply to blunt Java-browser cross-platform momentum, but to destroy the cross-platform threat entirely," the suit said. Microsoft CEO Bill Gates called the lawsuit "a step backward for America, for consumers, and for the personal computer industry that is leading our nation's economy into the 21st century. How ironic," he added, "that in the United States—where freedom and innovation are core values—that these regulators are trying to punish an American company that has worked hard and successfully to deliver on these values."

Although most of the technology industry ducked the issue, preferring not to take on the Redmond powerhouse, Sun has been vociferous in its support of the lawsuit. Indeed, it is widely rumored within Silicon Valley, though not acknowledged by Sun, that the company helped support research by local attorney Gary Reback that provided some of the theoretical basis for the government's antitrust allegations. Microsoft is a new type of monopoly that takes advantage of technology users' desire to standardize on a single platform, goes the theory. Once it achieved near-total dominance with Windows as the operating system for PCs, Microsoft was able to compel computer vendors to buy other Microsoft products as a condition for installing Windows, thus realizing increasing returns from its monopoly ownership of a key technology.

McNealy, like many executives in Silicon Valley, is a libertarian who generally decries government interference with the free market. Yet, he makes an exception when it comes to Microsoft, contending that the government is the only one with the power to check its monopoly. "I am a raging libertarian in many ways," he says. "We have a government doing all kinds of things it shouldn't be doing . . . but one thing it should be doing is stepping in when competition is being stifled by monopoly power. You've got to remedy a situation when there's a monopoly." In an opinion piece in the November 23, 1998, issue of the *San Francisco Examiner,* McNealy compared Microsoft of the 1990s with AT&T of the 1980s, before it divested the Baby Bells.[5] He points out how consumers benefitted from more choices— they could turn to MCI or Sprint—after the government-enforced breakup of AT&T. "The right thing in the Microsoft case is to take whatever action is necessary to restore competition and innovation in the software industry," he wrote. "It is clear . . . the government has done the right thing by challenging Microsoft's business practices. Let's hope that when the dust finally settles and the ruling comes in, it is just as right."

Whether the government wins, the antitrust action "is a big distraction for Microsoft," notes Bill Raduchel, Sun's chief strategy officer. "In the end there's only 168 hours a week even in Bill Gates' life, and he has to spend some hours of that dealing with the antitrust issue." Raduchel likens Gates to John D. Rockefeller and his oil monopoly, which Rockefeller lawyers argued should not be checked because it was a vital high-tech industry. Microsoft has the same sense "that they have a God-given right to this power and it's for the good of the world," Raduchel says. "Gates doesn't understand what the real issues are because nobody inside Microsoft is a critic." By speaking out against Microsoft, he asserts, Sun has helped to create an environment in which the issues, such as coercion and lack of choice, can be publicly explored.

Sun has found one unexpected ally in the Washington-based Software Publishers Association (SPA),* which represents 1,200 software companies, including both Microsoft, its largest dues payer, and Sun. In February 1998, the SPA released a set of "competition principles" that, though they did not cite Microsoft by name, were clearly aimed in that direction. "Established incumbents should not be permitted to exploit their market power . . . in ways that foreclose rivals' opportunities to reach consumers through essential distribution channels," the SPA stated. Ownership of a dominant operating system "should not be used [by the vendor] to unfairly favor its own products and services . . ." Later that year, the SPA released a 40-page report suggesting that Microsoft was using the same anticompetitive tactics it employed in the PC market to establish Windows NT as the dominant operating system in the corporate enterprise market. "This [question of monopoly power] is the most important issue facing our industry," says SPA President Ken Wasch. "We had to speak out. People don't understand that Microsoft is also going to have a monopoly on the workstation/server business in 18 months."

When the antitrust trial recessed on February 26, 1999, experts agreed that the Justice Department had done a credible job in presenting its case, whereas Microsoft had stumbled. Still, not many expected the government to seek the most radical remedy, breaking up Microsoft. Instead, expert observers speculated that the government might seek to compel Microsoft to open up its alleged monopoly, the Windows operating system, by requiring it to license

---

* On January 1, 1999, the SPA merged with another association to form the Software & Information Industry Association.

the source code to other companies. With the trial set to resume in May, Microsoft and the Justice Department were conducting secret negotiations that could lead to a settlement. Indeed, the presiding judge in the case, U.S. District Judge Thomas Penfield Jackson, asked both sides to try to settle. Whatever the outcome, evidence presented during the trial bolstered Sun's contention that Microsoft wielded its power unfairly and unlawfully in some cases. For example, Intel Vice President Steven McGeady testified that Microsoft pressured the chipmaker not to develop products that would support Java. Sums up Sun President and COO Ed Zander: "It's every entrepreneur's dream to be a monopoly, but when you are there are rules you must follow." Microsoft didn't follow those rules, he adds, and now, "people understand what we've been saying all along."

■ THE INDUSTRY FIGHTS BACK

At the close of 1998, market forces reasserted their influence on the future of the technology industry. America Online (AOL)—the Dulles, Virginia–based on-line giant—brokered a complex deal in which it would acquire Netscape for $4.28 billion in stock and enlist Sun as a partner to jointly sell and service Netscape's corporate software. The deal, expected to conclude in early 1999, had far-reaching implications. Sun's position as the preeminent anti-Microsoft bastion was enhanced when AOL sought it out to seal the acquisition of Netscape. Without Sun's involvement, the deal would probably not have occurred, because AOL has limited expertise in the corporate world and urgently needed a partner. Sun filled the bill because it was both opposed to Microsoft and skilled in the areas where AOL was not. Sun got AOL to back Java and promise to buy Sun servers. On the other hand, the transaction bolstered Microsoft's contention that the technology world was changing so quickly and radically that any supposed monopoly would be short-lived. After the deal was announced on November 24, Microsoft's lawyers indicated they would ask the Justice Department to dismiss its antitrust suit at the conclusion of testimony.

Sun's three-year partnership agreement with AOL appeared to have no more than modest risk for Sun. The two companies said they would work together to develop comprehensive solutions, using Netscape's existing software plus Sun's servers, that enable corporations and Internet service providers (ISPs) to do electronic commerce. As part of that deal, Sun guaranteed that AOL would receive $975 million in revenue over three years from sales of Netscape software. Through 2002, AOL is committed to buy $500 million worth of Sun products, while it will in turn receive $275 million in licensing fees from Sun. On the consumer side, the two companies will collaborate in developing Java-based devices that can be used to access AOL's on-line service and the Internet anywhere and any time. The agreement marries Sun's expertise in the corporate world with AOL's consumer brand to push the concept of widespread electronic commerce as the next great wave of technology.

Following the deal announcement, AOL's CEO Steve Case and McNealy held a press conference via telephone. In the conference call with reporters, Case promised that the AOL-Netscape-Sun combination will usher in a "new era in e-commerce." AOL/Netscape will bring in the consumer traffic, while Sun and AOL will provide the infrastructure to support on-line shopping and transactions. McNealy likened the combined offering to "ISP in a box," meaning that companies who bought the AOL/Sun products could quickly establish themselves as e-commerce providers. "We are trying to build a medium that could be as important as the TV or the telephone," he said. In doing that, Sun will service and support its own products, like Solaris and Java, along with Netscape's corporate software. Netscape's software, which runs on top of Solaris and other operating systems, competes directly with IBM's Lotus division and Microsoft in helping corporations set up intranets and extranets. Case and McNealy envisioned a broader appeal to the emerging market for e-commerce, in which all three companies—AOL, Sun, and Netscape—want to play.

McNealy couldn't resist a characteristically caustic comment during the conference call. First, he noted that the Sun victory in the Java lawsuit, coupled with the AOL endorsement just a week later, sends a clear message to developers—"write to the 100 percent compatible platform" (i.e., Sun's version of Java). Java, he added, has achieved "critical mass . . . I have to discount printer companies [a reference to Hewlett-Packard] and any large software companies in the Northwest [i.e., Microsoft] when they complain" about Sun's specifications on Java.

At least one key observer saw the deal as so portentous that it could signal a fundamental change in the power structure of the technology industry. Consultant Patricia Seybold says all three participants stand to benefit. Netscape, which had been seriously hamstrung by competition from Microsoft, will be revitalized by AOL's financial clout and strategic vision. With its acquisition of the Internet pioneer, AOL, which began life as a proprietary online service, gains the cachet of becoming an Internet leader. In addition, with its preliminary win in the Java lawsuit and its partnership with AOL, "Sun has substantially advanced its position to make Java a de facto window to the Web and an alternative to the dominance of Windows," she says. "The combined marketing and financial muscle of AOL and the product development skills of Netscape may just help to turn the tide against the Microsoft juggernaut, whatever the final resolution of the antitrust suit . . . Java and a fundamental commitment to open standards openly arrived at may finally rule the day and help to bring Microsoft to heel."

In fact, Microsoft's lawyers were making just the same kind of statements outside the Justice Department courtroom the day the deal was announced. Lead attorney John Warden—quoted by the *Wall Street Journal Interactive Edition* on November 25, 1998—charged that the AOL/Netscape merger shows the "utter vacuity" of the government's contention that Microsoft could gain a choke hold on the Internet.[6] It's time for federal and state governments that brought antitrust charges to "recognize commercial reality and the pointlessness of beating up" on Microsoft, he said. "These people (AOL, Netscape, and Sun) aren't running scared, they're running hard against Microsoft." Although it was unlikely the case would be dismissed, lead government lawyer David Boies conceded in the same article that the court would have to consider the AOL-Netscape-Sun alliance in weighing possible remedies against Microsoft.[7]

■ BATTLE OF THE TITANS

It's clear that Sun is not going to vanquish Microsoft the way it did Apollo or Digital. Microsoft is too big, too dominant, and Gates is too smart. But, neither is Sun going to lose, certainly not in the immediate future. The battle promises to be a long and protracted one, and the outcome won't be clear for several years. The AOL-Netscape-Sun deal almost guarantees to prolong the intraindustry fighting, by making it less likely that the government will seek or get an extreme remedy against Microsoft. Some analysts had speculated that Microsoft, like AT&T, might be broken up into a number of smaller pieces, dubbed "Baby Bills." But the emergence of an impressive coalition of non-Microsoft powers—Sun, IBM, Oracle, and now AOL—lends credence to Microsoft's argument that the market can choose who will govern the Internet, and it won't be any single company. Seybold foresaw a new balance of power emerging in the technology industry, composed on the one side of Microsoft and its allies, and on the other, of Sun, AOL/Netscape, IBM, and others. Companies now have "two positive poles around which to ally themselves," she says, rather than being simply pro- or anti-Microsoft. "For customers and businesspeople, this should assure a set of standards-based solutions rather than the dominance of one player."

Sun has now firmly rooted itself as Microsoft's chief obstacle, with a late boost from AOL and a lot of support from IBM. As with any multifront, far-reaching war, there will be plenty of victories and defeats for both sides before it's over. Microsoft's NT technology will continue to eat away at Sun's traditional markets, especially workstations. At the server level, Solaris has a longer life span, but NT will inevitably intrude here as well. Java is the secret weapon that scares even mighty Microsoft, but Sun has to figure out how to use it more effectively than it has so far. Java is more than a Microsoft-killer; it could be the path to a new world unclaimed by any reigning power, although the AOL deal is an early attempt to plant one flag. As we'll see in the next chapter, Sun is positioning Java and a newly introduced sister technology, Jini, as the solution for the world of ubiquitous computing. (Ubiquitous meaning turning everyday products, from cars to credit cards, into tiny digital devices.) Meanwhile, Sun continues to wage a withering battle of words and legal actions, hoping to delay Microsoft's own penetration into the new world.

Says McNealy: "There are no other competitors to Microsoft left except Sun. When we stop competing with Microsoft you have lost your choice." The world of computing is narrowing to Intel/Microsoft and SPARC/Solaris/Java, he maintains, in one of his characteristic sweeping generalizations. Other computer vendors such as Hewlett-Packard and IBM do offer alternatives to Microsoft, although they also use NT and Windows. Because McNealy said this before the AOL announcement, he may have to change his tune slightly. But he is correct in his point that companies like Sun, which develop new operating systems and related tools, are dwindling, while nearly everyone else is using intellectual property developed elsewhere. "At some point you can't OEM your engine, doors, chassis, and drive train, and call yourself a car manufacturer," is McNealy's analogy. Most computer vendors have become car dealers rather than manufacturers. "The industry is hollowing out into dealers," he maintains.

General Motors technology officer Dennis Walsh reflects on the dilemma faced by many who don't want to take sides: "Sun has shown a lot of courage in speaking out against Microsoft. People want competition but they're afraid to say something that angers Microsoft." On a personal basis, he adds, "I respect McNealy." On a company level, "we have 137,000 copies of Microsoft software." That's also the dilemma for Sun. Despite all the promises emerging from the AOL/Netscape deal, Sun's technology remains an island in a Microsoft sea. By refusing to become a Microsoft "dealer," McNealy has undoubtedly focused Sun internally and raised awareness externally. But, he has also locked himself and Sun out of a huge and growing portion of the existing technology world. Sun may yet be able to wrest some ground from Microsoft, but McNealy, like any good general, is also searching for alternative routes around the enemy. If Java can lead Sun into a new world, that is the company's best hope for victory.

Changing the Rules (Again)

Scott McNealy has always emphasized focus—which he instills by fixing Sun's sights upon a designated enemy and
then rallying the troops. But, in mid-1998, Sun was in danger of losing its focus. McNealy's zeal in targeting Microsoft set up an us-against-them mentality that did not
always serve customers, allies, or Sun itself very well. In
setting off into the new world of computing, even McNealy
realized that Sun had to get its internal house in order. He
finally disbanded the planet structure, which was wearing
thin and contributing to the company's inability to fashion a clear strategy for Java, and replaced it with more
coherently stratified divisions. By naming the pragmatic
Ed Zander as the executive in charge of these divisions,
McNealy signalled that he was ready to at least tone down
the Microsoft rhetoric and allow Sun to concentrate on
more realistic aims, like shoring up its existing business
and taking aim at new markets. "I want to talk about what
Sun is, not what Microsoft isn't," says Zander. "I want to
talk about the value we provide."

In zeroing in on Microsoft, Sun for awhile forgot the adage that made it great in the first place: change the rules. You don't beat an entrenched competitor by picking on its strength—in Microsoft's case, the desktop. Rather, you change the rules so that you're no longer fighting on your enemy's turf, and the home-field advantage is negated. As we saw in Chapter 9, Sun harnessed Java in an effort to develop a network computer that could take the place of PCs. This was not only a lost cause, but Sun lost time in setting out on a course that could lead to victory. It almost repeated the company's mistake a decade ago in going with the 386i rather than working on the then-new technology of routers. Today, Sun has a similar opportunity with Java.

What makes the opportunity so real for Java is the proliferation of that universal network, the Internet, coupled with the availability of powerful microprocessors that can reside anywhere. This combination is opening up vast new territory to the digital revolution. No longer is computing confined to bulky machines that sit on your desk or in corporate data centers. There can be smaller devices that do specialized things, like a smart phone that remembers numbers and receives faxes and even surfs the Internet, or a smart card that carries all your medical information or identification to get you inside a building or a computer network. Even cars and home appliances can be networked, so that you ask your automobile to display a map showing the way to your chosen destination, or call up your oven and tell it to turn itself on at 5:00 P.M. so the roast will be ready when you walk in the door at 7:00. The potential here is so great that everyone from banks to telecommunications companies to utilities are searching for ways to make themselves relevant to the digital world/home/car.

Neither Microsoft nor Sun (nor anyone else) owns this market, although they'd like to. Microsoft aims to get there by offering streamlined versions of Windows lightweight enough for the new environment. For Sun, it's ideal territory for Java. The ever-optimistic George Gilder believes that the rise of such devices as the smart phone "makes Windows less significant every day." Microsoft, he asserts, is at the pinnacle of its influence, like IBM in the early 1980s, and is about to give way to Sun and others in the digital world. The difference in this environment is that there is no entrenched operating system and Microsoft has no built-in advantages except by virtue of its talent and its resources, the same as Sun. McNealy in 1998 refined Sun's organizational structure to make better use of its resources. And externally, Sun is learning how to build alliances that take Java and its other technologies to places that Sun alone could not reach.

■ SMASHING PLANETS

Sun's internal dissent, especially as exemplified by the planet structure, has long been a two-edged sword for the company. There's no doubt that the planets heightened the internal focus on each individual business—such as Java, Solaris, SPARC, and workstations/servers. New kids on the block, like JavaSoft, got as much or more attention as old reliables, like SunSoft or the computer company. Java, as frail as it was initially, might not have survived if it had been buried in the Sun bureaucracy rather than turned into a planet. But the planets were increasingly unpopular with customers, who complained that they didn't know who to contact when they had a problem, and with partners, who got bounced around between internal Sun organizations with sometimes-competing aims.

Dealing with different customer support groups in each Sun planet, "you started feeling like you were on a merry-go-round," says Mark Biser, manager of technical support for the Volvo Group in Greensboro, North Carolina. When the automaker did a complex installation that required new software and hardware, he had to deal with four consulting organizations inside Sun. "I never did figure out who belonged where," he says. "I finally called my account rep [at Sun] and said you figure this out." Netscape's Brian Bennett calls Sun "the most frustrating partner I've had to deal with." He blames the planets. One example of the problem: Netscape wanted to sell communications software to Sun for packaging with its Internet servers, which required dealing with the software arm, SunSoft. Netscape might offer a 60 percent discount on a $1,000 product, meaning SunSoft paid $400, which it then resold to Sun's hardware arm, SMCC, for $700. "They didn't want us to deal directly with SMCC," says Bennett, because "there was this battle going on between SunSoft and SMCC." SunSoft wanted to boost its profit by reselling the Netscape software, whereas SMCC's aim was to put more value into its hardware with new software features. Netscape went over the heads of the two planets and appealed to McNealy, eventually obtaining an agreement under which SunSoft would resell the hardware to SMCC with no profit margin.

In late 1997, over the Christmas break, high-ranking Sun executives realized that the planet structure had outlived its usefulness and began plotting a reorganization, which was announced in two phases: January and April 1998. The first step was formation of an executive committee, reporting to McNealy, composed of Ed Zander as COO; Mike Lehman as CFO; and Bill Raduchel as chief strategy officer. The second step was to replace the planets with divisions overseen by Zander. In the process, Sun added two divisions, to focus on new lines of business in the consumer and storage markets, resulting in a total of seven: computer systems (workstations and servers), microelectronics (SPARC), Solaris, Java, customer services, storage, and consumer/embedded.

Even though they lost some of their autonomy under the new structure, most Sun executives were relieved. "The planets placed too much visibility on each entity," says Larry Hambly, who is chief quality officer for Sun and president of Sun Enterprise Services, the customer service division. Under the planets, the salesforces competed with each other, while the people who were supposed to give customer service passed the buck. "There was too much of, 'I don't know; that's somebody else's problem'," says Hambly. With any structure in place for seven years, "calcium deposits get formed and everything slows down," adds Masood Jabbar, president of the computer systems division. "You have to do some tinkering."

Zander was the driving force in the reorganization. "The last thing I wanted to do was reorganize," he says, but as the executives were doing the planning for 1998, "I said to Scott, 'You know it would work better if it was this way'." Zander went away one weekend and drew up an outline of how the new divisional structure might work. "All of this affected about 5,000 people at Sun," he says, some of whose job titles changed or were shifted into new divisions or wound up reporting to new bosses. About 200 jobs were eliminated, although Sun also made 700 new hires in the process of adding divisions.

Zander believes the reorganization will enable Sun to present "one face to the customer," something it hasn't done for a long time. "The worst thing you can do is confuse a customer," he says, and that's what the planet structure did. "We let our organization spill out into the marketplace outside these four walls. It was JavaSoft and SunSoft, rather than Sun." Internally, "the attitude was, 'my opco [operating company or planet] is better than your opco.' " As COO, Zander spends time with each of the division presidents to encourage cooperation. "We have eliminated the fiefdoms. It's all for Sun now." Previously, he says, Sun's adage was "loosely coupled, highly aligned," to describe its organizational approach. "We were good on the first part and lousy on the second," Zander says. "My goal is to emphasize 'highly aligned.' " In mid-1998, customers said they could begin to see the impact of the organizational changes. "I sense that internally, there's still confusion as to where everybody's going to land and who's reporting to who," says Volvo's Biser, "but from my viewpoint, the re-org is definitely a step in the right direction. In terms of support, the number of people I have to deal with is diminishing and I have a single account rep."

Although the division structure consolidates sales-forces and eliminates separate logos, each of the seven divisions is still responsible for its own P&L, research, marketing, manufacturing, and product delivery. Sun did not want to lose the sense of decentralized, entrepreneurial units entirely. Thanks to McNealy's fondness for the planets, the company held onto the structure longer than it should have. But in the end he recognized that the planets were doing more harm than good. The reorganization also highlights Zander's expanding role at Sun. McNealy obviously listened to his COO's advice and went along with a retooling of one of his most cherished innovations.

➤ The Scott and Ed Show

Many observers speculated that the purpose of the reorganization was twofold: the public one of reducing the internecine arguing that had frustrated customers and partners; and the private one of keeping Zander, who was being courted for the top job at companies like Apple and Silicon Graphics. "It's the end of one era and the beginning of another—the Ed Zander era," proclaims former Sun executive Eric Schmidt, who was himself recruited into a CEO job at Novell. "Scott [McNealy] wants to fight the great fight against Microsoft," says Schmidt. To do that, he needs a strong second in command with an operational focus, namely Zander.

In April 1999, Sun gave Zander the additional title of president, although his responsibilities weren't expected to change much. The elevation came just after two of Sun's primary competitors, Compaq and Hewlett-Packard, started well-publicized searches for new CEOs. Zander, no doubt, was on a short list at both companies, and the promotion made it clear that McNealy was determined to keep him at Sun. McNealy relinquished the title of president, but remains chairman and CEO. In a press release, he lauded Zander's contributions: "Sun is racing down the highway with a full tank of gas and precise directions on where the industry is going. There is no company in our industry that is better positioned to deliver the right products, services, and technologies to dot.com the world (a reference to Sun's ongoing advertising campaign). Ed has been a key leader for Sun and deserves the recognition for driving the operations of the company to this point."

It's not easy playing second banana to Scott McNealy, but Zander has a self-effacing humor that helps him carry it off. At last year's JavaOne conference, he told the assembled crowd of thousands of programmers, journalists, and analysts: "I'm the warm-up act for Scott—it's like warming up for the Pope." Replacing McNealy at a company function in June 1998, he stepped out in front of the expectant audience and announced: "I apologize. Scott McNealy was supposed to be here and I'm not Scott McNealy. He's in Washington being nominated for a Smithsonian award, so you've got me instead."

Zander is quite a contrast to McNealy both physically and psychologically. Relatively short, slender, and balding, his competent, businesslike image is far from the jock facade that McNealy cultivates. Zander always wears a suit (usually Armani) and tie, while McNealy rarely dons formal attire. Almost a decade older than McNealy, Zander spent 14 years at button-down hierarchal companies, Apollo and Data General, before joining Sun in 1987. Zander provides a much-needed balance to the capricious CEO: he is more attuned to everyday business requirements than religious campaigns. Were he to leave Sun, it would be a serious blow to the company's effort to shore up relationships with important customers and partners. Zander is cagey about prospects outside of Sun. "People in my capacity always get calls. Personally, I'd love to be the top guy, to run my own thing," he says. "On the other hand, Scott gives me a lot of leeway. We have a good relationship and it has been a good ride."

Jeremy Barnish, the executive speechwriter who works for both McNealy and Zander, says the two complement each other in many ways. McNealy is unpredictable in his approach to an issue. "You really never know how Scott arrives at something." At the opposite end, "Ed is clarity through attrition. He works all the edges off a problem until he gets it down to size." Barnish says McNealy is impatient with details and likes to get at the big ideas, whereas Zander "wants to work through everything with you four or five times." Zander's style is like "filleting a fish," he says. "You can see all the steps of a process."

Zander does share characteristics with McNealy: he will play the fool to get an idea across for Sun. At one event, he walked out of a huge JavaStation and said, "It takes a thin man to walk out of a thin client." And he can be as intense as McNealy, like screaming across the company cafeteria, "What have you done for me today?" If you spot Zander at a public event, good luck catching up to him, because he's almost always in a rush. At the 1997 Internet World trade show at Jacob Javits Center in New York, Zander finished a presentation and dashed through the corridors ahead of everyone else. "He runs up the escalators and can't find his limo, so he jumps in a taxi and is gone," Barnish says. A moment later, the company limo shows up, and everyone else piles in, except Zander, who couldn't wait.

Zander, who has run two of the planets, SunSoft and SMCC, is now the day-to-day manager at Sun. "Scott has been the company's visionary, spokesman, and guiding light," says Raduchel. "But the job of being CEO, chairman, president, and COO, which Scott was, is an unwinnable job. Scott doesn't have the bandwidth to handle everything." With Zander managing the business, McNealy can concentrate more on the public persona. However, it's not quite as cut-and-dried as Mr. Outside and Mr. Inside. Zander's emphasis is on operations, but he frequently appears in public forums, whereas McNealy still gets involved in most internal decisions. Says Zander of their respective roles: "Scott is Sun. He is the soul and inspiration of the company. Clearly my function right now is to make sure things work around here: We hit our numbers, deliver on our products, meet our goals and commitments."

Regarding Microsoft, the two differ in approach but not in conviction. "Scott's goal is about bringing the world to an understanding that Microsoft is a problem and that there's a difference between us and them," says Zander. "I don't personalize my opposition. Microsoft is a company that I'm competing with. When I talk, it's to dispel myths about NT, to talk about Microsoft's inability to deliver at the enterprise level." Zander is hardly low-key, but he comes off as cool and level-headed compared with the mercurial McNealy. His presence is reassuring to Wall Street, to customers, and to Sun allies.

■ INTEL OUTSIDE

Another sign of Sun's new pragmatism is its attempt to move closer to Intel, whose long-standing partnership with Microsoft is summed up in the technology industry's neologism "Wintel," which refers to Windows running on an Intel microprocessor. In late 1997, about the same time that executives were plotting how to deconstruct the planets, Sun made a startling announcement: It would develop a version of Solaris for a new Intel microprocessor called Merced. This was intriguing on a number of fronts. First, it was a last gasp of the planet structure, because SunSoft, which oversaw Solaris, decided to collaborate with Intel to the dismay of the microprocessor group at Sun, for whom Merced is major competition. Second, Sun could be hedging its bets regarding its own ultraSPARC technology by putting Solaris on Merced. The Solaris/ultraSPARC combination currently powers all of Sun's hardware products except the JavaStation, and will compete with NT systems that will switch to Merced when it is available. Third, on Intel's part, Merced, which is a radically different design than the chips that power PCs, represents an attempt to reach out to the Unix world and reduce its dependence on Microsoft. By helping Intel become a platform for Unix operating systems such as Solaris, Sun could help drive that wedge between Intel and Microsoft. Says a hopeful McNealy: "Maybe Microsoft and Intel will split. Maybe the marriage will break up."

Sun's collaboration with Intel was not entirely without precedent. Since the days of the 386i, it had offered a version of Solaris on earlier Intel chips that it licensed to vendors like Fujitsu and NCR, although the Solaris/Intel combination never found widespread acceptance. "People look at Solaris on Merced as a discontinuity," says Mel Friedman, president of Sun Microelectronics, the division that oversees SPARC. "No more than Solaris on Intel x86 [the PC-based line of chips]." Friedman points out that he can license SPARC to other software vendors in the same way that Solaris is licensed to other hardware vendors. "I have to compete with Solaris on Merced by offering better performance and better scalability [with Solaris on ultra-SPARC]." To that end, Friedman notes that the Solaris/SPARC combination has seven years of development history, whereas Merced isn't even expected to reach the market until mid-2000.

John McFarlane, president of the Solaris software division (formerly SunSoft), says Sun will be more aggressive in pushing Solaris on Merced than it was with earlier Intel incarnations. "In terms of Merced readiness, Sun is the only vendor with this depth of Intel experience," he says. "We've been running Solaris on Intel since 1988." The Solaris/SPARC and Solaris/Merced combinations will be compatible, he says, so that application developers can easily write for both of them. "We have a single Solaris—whether on Intel, Merced, or SPARC." By partnering with Intel and licensing Solaris to other computer vendors, "we're bringing on top-notch world-class companies to help in the evolution of our operating system," he says, furthering Sun's goal of making Solaris one of the leading operating systems in the network computing environment of the future.

Intel has a different vision, which is to have its microprocessors running everything from the PC to the server. "I don't see Sun as a microprocessor vendor," says John

Miner, corporate vice president and general manager for Intel's enterprise server group. "Sun is a systems vendor and they're trying to move up in the value chain. Sun's customers wanted Solaris on Merced. There was the desire on Intel's part to assure that Merced's customers would have the OS of their choice." As for Intel, "our strategy isn't driven by what Microsoft is trying to do," Miner maintains. There's a performance gap between what Intel's microprocessors offer and what PC software can deliver, so Intel wants to enlarge the market for its technology. "We've been at the client [desktop] and then in entry-level and mid-range servers," he says. "We believe there's great benefit in having a unifying architecture top to bottom in the enterprise," which would, of course, be Intel. Even though Miner insists that Intel is forging its path independent of Microsoft, their two views of the corporate enterprise are parallel: one integrated technology everywhere, be it software or microprocessor.

Although McNealy and everyone else at Sun swear up and down that the company would never abandon SPARC, some knowledgeable observers wonder. With Merced, Intel is trying to close the gap between its microprocessor technology and the RISC technology that has powered Unix workstations and servers for years. "The expectation is that Merced will offer the same level of performance as ultra-SPARC," says Linley Gwennap, editorial director of the industry newsletter *Microprocessor Report,* in Sebastopol, California. "If Merced does meet that goal, why would Sun need to keep developing its own processors? If they go to Merced they could buy high-volume, commodity chips," saving about $100 million a year in R&D on SPARC.

Weighing against that argument is that staying with SPARC differentiates Sun in the market. There also is a sizable installed base that would be forced through a painful transition if Sun dropped SPARC. Gwennap expects Sun to stick with SPARC for the foreseeable future, but adds that it will be increasingly isolated. As with NT on the software side, the other workstation/server vendors, such as IBM and Hewlett-Packard, are moving to Merced. In the early

2000s, Gwennap projects, Merced will have a 60 percent share of the market for this type of chip, and Sun will have around 20 percent. "Intel can outinvest Sun," whose strategy is vertical integration with Solaris/ultraSPARC. "But the rest of the computer industry is going to a horizontally layered, value added strategy," he says.

Zander discounts the Merced threat. "I've been hearing Merced is going to clean my clock for years. One of the things you'll hear at Sun is 'Don't live in the future.' I am almost ready to bet you'll never see Merced." Thus, Zander professes to be comfortable with the fact that, on one side, Sun's microelectronics engineers are working feverishly to stay ahead of Merced and maintain ultraSPARC's edge in the marketplace. On another side, Sun will put Solaris on Merced because the goal is to make Solaris ubiquitous. Zander hastens to point out that Sun will not sell Solaris on Merced itself, but only license it for resale by partners such as NCR. Nonetheless, Sun could wind up competing against itself as it sells Solaris/ultraSPARC against a vendor selling Solaris/Merced. With its overlapping SPARC and Merced strategies, Sun is playing out a very tricky hand. If it continues to succeed with Solaris/ultraSPARC in the corporate marketplace, that will intensify the confrontation with NT and Unix vendors using Intel's Merced. In late 1998, IBM teamed up with a couple of other Unix companies to develop a new version of the operating system for Merced, indicating that Solaris won't have the Unix market to itself any time soon. If Solaris/ultraSPARC falters, that will put pressure on Sun to join the crowd and adopt Merced as its primary microprocessor, a move that McNealy would have to be dragged to kicking and screaming.

■ AN ENTERPRISING COMPANY

Even as Sun insists that it won't follow competitors into the NT and Intel world, in one area it has been forced to become more conventional, and that is in service. Historically, Sun had a poor reputation for customer service. It was a company driven by engineers selling cool stuff to other engineers. If those engineers had a problem, they solved it themselves. For much of Sun's existence, "service was a secondary issue," says Hambly. "What early customers cared about was performance and price." But then Sun, as described in previous chapters, moved away from selling only workstations to emphasizing servers, a refocusing that started in the mid-1990s in response to the encroachment of NT on the workstation market.

When you're selling a server, a very costly (Sun's top-of-the-line model goes for $1 million-plus) machine that is critical to the operations of the entire corporation, you have to provide lots of hand-holding along with it. For years, IBM in particular has derived billions of dollars in revenue from ongoing service contracts on its mainframe computers, the machines that Unix-based servers are often displacing. In the past, Sun might designate an engineer or two to handle customer "trouble" calls, but it had no formal structure for dealing with after-sales support. The situation was exacerbated by the planet structure, which allowed customer inquiries to fall into the gap between the various operating companies.

All that is changing, and here again, Zander's influence is apparent. He came from companies that stressed service as well as products and is trying to edge Sun away from its purely product-centered mentality. "Ed is a very market-savvy person," says Hambly, "and there was pressure from the market [for more service]. Ed is good at observing market trends and distilling them." Sun created a formal customer service organization reporting to McNealy (now to Zander) in 1993; before that, service had been buried a couple of management layers down in the computer opco. As it became clear that Sun's future growth would come from selling high-end services to the corporate enterprise, the service organization has flowered. Over the past couple of years, it has added almost 2,000 people and now represents about 15 percent of Sun's revenue.

"We had to extend upward into the enterprise," says Hambly, who chaired the product strategy committee that foresaw the transition from a workstation- to a server-centric company. "We saw that this was an opportunity and began to invest in developing more products and services to support it," he says. "NT was having an impact on our traditional marketplace. We don't want to contribute to the inevitability [of NT] by abandoning that market, but at the high end we have an opportunity to be more successful."

Hambly distinguishes Sun's strategy from that of its chief competitor in the server arena, IBM. "They will deliver a total solution, cradle to grave," he says. Sun will deliver key services related to its own products, SPARC, Solaris, and Java, and then partner with consulting firms and system integrators to do the rest. "You're either a product-focused company or you're a solutions company focused on delivering to customers," he says. "Our strategy is to remain product-focused and build core service competencies around our platform." Daniel Kunstler, who follows Sun as a managing director of J. P. Morgan Securities in San Francisco, agrees that even with the expansion of its service division, Sun is not going down the same road as IBM. "IBM will provide whatever product or service its customers want, but in doing that they've forfeited the idea of promoting their own intellectual property [IP]," he says. "Sun still sees itself as promoting its own IP."

Here again, McNealy has drawn a line in the sand between Sun and the rest of the computing world. Sun has tempered its all-Sun-or-nothing approach to where it will, for instance, provide linkage to NT and offer better customer support to corporations who are running multiple systems. But, unlike competitors such as IBM or HP, it won't sell or service another company's intellectual property, like Intel's or Microsoft's, as part of the "Sun solution." When you buy from Sun, you get Sun, and Sun only. In the corporate computing world, that is a lonely—but so far, defensible—stance.

➤ Java Everywhere

As Sun reorganized and strengthened its traditional business, it was at the same time pushing Java as its entree into what's called ubiquitous computing. McNealy harps on the concept of webtone to describe his vision of how this unfolds: Rather than take your laptop computer with you everywhere, you simply carry a card or a ring or other device that allows you to access technology on demand. He is prone to pulling his Sun access card out of his pocket and announcing, "This is all the computer I need." The idea is that he can put that card into any computer running Java and gain admittance to Sun's corporate network. There are still shortcomings to this approach. I've seen McNealy run the demo and fail, because he messed up the password or the computer link just wasn't there. Similarly, Sun has invented the "Java ring," which can be plugged into a Java-enabled computer via a specialized interface to allow the wearer to interact with the system and everyone else on it. So far, the Java ring is more proof of concept than real product, but it is one more piece of McNealy's propaganda campaign to establish Java as the centerpiece of this new world of computing. Microsoft has its own campaign on behalf of Wintone, or Windows everywhere, in a stripped-down version called Windows CE that is more suited to small devices.

In several arenas, the campaign is more than propaganda. Sun has signed agreements with leading cable, cell phone, and credit card companies who plan to embed Java into their products to enrich the consumer experience. In May 1998, Tele-Communications Incorporated (TCI) agreed to use a version of Java called PersonalJava to program interactive features into its forthcoming digital settop boxes. The Englewood, Colorado–based cable provider intends to roll out digital boxes to its 18 million subscribers over the next three to five years. Those boxes would allow consumers to do such things as bank from home, exchange e-mail, and surf the Web. But, TCI also signed agreements with Microsoft to use Windows CE as the operating system on at least five million of those boxes, although PersonalJava will be the programming language even for those. Another form of Java could be the operating system on digital boxes that don't run Windows CE. Although both companies heralded their pacts as victories, each would have preferred TCI to lock out the other. By pitting the two against each other, TCI Chairman John Malone is trying to ensure that there will be no monopoly of his world the way there was of the PC.

"The operating system is very fundamental to the box," says David Beddow, a TCI senior vice president who oversees the digital box effort. "We don't want to be in a situation where you can run only one OS because that gives the vendor too much control over your box. We made a decision a long time ago that we're not going to be single-source in this endeavor. We're not singling Microsoft out; it's just one of multiple vendors." Beddow says TCI didn't really have to play Microsoft and Sun against each other; "they did a pretty effective job of that by themselves." He scolded the two squabbling technology companies as acting like a "group of unsupervised children," adding that competition is healthy, "but animosity and open feuding doesn't help things at all."

Scientific-Atlanta, the Atlanta-based manufacturer of cable boxes, has also licensed Java technology, for its Explorer 2000 series of digital settop boxes. H. Allen Ecker, Scientific-Atlanta's president of subscriber systems, says the choice of Java resulted from customer requests. Starting in 1999, Scientific-Atlanta expects to manufacture about 1 million digital boxes a year to start replacing standard cable boxes. "We'll give customers the ability to have PersonalJava on all of them," he says. "They make the choice." Like TCI, Scientific-Atlanta will pay Sun a licensing fee for every box with Java that it sells. In turn, Scientific-Atlanta's customers, the cable operators, determine pricing to consumers for the additional services they can offer on digital boxes. Ecker says he's staying out of the battle between Microsoft and Sun. "That's between Scott McNealy and Bill Gates." Scientific-Atlanta "will respond to our customers. If a customer wants to use Windows CE, we'll put it on."

➤ Smart Cards and Phones

In another realm of advancing technology, smart cards, Java has a head start, thanks to a partnership with Visa International, the San Mateo–based credit card company, but Microsoft as usual is coming on with a rush. Smart cards contain a tiny embedded chip and an operating system that allow them to be used for everything from identification to storage of information such as your medical history to electronic money. In 1996, Visa approached JavaSoft about developing a smart card technology, says Philip Yen, senior vice president of Visa's chip platform. Visa had scouted out other possibilities, including IBM, and determined that nothing really fit what it would need in a smart card. "Sun had no experience in smart cards, but they had established Java as a broad technology with an open approach," says Yen. "That was most attractive from a commercial aspect because we wouldn't be locked into something that Sun controls." He praises Sun for being willing to make the investment and develop a technology called Java Card. "They were very quick to respond to our initiative and get the marketplace behind them," says Yen.

In January 1998, Visa and Sun formalized their partnership to jointly develop and promote Java Card as the standard smart card environment. Yen says this will follow Sun's Java model in that all smart card manufacturers will provide input, but Sun has ultimate responsibility for incorporating changes. "There is a mechanism for Sun to continue to innovate," he says, while customers "have a forum for comment." This provides a check and balance on Sun. "If it doesn't deliver what we need, then over time the licensees will do things on their own." To date, says Yen, this approach is working well. Visa expected to roll out its first smart cards in mid-1998 in Asia and by the end of the year in the United States.

Java seemed to have clear sailing in the smart card world until October 1998, when Microsoft unveiled a Windows-based product aimed at the same market. At a conference in

Paris, Craig Mundie, senior vice president of consumer platforms, said Microsoft should be ready to test its product in the first quarter of 1999 and to ship it later in the year. Two European-based smart card manufacturers, Gemplus and Schlumberger Industries, had already signed on to use the Microsoft product. Market researcher Dataquest forecast that the worldwide market for smart cards would reach $6.8 billion in 2002.

Sun scored another victory in early 1998 when Motorola, of Shaumburg, Illinois, announced plans to license Java for use across its wide portfolio of products, including automotive components, cell phones, smart cards, and other electronics systems. "Java has been widely accepted by various industries, our software development partners, but most importantly, our customers, as an open software solution," says Motorola CEO Chris Galvin. Like IBM, Motorola has a host of disparate products that Java can help to communicate. With its ability to be used in a wide range of simple to complex products, "Java is a sought-after alternative for us and our customer partners," says Galvin. McNealy trumpeted the agreement as the largest technology license in Java's history, anticipating the technology's inclusion in "tens of millions" of Motorola products.

One place where a so-called Java appliance is already working is inside stores operated by the giant Home Depot chain of Atlanta. For a new line of business, in which Home Depot rents tools to consumers, the chain is installing a Java-based, touch-screen system on which consumers can select the tool they want to rent. The system will also verify credit card information. "We went live in 1998" in about 60 stores, says Mike Anderson, vice president of information systems. He expected to have the system running in all of Home Depot's 700-plus outlets in 1999. One of the reasons Home Depot selected Java is because it's easy for employees and consumers to use. In fact, Anderson says, Java is so popular at the local universities that 80 percent of computer science graduates learn to program with it, so Home Depot can hire the talent it needs to develop even more applications in Java.

■ READY FOR THE FUTURE

Sun made a smart move when it placed Java applications, such as smart cards and cell phones, into its new consumer/embedded division, formed when the planets were phased out. Some potential Java licensees in consumer electronics had complained that Sun had little understanding of their world, which relies on high volume and low prices—the opposite of the corporate market. By creating a new division that would focus only here, Sun could dispel the notion that decisions on consumer devices would be driven by the same strategy it used in selling big-ticket servers and workstations.

"Customers are coming to us that we've never seen before," says Bud Tribble, Sun's vice president of architecture and technology. "We can play at two levels: both the device the consumer is interacting with and the infrastructure to support it." In other words, Sun can license Java to, say, Visa, to run on a smart card and also sell Visa an expensive server for all those smart cards to interact with. Even though many competitors would like a piece of the action, Tribble does see it coming down to Sun versus Microsoft. "The consumer market historically has been fragmented," he says. "Java could correct that. You can have a variety of chips and devices but a unified programming model." With Windows CE, "Microsoft has the same idea, except everything would come from Redmond. Java allows more diversity."

Tribble shares McNealy's propensity to define the world simplistically. In fact, there will be multiple competitors. AOL, for example, by acquiring Netscape put its stake into the ground. 3Com Corporation, manufacturer of the hugely popular Palm Pilot, could expand that gizmo's operating system into the same areas that Java and Windows CE are eyeing. Because this world of ubiquitous computing is so much larger and more expansive than desktop computers, it's extremely unlikely that any one vendor will be able to dominate it the way Microsoft did the desktop. In that sense, Sun had won before it even began, but the habit of picking Microsoft as the lone enemy dies hard. McNealy and other Sun executives must take off their blinders and see the world in full—as an array of sometimes-competing, sometimes-cooperating companies who aren't going to choose up sides like kids in a schoolyard. Rather, each company will seek to build upon its own strengths in entering the new market. To paraphrase Zander, Sun will have to sell Java to these potential allies for what it is, not for what it isn't (i.e., Windows).

The failure of the network computer to take off as expected may have forced Sun onto the correct path with Java. In a way, the technology is returning to its roots, for it was initially envisioned as an operating system for the cable settop box. Now the setting is not only the settop box, but almost any consumer electronics device to which you want to add smartness. As we'll see in the next chapter, whether it all works depends upon a myriad of factors, everything from how the Department of Justice resolves its antitrust suit against Microsoft to consumers' willingness to embrace interactive appliances. In developing partnerships with companies like TCI, Motorola, and Visa, Sun is definitely moving in the right direction, but no one knows yet whether the products that result will go the way of the VCR or New Coke. In entering the consumer world, Sun has broadened its horizons, but it has also lessened its control. It must depend upon a group of companies and customers that it has never dealt with before. If Java triumphs here, it will be a tribute not just to Sun's capacity for innovating technology, but to its ability for adapting that technology to dreams that come from outside itself.

Chapter

12

The Millennial Sun

If Sun were an introspective company, how might it take stock of itself as it approaches the twenty-first century and its 20th anniversary in 2002? It's certainly a very different organization than the one founded 17 years ago by four kids from Stanford and Berkeley who had stumbled upon an appealing technology for people largely like themselves. That Sun sold one product to a handful of specialized niche markets in which everyone pretty much knew everyone else. The Sun workstation was aimed at engineers, who designed complex products or did mind-boggling number-crunching that required a powerful, fast computer light years beyond the nascent PC. By contrast, the Sun of today sells to corporations around the globe, with an array of products reaching from the individual to the data center. Like digital spiders, Sun servers sit at the center of webs of electronic interconnections, handling everything from Internet surfing to auto manufacturing schedules. Sun workstations, though challenged by entrants running Microsoft's Windows NT (renamed Windows 2000 in late 1998), are still highly favored by top-tier users for their reliability and scalability. In its most recent transition, Sun is reaching out to the consumer market with its Java technology by forging alliances with new partners such as America Online, Motorola, Visa, and TCI.

So, the Sun of today is bigger, more diversified, and financially robust. Although other computer makers stumbled in hitting quarterly earnings targets in 1998, Sun was consistently ahead of Wall Street estimates. And yet, the whispers about Sun's impending demise are never stilled. For the Sun of today, and tomorrow, faces challenges those four kids from the university never conceived of when they blithely launched their start-up workstation company. In the intervening years, technology has become big business, no longer the purview of social misfits folded over glowing computer screens in university labs. Those one-time misfits now preside over empires whose market value is greater than a lot of countries' GNPs. Partly by its own doing and partly as a result of market trends, Sun finds itself pitted against that social misfit-turned-(alleged) monopolist, Bill Gates, and his Microsoft empire.

But for Sun to succeed in the twenty-first century, it will have to draw on its past. Even as the company has grown and prospered, it remains, in many ways, a throwback to that more innocent era of the past, when technology was for creating "fun stuff." Sun stands almost alone now in sticking with the strategy of "innovate, and they will come." For most of its competitors, it's "integrate [solutions from everywhere], and they will come." Scott McNealy's bet-the-company strategy is to wager that Sun can come up with innovations that will change the nature of computing and level the playing field with Microsoft, maybe with a little help from the courts. Sun turned to its most storied innovator of all, Bill Joy, to unwrap yet another technological breakthrough in mid-1998, called Jini, which expands on the Java legacy. With Jini and Java, coupled with the old reliables, Solaris and SPARC, Sun believes it has what it takes to shine on as the new millennium dawns. Let's see.

■ I DREAM OF JINI

Jini (pronounced *genie*) is new software that allows any digital device—from cameras to printers to stereo sound systems to air conditioners—to hook into a computer network and identify itself and its parameters. Once that occurs, each device can communicate with each other—for instance, a digital camera could print a photograph to a color printer. This advances on Java by applying the principle "write once, run anywhere" not only to computers, but to all electronic devices. With the announcement of Jini, the hype machine was back in full gear. "Poof! There goes the desktop computer," opined the August 1998 issue of *Wired* magazine, graced with a cover photo of a relaxed, blue-jeaned Bill Joy sitting in a chair holding a cup of java, er coffee.[1] *Wired* described Jini as a "global nervous system," and predicted that it might achieve "the irresistible dream" of the magazine's patron saint Marshall McLuhan: one huge computer formed by thousands of interacting machines networked together. "A means of thinking, creating, and communicating that is everywhere at once." The *New York Times* also found the concept irresistible; a front-page story on July 15, 1998, tapped Jini as "Taking a Step Toward Converting the Home into a Supercomputer."[2] The *Times* duly noted that Microsoft is working on a system of its own, called Millennium, but proclaimed that Sun has the lead because it has already established Java as the standard for exchanging software code.[3]

Joy and his Aspen-based research group have been quietly developing Jini for four years, in a project reminiscent of Java's start-up. Jini, explains the proud papa, enables groups of disparate electronic devices to participate in a real-time "conference call" that allows them to collaborate. This encompasses the notion of "Java Tone"—you can plug in any device and the system recognizes it and can connect it to any other device, just like the phone system. "It's kind of magic," says Joy excitedly. "Small simple things enable complex behavior. With Jini you can build a bunch of simple devices and they combine to make a complex system—like ants in an anthill." He also compares Jini with an electric plug, where "any company that works with Jini can build a device and know it will work with any other." One announced customer for Jini is Quantum Corporation, a Milpitas, California–based company that makes computer disk drives. Quantum plans to use Jini to build network connections within disk drives, rather than relying on the computer's operating system to handle that complex task.

Thanks to its experience with Java, Sun doesn't have to stumble around trying to figure out what to do with Jini. It intends to commercialize Jini, which runs on top of a Java Virtual Machine (the Java equivalent of a computer in software), by enlisting allies to make the technology as widespread as possible and as quickly as possible. In early 1999, more than 30 companies had endorsed Jini, including 3Com, IBM, Canon, Computer Associates, Cisco Systems, Kodak, Motorola, Nokia, Novell, and Sony. Sun's consumer division, which also handles the embedded Java technology described in the previous chapter, will take charge of Jini, with a lot of help from Joy. According to him, Sun will license the source code needed to create Jini programs for no charge or a very nominal one in an effort to establish it as a standard for interactive devices. "Jini needs to be more widespread even than Java because there are more device makers than computer companies," he says. Sun will make money by developing products and services surrounding Jini. Again, if you're going to have a bunch of devices talking to each other, they all have to speak the same language (Jini) and have a place to interconnect, like a telephone switching center. Sun figures its servers can play the role of switching center.

To Joy, Jini represents the next generation of computing, in which instead of having one complicated machine—the personal computer—trying to do everything, "you have different devices with different capabilities." He hastens to add that, contrary to the *Wired* headline, "I don't think it's going to replace computers. It's going to augment devices that work with PCs." Joy has evidently learned the lesson of the JavaStation and is shifting the competitive turf from PCs to the larger, more diversified world of electronic devices. "You can't afford to have a system where when one thing fails, everything fails," he says. Jini can help consumers or businesses identify which device has a problem and which ones are working properly. Microsoft's Millennium, which so far is only a rumor, "may try to solve the same problems that Jini's trying to solve, but if Microsoft's involved, it's going to be too monolithic and too one-world," he sniffs.

■ JINI'S OUT OF THE BOTTLE

Bill Joy assures me that Java and Jini represent only part of Sun's strategy for ubiquitous computing, which will gradually be revealed as new pieces are added. But, there's enough out there to take a stab at assessing whether Sun has a realistic chance at reshaping itself beyond its current mainstay businesses, workstations, and servers. Experts inside and outside Sun agree that Java/Jini and related technologies, though they bring in little real revenue today, must succeed in becoming high-volume products for the company to have exciting growth prospects in the twenty-first century.

George Gilder, for one, believes that the Java division will eventually be Sun's largest. Java, he notes, is what Clayton Christensen of the Harvard Business School calls a "disruptive innovation," which creates new markets, attracts new customers, and fosters new distribution channels. By contrast, Sun's servers and workstations are sustaining innovations, which support existing product trends. Java has changed Sun's image from workstation company into Internet technology leader, with 1 million developers now using Java as the programming language of the Web. "Did the most wild-eyed Java enthusiast expect such a rapid triumph?" Gilder asks. He sees the newer, fast-moving Java world interacting with Sun's traditional businesses in a way that benefits both. Sun servers and workstations are revitalized by the infusion of Java technology. The selling point for Sun is that, as the creator of Java, its other platforms will run the new technology better than anyone else. Ultimately, says Gilder, Java succeeds because technology users are rejecting "bloat" in favor of a networked world in which they access what they need when they need it. "Java will probably be the basis of this new paradigm," he says, although there are no guarantees.

David Gelernter, a professor of computer science at Yale University who takes credit for some of the theories that spawned Jini, agrees with Gilder. "The Microsoft Windows view of computing . . . is obsolete," he states in an opinion piece in the October 26, 1998, *Wall Street Journal*.[4] "It dates from a long-dead era when most people owned only a relative handful of computer files, since they hadn't been computer users for very long; when e-mail and the Internet were largely unknown; when memory and computing power were expensive." In what Gelernter calls the "New View" of computing, files are stored not on a hard drive, but in cyberspace, where they can be accessed from any network-connected machine. "It's the system's job to get you what you want," he says, "but unlike most of today's systems, it won't have a million options and switches and 'features'; your mother, or even a CEO, will be able to master the controls in five minutes."

These are the optimists, where Sun's concerned, and they segue neatly into Scott McNealy's visions of a diverse world of technology content knit together by Java and Jini. The pessimists, however, have another view: of Java fragmented, like Unix, and of Microsoft's continuing dominance. Tom Kucharvy, president of Summit Strategies in Boston, says Sun has spread itself too thin with all its various Java implementations—like ones aimed at the network computer, smart cards, embedded devices, and so forth—leaving room for someone else to slip in and grab important chunks of the market. Kucharvy nominates not Microsoft, but IBM.

"IBM has the most to gain from Java and is certainly in the best position to be the winner if Java becomes a major factor in the business world . . . IBM lends credibility in the marketplace and has a tremendous number of developers and the discipline necessary to turn Java into a true enterprise-class environment," he says. Although Sun and IBM are allies today because they're both concerned about stopping Microsoft, "IBM is in a strong position to co-opt Java. The more successful Java becomes, the more incentive there is for vendors to diverge." And IBM has more developers, more salespeople, and more money to put into Java than Sun. After all, IBM turned to Java because it could integrate Big Blue's different computing platforms, from mainframes to network computers. IBM would certainly like to optimize Java for its own environments, not watch a smaller sometime competitor, Sun, decide where this key technology is headed. Watch out for IBM, like Hewlett-Packard, to develop its own versions of Java in the future, Kucharvy suggests.

If Java becomes wildly popular, the second winner is Microsoft, he believes, because most developers will write for its version of the technology, not Sun's. Software developers "don't write to dollars; they write to units," he says, and Microsoft's Windows NT had 40 percent of the server market (mostly on the low end) in 1998, headed toward 50 percent in 1999. Kucharvy sees Sun, then, as no more than third in the business market for Java applications and operating systems, behind IBM and Microsoft. In a December 2, 1998 appearance in New York before the Manhattan Institute, Bill Gates insisted that the "PC model has defeated every other model," and dismissed Sun's view of a network-centric world as a mere "sales slogan," according to a December 3 article in the *New York Times*.[5] He predicted that PCs would eventually be able to handle functions now performed by mainframes and Unix servers. "The PC model will take over the rest of the industry."

■ ROSE-COLORED GLASSES?

Sun's executives, of course, are numbered among the optimists. Chief Technology Officer Greg Papadopoulos sees two fundamental shifts taking place in technology, both of which play to Sun's strengths. The first is the rapid consumerization, and simplification, of network access by means of appliances like a telephone or a settop box. "Computing is way too complex and PCs are excruciatingly difficult for people to use," he says, echoing Gelernter. "I no longer live on my PC. I live on the network. In the future, you will have your own Web site on the network. You will have an agent acting on your behalf on the network." The second shift is the reconsolidation of computing around massive data centers inside corporations, which shifts the balance of power back toward centralized computing and away from the desktop. The difference between this concept and the old mainframe-centric, punchcard world is that information and the ability to innovate are distributed to the individual desktop, not locked away in a machine only an information technology (IT) professional can access. Instead of being the guardians of computing, IT departments become service providers, like the telephone operator who assists you in placing a call.

Sun has departed from its original business model, Papadopoulos concedes, which was to take readily available components such as the Unix operating system and someone else's chips, and put them together in a way that added value. That worked in an environment in which all the competitors were more or less starting from the same place, he says. Today, with technology companies aligning themselves into two major camps, it takes a different strategy to succeed. Sun puts its own intellectual property (IP)—like Java, Jini, Solaris, and SPARC—at the foundation of its product offerings, and enlists partners to create value on top of that. "By drawing the line [on IP] at the right place, you can build a sustainable model and capture the value of your own R&D," he says. For example, Sun will never build a fabrication plant to manufacture chips, but does its own design work with SPARC. On the software side, Solaris and Java are the operating systems, but application developers are indispensable partners. Bill Raduchel, Sun's chief strategy officer, likes to explain Sun's strategy the way he might to one of his former students. By controlling an integrated computing system—from the microprocessor to the server and client operating systems—Sun can "build the whole house," he says, while other vendors "just give you a prefabricated living room."

Sun is fortunate because, unlike Netscape or Novell or other would-be Microsoft opposition from the past, it still has an entrenched market in which Microsoft products are becoming increasingly important but, so far, not taking over entirely. Sun is fighting a war of delay and attrition, and it's hard to say when NT and Merced will achieve parity with Solaris and SPARC in the corporate enterprise. What you can say is that, with Microsoft and Intel, respectively, behind those technologies, NT and Merced will gobble up pieces of Sun's traditional markets even as Sun works feverishly to open up new vistas with Java and Jini. With those two technologies, "we're evangelizing a new way of doing things," says Ed Zander, that isn't going to yield substantial revenues in the near future. Solaris, ultra-SPARC, and Sun's workstation/server business will have to pay the price for moving into that future. "We'll be doing missionary work for years," says Zander. In the 25 years he has been in the technology industry, there have only been a handful of dominant platforms built, including IBM's mainframe operating system, Digital's minicomputer operating system, Apple's Macintosh, Microsoft's Windows, and now Java. "The whole basis of our bet is to move the world away from this Windows-centric model. We're the change agent." Microsoft has been reduced to a reactive role, Zander asserts, in responding to developments like the Internet and Java. "I'm helping to set the agenda." Indeed, in early 1999, Sun's ally Oracle announced agreements with Hewlett-Packard and Dell Computer to sell server appliances that bypass Windows in accessing Oracle's database.

■ HOW SUN CAN WIN

What must Sun do to head off the pessimists and achieve the rosy world of ubiquitous computing foreseen by the likes of Joy, Gilder, and Gelernter? Bottom line: Sun dominates the market for Unix workstations and servers, and walls off the high end against the NT/Merced encroachment for at least five years. In those five years, Sun establishes Java/Jini as the centerpiece in the world of ubiquitous computing and begins to accelerate sales of its servers because they're needed to run all these new devices like smart cards and digital settop boxes. To do that, Zander must get the new Sun divisions working together, in a way the planets never did, to create systems in which Java/Solaris/ultraSPARC offer the highest performance of any combination anywhere. Solaris, for example, has to be the best enterprise operating system for running Java applications. If it's a system from IBM or Hewlett-Packard or someone else, Sun has lost.

Secondly, Sun has to handle Java/Jini in a more credible fashion, not treating the technology like a matter for religious conversion, but realistically assessing what can be delivered and when. With Java, "Sun promised too much too early and lost a lot of credibility" when the technology didn't perform as well as expected, says Colin Mahony, an analyst with The Yankee Group in Boston. Sun has to tone down the hype machine until it's ready to deliver on the promises it's making now with Jini. Then too, Sun can't depend just on fees from licensing Java or Jini to various customers. To reap big bucks from its innovation, it must provide the infrastructure in which Java functions. So vendors don't just buy a programming language, but servers and software that run the Java operating system and related applications, dishing it up to those proliferating consumer devices. When you open up your cell phone to check your e-mail or pull out your smart card to load up on electronic money, a lot of the time you'd be contacting a Sun machine. Sun is in your handheld device, but it's also in the nerve center that makes that device useful. "Java is successful if it becomes so pervasive, you don't even know it's there," says analyst Bret Rekas.

Based on the number of employees in the Java division, Sun is spending an estimated $180 million to $200 million a year on salaries and infrastructure to support those people. Beyond that, there are the sunk costs for all the R&D. Analysts speculate that Sun may have pulled in enough fees from licensing the Java programming language in 1996 and 1997 to break even on ongoing costs, but a licensing model cannot be sustained indefinitely. To be successful, Java needs to bring in revenues from product sales, which remain a couple of years away. By 2001, the Java division would be successful if it were making about $100 million in operating profit on $300 million in revenue, suggests Daniel Kunstler, managing director of J. P. Morgan Securities in San Francisco. That would give Java margins similar to those of a successful software company. He believes that's possible if Java technology proves itself in models like the Visa and Motorola deals, and Sun is able to expand on those.

On the people front, Sun must continue to provide a culture in which the Bill Joys and James Goslings can innovate. There will always be tension between the needs of the outside world—customers and allies who want incremental improvements to existing technology—and the demands of resident geniuses who want the freedom to come up with that next breakthrough. Sun has done a fair job of treading the line between order and chaos, tilting toward the latter. As the company grows and instills processes, it can't give up on the near-anarchy that allowed Java to hang on until it found a purpose and helped Jini to be born. At the same time, McNealy, Zander, Alan Baratz, and the rest of the top executives have to develop coherent strategies to turn Java and Jini into successful businesses generating real returns, not just headlines.

McNealy also needs to stop obsessing over one opponent at a time, which causes him to lose sight of other competitors. "One of the weaknesses I've always seen in Sun is their tendency to be too focused on one competitor, in this case Microsoft," says Michael Goulde, vice president of research for the Boston-based consulting firm, Seybold Group. "The technology industry is a collection of sporting events and every company is playing their own game. While Microsoft is playing three-dimensional chess, Sun is playing ice hockey." Within the corporate world, "the real target for Sun needs to be how can they beat IBM," he adds. Another looming target is Compaq Computer, which, with its takeover of Digital, is moving aggressively into higher-level markets that used to be the purview of the Unix vendors.

Sun is moving to offer customers the ability to interoperate its platforms with other technologies. So, it no longer forces customers to choose between Sun and everyone else. This is one area in which Sun retains a lead over Microsoft, which is more accustomed to dealing with individual desktops than the enterprise as a whole. Sun must keep that advantage as long as it can by making its own technology more friendly to NT and by partnering with full-fledged solutions providers like IBM and consulting/accounting firms. It's a complicated world, and your friend in one arena may be your competitor in another. As in the fantasy movie *Pleasantville,* Sun's vision has been of a black-and-white universe; it is now learning to see the world in various shades of color.

Outside the business world, in the emergent paradigm of ubiquitous computing and embedded systems, Sun has a lot to learn, as Hewlett-Packard complained when it decided to develop its own verson of Java to serve the market. But everyone else is learning, too, including Microsoft. The field is wide open and Sun, with Java and Jini, has as good a shot as anyone of becoming a contender. What Sun must do here is loosen its grip on Java and Jini enough to let a thousand flowers bloom—that is, to allow partners and software developers and consumer electronics vendors to advance these technologies in a way that encourages new markets. It's a tightwire act for Sun, which is rather schizophrenic on the issue of control. While deriding Microsoft's iron hand on Windows, Sun is trying to find a middle ground with Java that allows outsiders to innovate while Sun makes the final call on what is acceptable innovation and what isn't. Sun may have to cede more control than that, and bow to the consensus of a third-party coalition of major Java partners like IBM. Sun doesn't want to trod the same path that IBM and then Microsoft did—exerting so much control that there's a backlash, from customers, partners, not to mention the government. That explains why, even though so many companies owe their success to collaboration with Microsoft, they're now turning on their one-time partner in court.

The stakes in both the Java lawsuit and the Justice Department lawsuit are high for Sun. With the Java suit, Sun has stopped Microsoft from using the Java logo on its Windows-friendly version of the technology, and will possibly get a damage award in 1999. So Sun can certainly brag that it won. As for the federal suit, the Department of Justice seems to be expanding it beyond the original narrow issue of whether Microsoft sought to undermine Netscape's browser to look at other technologies such as NT and Java. McNealy has argued for a breakup of Microsoft similar to the one that split out the Baby Bells from AT&T. Even if the government doesn't achieve that, its lawsuit is aiding Sun—and every other competitor of Microsoft—by compelling the Redmond giant to devote corporate brainpower and resources to fighting the suit, and by exposing a lot of pretty dirty, if not downright illegal, tactics on Microsoft's part. Says former Sun executive Chet Silvestri: "Somebody has to slow Microsoft down. That's why Sun is prodding on the DOJ. If Microsoft doesn't slow down, Sun can't win." Analyst Evan Quinn applauds Sun for playing hard and mobilizing the government. "Microsoft is hell-bent on domination," he says. "For Sun, it comes down to a question of survival. Microsoft has shown absolutely no propensity to let others have a piece of the pie—it's winner-take-all, loser-take-nothing. Sun had to use practically any stone to turn public opinion, government, and vendors against them."

However, it is now time for Sun to back off on the Microsoft bashing, which is getting old and making McNealy sound like a whiner. He is no longer a lone voice in the wilderness decrying Microsoft's bullying tactics. The Sun CEO should abandon his frat-boy approach for a more sophisticated outlook. After all, like it or not, McNealy is now an elder statesman in the young technology industry and should embrace that role. With its success in the Java lawsuit and its alliances with AOL/ Netscape, IBM, Oracle, and others, Sun has become the pivotal company in the coalition seeking to guarantee consumers and businesses an array of technology choices in the twenty-first century. If he chooses, McNealy could be an articulate spokesman for this coalition. The goal should not be to dethrone Microsoft, but to offer compelling alternatives that people want to buy. For Sun, it's get back to basics and give your customers what they need: not pulpit-pounding oratory, but a Java operating system for the network computer that works, a Solaris that really does run NT applications, an ultraSPARC that blows Merced away. The start-up Sun of the 1980s didn't need bombastic rhetoric to beat Apollo and Digital; it just aggressively delivered equivalent or superior technology at a better price. The task today is not so very different: Win on what you do, not on what you say.

Chapter Notes

Introduction:
1. John Harwood and David Bank, "CyberSpectacle: Senate Meets Electronic Elite," *Wall Street Journal,* March 4, 1998, p. B1.
2. *Fortune,* "Javaman: Sun's Scott McNealy Must Stop Bill Gates from Dominating the Corporate Universe! Will the Magic of Java Save the Day?", October 13, 1997, cover.

Chapter 1:
1. Scott McNealy, "Standardizing the Industry; Open Approach Could Halt High-Tech Slump," *Computerworld,* December 16, 1985, p. 17.
2. Mark Hall and John Barry, *Sunburst: The Ascent of Sun Microsystems,* Chicago: Contemporary Books, 1990, p. 14.
3. Ibid, pp. 14–15.

Chapter 2:
1. *Golf Digest,* June 1998, as reprinted in *New York Times,* "Duffers Need Not Apply," Adam Bryant, May 31, 1998, pp. 1, 9 (business section).
2. Brent Schlender, "The Adventures of Scott McNealy, Javaman," *Fortune,* October 13, 1997, pp. 70–84.
3. John Heilemann, "The Sun King," *New Yorker,* March 16, 1998, pp. 30–35.

4. Ibid.

5. Interview by Maryfran Johnson, "Witty Warrior," *Computerworld,* June 22, 1992, p. 36.

6. *Golf Digest,* June 1998, as reprinted in *New York Times,* "Duffers Need Not Apply," Adam Bryant, May 31, 1998, pp. 1, 9 (business section).

7. John Heilemann, "The Sun King," *New Yorker,* March 16, 1998, pp. 30–35.

8. Gerald F. Seib, "Freedom Fighters: Antitrust Suites Expand and Libertarians Ask, Who's the Bad Guy?", *Wall Street Journal,* June 9, 1998, p. A1, A10.

Chapter 3:

1. Mark Hall and John Barry, *Sunburst: The Ascent of Sun Microsystems,* Chicago: Contemporary Books, 1990, p. 151.

2. Nick Arnett, *San Jose Business Journal,* "Sun Micro Said to be Shining in Apple's Eye," December 16, 1985, p. 1.

Chapter 4:

1. James Martin, "Sun Finishes Scorching Year, Passes $500M Milestone," *Computerworld,* August 3, 1987, p. 59.

2. Annalee Saxenian, *Regional Advantage: Culture and Competition in Silicon Valley and Route 128,* Cambridge, Massachusetts: Harvard University Press, 1996, p. 128.

3. Cordell Koland, *San Jose Business Journal,* "Six Bay Area Firms Near $1 Billion Revenue Mark," November 16, 1987, p. 1.

4. Eric Nee, "Sun Challenge: Keeping Manufacturing, Support Up with Sales Growth," *Electronic News,* May 19, 1986, p. 21.

5. Kathleen K. Wiegner, "They Are Not There Waiting for the Plane to Land," *Forbes,* June 27, 1988, p. 49.

Chapter 5:

1. Juli Cortino, "Sun Struggling with Own Success," *PC Week,* June 19, 1989, p. 6.

2. Michelle Levander and Steve Kaufman, "Another Top Official Turns His Back on Sun," *San Jose Mercury News,* June 16, 1989, p. 14D.

3. Lawrence M. Fisher, "Hiccup for a Computer Superstar," *New York Times,* June 2, 1989, p. 9.

4. Ibid.

5. Michael Krey, "Dickensian Times: Hewlett-Packard, Apple, Sun Were Served Doses of Humility in 1990," *San Jose Business Journal*, December 31, 1990, p. 8.
6. Lawrence Aragon, "Contrarian Sun Hikes Cost of Old SPARCs to Sell New," *San Jose Business Journal*, February 22, 1993, p. 1.
7. Mark Mehler, "Sun's Network Strategy Starts Paying Off," *Investor's Business Daily*, October 20, 1994, p. A1.

Chapter 6:
1. Mark Hall and John Barry, *Sunburst: The Ascent of Sun Microsystems*, Chicago: Contemporary Books, 1990, pp. 194–195.

Chapter 7:
1. David Bank, "Why Sun Thinks Hot Java Will Give You a Lift," *San Jose Mercury News*, March 23, 1995, p. 1.
2. George Gilder, "The Coming Software Shift," *Forbes*, August 28, 1995, pp. 147–162.
3. John Markoff, "Making the PC Come Alive," *New York Times*, September 24, 1995, p. 1D.

Chapter 10:
1. Scott McNealy, "Why We're Suing Microsoft," *Wall Street Journal*, October 5, 1998, p. A30.
2. Ibid.
3. Paul Maritz, letter, "Sun Is Trying to Break Our Windows," *Wall Street Journal*, October 21, 1998, p. A23.
4. David Bank, "Paneful Struggle: How Microsoft's Ranks Wound Up in Civil War over Windows' Future," *Wall Street Journal*, February 1, 1999, pp. A1, A8.
5. Scott McNealy, "Opening Windows of Competition," *San Francisco Examiner*, November 23, 1998, editorial page.
6. Brian Gruley and Keith Perine, "Microsoft to Request the Dismissal of Antitrust Suit Due to AOL Bid," *Wall Street Journal Interactive Edition*, November 25, 1998.
7. Ibid.

Chapter 12:
1. Kevin Kelly and Spencer Reiss, "Poof! There Goes the Desktop Computer," cover, and "Creating One Huge Computer," *Wired*, p. 128, August 1998.

2. John Markoff, "Taking a Step Toward Converting the Home into a Supercomputer," *New York Times*, July 14, 1998, pp. A1, C4.

3. Ibid.

4. David Gelernter, "Manager's Journal: The Computer of the Future," *Wall Street Journal*, October 26, 1998, p. A22.

5. Steve Lohr, "Gates Serves Up Playful Scorn for Prosecutors and Rivals," *New York Times*, December 3, 1998, p. C4.

Acknowledgments

I would like to acknowledge the untiring efforts of Anne Little, Elizabeth McNichols, and Susanne Vagadori in Sun's public relations office, who devoted many hours to setting up the dozens of interviews within Sun that made this book possible. I also appreciate the busy Sun executives, managers, engineers, and employees who took the time to sit down and talk candidly with me. Mark Hall and John Barry, who wrote an early book about Sun called *Sunburst,* provided invaluable assistance. I'm grateful to David Bunnell, who first hired me at *Upside* as executive editor and then gave me the challenge of starting Upside Books. Also, this would not have been possible without the backing of John Wiley & Sons and, in particular, editor Jeanne Glasser. Finally, I thank Eric Nee, who taught me how exciting the technology industry could be, for his friendship over the years, and particularly for his thoughtful editing of *High Noon.*

Index